TALES
GOOD AND EVIL,
HELP AND HARM

TALES OF GOOD AND EVIL, HELP AND HARM

PHILIP HALLIE

with a Foreword by JOHN J. COMPTON
and an Afterword by DORIS A. HALLIE

HarperPerennial
A Division of HarperCollins*Publishers*

A hardcover edition of this book was published in 1997 by HarperCollins Publishers.

HarperCollins books may be purchased for educational, business, or sales promotional use. For information please write: Special Markets Department, HarperCollins Publishers, Inc., 10 East 53rd Street, New York, NY 10022.

First HarperPerennial edition published 1998.

Designed by Alma Hochhauser Orenstein

The Library of Congress has catalogued the hardcover edition as follows:

Hallie, Philip Paul.
    Tales of good and evil, help and harm / Philip P. Hallie : with a foreword by John J. Compton and an afterword by Doris A. Hallie. — 1st ed.
      p.   cm.
    Includes bibliographical references and index.
    ISBN 0-06-018745-X
    1. Altruism—Case studies. 2. Ethics—Case studies. I. Title.
    BJ1286.A6H35   1997
    170—dc21   97-3998

ISBN 0-06-092901-4 (pbk.)

98 99 00 01 02 ❖/RRD 10 9 8 7 6 5 4 3 2 1

For Michelena and Louie
who both carry on their father's
intensity, compassion, and joy

One hand washes the other.

In the eye of a hurricane the sky is blue and birds can fly there
without suffering harm. The eye of the hurricane is in the very
middle of destructive power, and that power is always near, surrounding that blue beauty and threatening to invade it. . . .

In a world of moral hurricanes some people can and do carve
out rather large ethical spaces. In a natural world and a social
world swirling in cruelty and love we can make room. We who
are not pure ethical beings can push away the choking circle of
brute force that is around and within us. We may not be able to
push it far . . . , but when we have made as much room as we
can, we may know a blue peace that the storm does not know.

—PHILIP HALLIE, OCTOBER 1986

To turn Magda, Josh, etc., into heroic figures is to exonerate ourselves from participation in their powers and beauty—as if they
were not in our moral sphere. It would be like spending our
lives looking at great athletes doing great things and expecting
(somehow) that this would make *us* great athletes. Heroes are
beyond being ends-in-view, operative effective role models.
They are too far beyond us to be incitements to act like them.

The people in my hurricane book must be us, like us, close to us,
though in some ways better than us, if their beauty can touch us,
while their actions and passions can enliven us to act and feel. . . .

—PHILIP HALLIE, DATE UNKNOWN

CONTENTS

FOREWORD

John J. Compton

This is a book of stories—stories about real people who, often at great risk to themselves, chose not to ignore or to hurt but rather to help other people. Philip Hallie called these stories "tales of good and evil" because, in them, he meant to show us what he saw as our most precious human ethical possibility—life-affirming and life-giving openness to others.

We all live in hurricanes, struggling to survive, Hallie thought. For this very reason we face a profound challenge in the need of other struggling people more desperate than ourselves. How we respond is one measure of what kind of human beings we are. Hallie came to believe that, in each of our hurricanes, there is a quiet eye of generosity, however narrow, from which we are able to reach out to help others. He hoped that these stories would enter and enrich the emotional memories out of which we live, and would thus help to enlarge that eye.

Hallie meant these tales to speak for themselves, to let us enter directly into the lives of the remarkable people he came to know or know about—Magda and André Trocmé, who, with the villagers of Le Chambon, under the Nazi occupation of France, helped save thousands of Jews; Julius Schmähling, the German general overseeing the region of Le Chambon, who knowingly allowed the rescue to go on; Joshua James who, in an earlier era, spent his life as captain of a lifeboat crew, saving shipwreck victims off the coast of Hull, Massachusetts; and Kätchen Coley, a contemporary Middletown, Connecticut, woman who created and energized another sort of lifesaving institution, The Connection, devoted to rehabilitating drug- and alcohol-dependent young men and women. Hallie portrayed these helpers in intimate, personal depth as well as in their interplay with the communities and histories surrounding them. Never moral saints, all of them were ambiguous, sometimes difficult human beings struggling within their own very particular hurricanes.

As he tells their stories, though, Hallie is telling us his own as well. It too is remarkable, yet, unlike the others it emerges only obliquely, in bits and snatches, as he describes how he came upon these people, how they entered his life, and how and why they spoke to him and captured his passionate imagination. The fact that they and their stories moved and formed *him* seems to be as essential as they themselves are to the distinctive understanding of good and evil he offers us.

We have to see how strange this is. Here is Philip Hallie, a highly trained college professor of philosophy. Instead of writing technical tomes for his peers—although he did some of that too— he spent much of his life researching and writing history, and very curious history at that—personally narrated stories about people he personally selected, written not primarily for historians or philosophers but for human beings. There are no philosophical arguments here, nor any elaborate historical documentation. And we soon see that Hallie himself is at issue in these stories in a way in which, in their scholarly lives, philosophers and historians rarely, if ever, are. Yet it isn't that Hallie just liked to write stories, or that this personal style seemed appropriate to a wide audience. Somehow, through this style itself, Hallie is telling us something, and it is clear that he thought this something had human and philosophical importance. How are we to understand it? What was he up to? Because I knew Philip, and loved and argued with him throughout our philosophic lives together, it seemed appropriate for me to try to help his readers put this book in context.

Beginnings

The first thing to say, I think, is that writing stories such as those in this book—together with his teaching and his deep devotion to family and friends—were ways in which Philip sought to put his life together. He was always trying to overcome inner fractures and a sense of solitariness. No doubt something like this is true for every writer, perhaps for every one of us, but for Philip it had special force.

He was born in 1922, and, as he himself puts it, from his youth he lived in his own hurricane: the depression of the 1930s on the West Side of Chicago. There was nearly suffocating poverty. He grew up in a tenement he and his brother called the "Cockroach Building," with a dispirited, inarticulate father and a mystical, muddled mother, neither of whom could understand the other (or him). There were the neighborhood bullies who beat him because he was a Jew. Mercifully, there was also a loving uncle who taught him to fight back, and there were some mysterious moments of calm, on Friday evenings, celebrating the Sabbath. And then there was reading: His mother said he was *always* reading. It was a way out. So was school. So was the miraculous intervention of the summer camp offered by the ladies from the nearby Christian inner-city mission. So, eventually, was success at Herzl Junior College and winning an unbelievable scholarship to Grinnell. Philip's world was a street-tough one of need and struggle on the outside and a confusion of feelings within, a jumble of goods and evils, rising ambition, and a bit of hope.

His wartime experience only extended the boundaries of this world and sharpened his determination to try to make sense of it. At Grinnell, before the war, Hallie had discovered his intellectual power and passions—he devoured (and wrote) poetry because it enlivened his senses and fed his imagination; he prized physics for its beautiful conceptual clarity; and he came to see philosophy as a possible source of integrative thought. The army added to his arsenal. Pointing him toward intelligence work, it gave him language training, particularly in French, which would later open the whole of French history and culture to him. And then (of course!) it assigned him to the artillery. Throughout his months of combat, he kept a journal. He observed and reflected as well as fought; he wondered whether it would matter if he died, he expressed his passion for life and his love of beauty. Echoes of his reflections on both the raw brutality and the necessity of the fighting appear in the stories included in the present book. The war focused his mind.

One striking theme in the journals is the need, in life, for connections. On July 18, 1943, Hallie wrote, "I spoke of moral support by means of two foxholes connected by a trench. Life is very much like this: each man follows the configurations of his own personality, but in one wall there is a passage leading to his fellows." Much of what he personally struggled with, and much that he later came to write, is contained in the implications of this image: We live in little holes. How can we dig those "passages" that will link us to our fellows?

The search for intellectual as well as human connections shaped Hallie's development after the war. He needed to bring the conflicted feelings engendered by his personal experience, and fired by poetry and literature, together with the demands of a searching intellect that sought conceptual clarity. He thought at first that theoretical physics and cosmology would give him the comprehensive beauty he sought, so, after finishing Grinnell, he went to Princeton to study with the legendary cosmologist John Wheeler. He soon saw, however, that too much of his feeling life was left out. Perhaps it would be philosophy instead; so he got himself to Harvard's Department of Philosophy. There also he found sustenance for his logical side but none for the passional.

One afternoon in the fall of 1947, during a walk along a Cambridge street, the great philosopher-scientist Alfred North Whitehead asked him, "You say you love physics and poetry, but have you achieved a *wedding* of the two?" Hallie confessed that he had not. He went on to master symbolic logic, to absorb the rigors of empiricist philosophy of science, and to immerse himself in Wittgenstein's critical reflections on language. But he could not see how to "wed" these no-nonsense philosophies of pure critical reason with his poetic and ethical sensibility in any coherent way. It would be more than twenty years, and a journey that took him to England and to France to study, and then to Vanderbilt and Wesleyan Universities as a young professor, before Hallie could form an effective idea of such a wedding. And his way of achieving it would be far indeed from a speculative system like Whitehead's own. In the end it was the inspiration of a very much older philosopher—and a very unusual one—that gave him his clue.

The philosopher was Michel de Montaigne, the sixteenth-century French essayist. And the clue was to turn away entirely from abstract systems and jargony philosophizing, and toward common language and experience, toward actual human doings and sufferings and self-understandings, as the place where, if at all, he might seek humane wisdom and find a way to bring peace between the demands of reason and those of his passionate, poetic nature. What he would later write would be essays in the manner of Montaigne, stories like the ones in this book, as part of his personal search.

Montaigne

As scholars often do, Hallie discovered Montaigne while engaged in something else. Harvard had awarded him a traveling fellowship to Oxford, where he was working on the thought of the eighteenth-century philosopher David Hume. Hume's skepticism about abstract ideas and his turn to an analysis of human experience—and especially his respect for the place of sympathy and tradition in human life—appealed strongly. But Hume's readiness to "explain" all of our experiences as derived simply from fleeting, passively felt outward and inward sensations was, he thought, a serious error. Hallie's tutor at Oxford, H. H. Price, put Hallie onto the then (and still) largely unappreciated late-eighteenth- and early-nineteenth-century French critic of Hume, François Gonthier, called Maine de Biran.

Biran defended the view that there is much more to experience than Hume allowed—there is, crucially, the whole realm of internal self-experience, of thinking, feeling, and, above all, of voluntary bodily movement, the constant sense of oneself as an active agent that accompanies everything we do. Any true empiricist, Biran argued, needed precisely to point out such experiences rather than explain them away. Hallie made this argument the subject of his doctoral dissertation and his first book: *Maine de Biran—Reformer of Empiricism*, published in 1959.[1] The lesson that there are some "plain facts" of experience that are not to be explained away stuck with Hallie for the rest of his life. The experienced evil of hurting and being hurt, and the experienced goodness of helping rather than hurting, are some of the "plain facts" that Hallie is showing us in the present book.

The study of Biran led naturally beyond itself. Maine de Biran, Hallie found, had arrived at his focus on concrete, bodily self-experience by reading the essays of that earlier countryman of his Michel de Montaigne. So Hallie took his family and a Guggenheim fellowship to France to live with Montaigne. From this experience, from his close reading of the essays and actually staying, for a period, in Montaigne's chateau near Bordeaux, from a wide-ranging study of the political, religious, and philosophical conflicts in Montaigne's France, and moved by his intuitive sympathy for Montaigne's project to turn from philosophical debate to personal reflection, Hallie wrote *The Scar of Montaigne—An Essay in Personal Philosophy*, which was published in 1966.

What Hallie saw in Montaigne was a fellow philosopher, frustrated by his philosophical education (and the philosophical profession), forging a new direction. "Somehow," Hallie said, "in the twentieth century, at least in the English-speaking world, philosophy has come unstuck from living."[2] He wanted to show that Montaigne offers a helpful way of sticking them back together again. Montaigne's way of doing this, his style of thinking and writing, would become Hallie's own way of responding to Whitehead's question, his way of wedding intellect with the life of imagination and feeling.

Writing amid the turmoil of the wars of religion, and surrounded by scientific and philosophic controversy, Montaigne concluded that philosophers and theologians, and of course the political leaders who draw on them, all tend to presume too much. They claim to know what they cannot know. They think they can achieve a certainty and a universality of insight that are precisely belied by their continuing disagreements with one another and the strenuous efforts each makes to persuade the others that his own doctrines are, after all, "obvious." They think they can put aside their particular religious backgrounds and bodily natures, their feelings, and their daily lives, while talking grandly about faith, nature, body, feeling, and life. In effect, Montaigne believed, what such people do is proclaim their personal views to be necessary for everyone else. The human consequences are irresolvable public conflict and bloody war, as well as private confusion and, perhaps above all, a failure to be able to savor the genuine joys that are possible in life. One can almost see Hallie nodding in agreement!

We human beings are "mixtures," thinks Montaigne. We do have a ray of divinity in us, and we do have rational powers. But both are mixed with wide individual differences of circumstance, of tradition and practice, and are subject to powerful and unpredictable passions. So much so that one cannot untangle the mixture. As

Montaigne puts it, in a phrase that Hallie echoes again and again, the human condition is *"merveilleusement corporelle"*—it is a wonder how physical our nature is! Each of us is born with a particular body and a particular temperament, born in a particular nation and region, and born into a particular culture and language. That is why we have to be skeptical of any absolute claims. "There is no use our mounting on stilts, for on stilts we must still walk on our own legs. And on the loftiest throne in the world we are still sitting on our own rump."[3] If we are to live in keeping with our condition, we can only live with our particular "mixtures," accepting the differing values each of us has been brought up with. We can only try to exercise patience, prudence, and self-control, and do the best we can.

This practical skepticism is what Montaigne tried to follow in his own life and to show in his writing. In the *Essays* he makes it clear that he makes no grand universal claims. He is only "essaying" himself, he says at the outset: "Reader, I myself am the matter of my book." As he discusses public life, faith and reason, varying cultural customs, the meaning of friendship, education, and all the rest, he will simply be portraying his own style of life—his individual way of discharging public duties, yet keeping his freedom and enjoying friends and the healthy satisfactions of his natural appetites. And he will portray this style of life through the style of the essay itself. When Hallie sums up what he sees as Montaigne's message, we can hear him speaking for himself as well:

> Style is what a man can offer who does not claim to know The Truth nor The Way to it, but who does wish to live, to think, to feel, and to act vigorously. It is a particular way of living that can be communicated by a particular way of writing or speaking. It can be communicated by what a man *says* and by what a man *shows*, by what a man talks about and by his way of talking about it.[4]

If this is the spirit of the *Essays*, it is also precisely the spirit of the present book. We are to learn from the moral energy of the remarkable people Hallie tells us about, of course. But in presenting them Hallie presents them as they have energized *him*, and as part of his own growing self-understanding. His point is to communicate to us—by personal contagion rather than impersonal recitation—the force of what he has learned. And he counts on us to assess what we find and to use our own judgment as to what we will accept or reject. He offers "no proofs," he says; ethics admits of no proofs. As with Montaigne it is himself, Philip Hallie, whom he paints—it is his personal way of regarding things, his style, his perception of good and evil that he offers us in these stories.

Evil

Hallie was drawn to attend directly to ethical issues in much the way Montaigne was—by the press of events around him. While he was working on the Montaigne book, in the late fifties and early sixties, the civil rights revolution erupted. And during much of the same period, survivors of the Holocaust were beginning to find themselves able to speak. I remember his intensely personal response to both these courses of events—as a white man, he felt acutely the moral judgment of the victims of slavery and the subsequent generations of racial bigotry; as a World War II soldier and a Jew, he began to identify himself ever more strongly with the victims of the Nazi extermination machine. At the same time, again much in the spirit of Montaigne, he recognized that, although he had certain public responsibilities, he was no activist and that his role would have to be reflective, suited to his own manner of life as a teacher and writer.

The outcome, nonetheless, was a sort of conversion. In spite of his Montaignesque skepticism, Hallie became virtually obsessed with the problem of human evil, with the human penchant to control, maim, and destroy other human beings. Whereas before he preferred to take a distance from abstract ethical issues and, above all, from the kind of discussions in so-called metaethics about the meaning of ethical words, he now began seriously reading and teaching concrete, life-and-death ethics. He made it his personal mission to try to understand the dimensions of human cruelty and with that, perhaps, to see some ways of mitigating it.

The issue was how to proceed. It was Hallie's poetic and aesthetic sensibility that provided the inspiration: He would use images. He wanted to feel (and see) the very *experience* of cruelty, of "mortal maiming," as vividly as possible in all its horror. Why not, then, ask (and show) what cruelty means in pictures and stories that have been created precisely to express that emotional meaning?

This was the project for *The Paradox of Cruelty*, which Hallie published in 1969—as he rightly observed, "one of the few philosophy books ever written in which illustrations play a central role."[5]

A lifelong admirer of Hogarth, Hallie began the book with a painstaking analysis of two of the artist's most famous series of engravings—Marriage à la Mode and The Four Stages of Cruelty—showing the essential role of the victimizer's overwhelming power and the subtle as well as overt, the institutional as well as the personal ways in which that power crushes the victim. He went on, through the fiction of de Sade and the Gothic horror tale, to stories of black slavery and segregation, in particular the history of Frederick Douglass, using a marvelously fierce portrait of him and Douglass's own autobiography. Hallie underlined what all of them showed—that enforced isolation and passivity of the victims, kept in place through the purveying of soothing, self-deceiving abstractions about what is going on, are integral to perpetuating cruelly destructive relationships. Removing the *power* of the victimizer becomes the only cure for cruelty. His careful examination of these varied images of cruelty showed Hallie clearly what his main conclusion had to be:

> [The meaning of cruelty] is to be understood in relation to the resistance it calls forth, in relation to the actions that crystalize the otherwise quiet desperation of the weak. You can understand a force like cruelty best by seeing the nature and force of what can *stop* it. When the weak get strong enough they show the amount of power that has been exerted on them; in their outrage . . . they show just how destructive the cruelty they have experienced has been. . . . One of the key contentions of this book is one of the key ideas of Douglass's autobiography: the opposite of cruelty is not kindness. . . . *The opposite of cruelty is freedom.*[6]

This was hardly news, of course, although it has been all too easy (especially for those in power) to forget or subvert it. But Hallie had provided a spectacularly vivid, almost palpable demonstration of the idea. He knew that his initial use of artistic and literary fictions would have to be "tested in the history of flesh and blood."[7] With his study of Douglass, he felt he had done this and that he had helped himself and his readers to come to terms with the agony of the racial revolution going on around them. He dedicated the book to his student Edwin Sanders who, "even after all those cruelties, is black and beautiful" and who had become "a flesh-and-blood presence in my life."

There you have it: The philosopher as flesh-and-blood, writing out of personal experience, an experience inhabited by other flesh-and-blood, fired by imagination and history, and enlarged and clarified through his own reflective struggle. A fresh, but really very old, way of being a philosopher.

Goodness

In this way, in the book on cruelty, Hallie had done two things—he had offered a passionate and penetrating analysis of a crucial ethical reality, and he had begun to create his own style of philosophical work. He had found *his* way of wedding poetry and physics, imagination and reason, images and the nature of things. What happened next led him to enlarge his ethical vision still further and to take his writing in a fresh direction.

By the spring of 1975, Hallie felt himself near depression from years of immersion in accounts of cruelty, torture, and death, many of which now focused on the Nazis' destruction of the Jews. One day he happened on a brief account of the tiny French village of Le Chambon in World War II. There, during the German occupation, under the leadership of its two pacifist Protestant pastors, a handful of ordinary people had conspired to *save* thousands of Jews, many of them children. Hallie was so moved by this amazing life-risking, life-saving resistance to evil that he vowed to pursue the story behind it. He could not believe what he had read. Evil had come to seem almost inevitable in the human condition. He had to try to understand how such *goodness* could have happened.

Hallie grasped the project as a kind of redemption. It became part of him. By coincidence, I was in residence at Wesleyan at the time and, since I knew about the village, I was able to start him on his way. He began to study what documentary history there was and sought out everyone who knew the little that was to be known about Le Chambon.

He befriended Magda Trocmé, the widow of the dynamic pastor, André Trocmé, who had been the spiritual force behind the villagers' quiet conspiracy to hide and save the Jewish strangers. Magda became a flesh-and-blood part of Hallie's and his family's life; she taught them the power of the practical, stubborn, day-to-day human caring that sustained her husband's pure and intense commitment to the imitation of Christ. Edouard Theis, Trocmé's friend and associate pastor, took Hallie to Le Chambon. In their quiet way, Theis and the other villagers he interviewed taught Hallie how "natural" and far from extraordinary it had seemed to them to help the strangers who came to their doors. He came to see how the long history of Huguenot persecution had given their descendants in the Haute-Loire a healthy disposition to resist government authority. He also came to see how little effect the brave efforts of this village had on the outcome of the war, how the village could have been wiped out by the Gestapo at any time, how simply lucky they were.

And yet—what had happened in Le Chambon *was* good and it *did* happen. Experiencing it changed Hallie's life. It gave him utter clarity about his own deepest commitments:

> I, who share Trocmé's and the Chambonnais' beliefs in the preciousness of human life, may never have the moral strength to be much like the Chambonnais or like Trocmé; but I know what I want to have the power to be. I know that I want to have a door in the depths of my being, a door that is not locked against the faces of all other human beings. I know that I want to be able to say, from those depths, "Naturally, come in, and come in."[8]

Chambon made hope possible. Even though what happened there was precarious—perhaps, as Hallie much later reflected, "beyond all quotidian understanding"—and even though the precise circumstances that made it possible are not likely to recur, the very existence of Le Chambon "sets a precedent."[9] A certain kind of goodness, that of armed resistance to the Nazis' destructive power—killing to prevent further killing—was, indeed, necessary. Hallie himself had participated in it. But, he argued, there was in Chambon another kind of goodness, a purer kind, the goodness of helping rather than harming, even at great personal risk. This was a "plain fact." Real human beings had brought it about and other real human beings could hope to have the courage to emulate them.

Hallie saw *Lest Innocent Blood Be Shed* appear in 1979, an account that has been read and treasured by many ever since.

Without Philip Hallie, the dramatic story of Le Chambon would never have been told. Fortunately for us, he retells and extends this story in part 1 of the present book.

Stories

Le Chambon set Hallie on a course that he continued in all the work that followed. Well after writing about the village, however, as he thought about his own life, he realized that he could not truly identify with the Chambonnais. They awed him, but they seemed set apart. Their goodness had to be called (by us, if not by them) a heroic, almost superhuman virtue. He felt that he had to find other exemplars far closer to his own troubled condition of mixed feelings and motives. He knew the many faces of evil by heart; he would have to try now to explore some of the many faces of goodness.

With great trepidation, Hallie decided to study the German general, Julius Schmähling, who oversaw the region of the Haute-Loire and yet who seemed to have permitted Chambon to do its work. Here was a truly ambiguous goodness—a faithful German soldier who protected Jews! Despite misgivings, he had to try to come to terms with this man. At the same time, Hallie, himself a lover of sailing and the sea, became fascinated by the American sea-man, Joshua James, who spent his life rescuing shipwreck victims in the teeth of (real) hurricanes. Here was another sort of goodness—disciplined helpfulness and skillful courage, taken up as a way of life. Pursuing James allowed Hallie to explore our varied human relationships to the forces of nature, relationships which have all too rarely entered the purview of ethics. Finally, coming home, out of his own work with a Middletown drug and alcohol rehabilitation program for young people, Hallie found himself asking how its visionary and tireless founder, Kätchen Coley, came to devote her-self to her seemingly impossible dream.

What is it, inside these people and in their worlds, that allowed *their* kinds of goodness to happen? This was Hallie's driving ques-tion. He was still wrestling with his accounts of these people in the last months of his life. It is thanks to the labor and love of his wife Doris, with whom Philip shared everything, that we are able to have the results of his efforts in the stories of the present volume.

How should we read them? Very much, I think, as we read

those in *The Paradox of Cruelty* and *Lest Innocent Blood Be Shed*—as essays, in the spirit of Montaigne, in which Philip is seeking to show what he, Philip Hallie, given his very particular nature and history, has found exemplary in the lives and work of these other, very particular people. We will learn how these people affected him, and what he has come to believe about human good and evil after living with them as he has. If he's done his job well, we will *enjoy* reading about these people too. We will have been enlivened by their stories and induced to make our assessments of them—and their author—part of an enlarged ethical reflection of our own.

Ethics

Ethics, as Hallie saw it, particularly life-and-death ethics, is rooted in a belief in the preciousness of all human life. We can express this as a general principle—one to the effect that we ought to respect and care for each and every human being—just as we might formulate other ethical principles or rules. Such formulations are indeed useful in certain ways, but they are abstract. About them, about how to justify them or to apply them, endless theoretical debate is always possible (even necessary). The belief that *founds* ethics, on the other hand, is *not* an abstraction, not a general principle, a doctrine or a teaching, but something concrete—an "imaginative perception of the connection between the preciousness of my life and the preciousness of other lives."[10] It is a perception that enters and helps form a person's *ethos*, or character. A vital perception which infuses feeling and motivates action. The challenge of the ethical life is "keeping that perception green."[11]

Here is where stories come in. In an article he wrote during the time he was working on the stories in this book, Hallie explains their role:

> True narratives of the deeds and passions of particular human beings are especially revealing . . . not because they lead to statistics or other large generalizations . . . [but] because they *show* us something, something particular, and yet something of large significance. . . . In stories, the ethos of a particular human being can seize you. . . . In a true story, a part of history is captivating now and memorable afterwards.[12]

That's the point: It is stories—better yet, true stories—that can seize the imagination, captivate it and, entering our memories, help to form who we are and how we act. Our ethical formation depends on them. That's why biblical stories and family stories are so powerful, and why the stories about Julius Schmähling, Joshua James and Kätchen Coley can be important to us. That's why the stories of Frederick Douglass and Le Chambon, or of Adolf Eichmann, for that matter, are important—they "involve an awareness of good and of bad things that goes beyond the awareness of general ethical rules or ideas." Beyond the generalities of mere "cautionary tales" too, such stories give us an awareness that is rich in the detail and messiness of real people living real lives, an awareness at once aesthetically pleasing and practically effective. And crucially: "Not being bullied out of this awareness means not forgetting the stories."[13] Remembering, telling and retelling them, keeps the awareness of good and bad things alive.

Remembering, telling and retelling tales of good and evil, moreover, is what helps to create and sustain an *ethical community*. Hallie never quite put it this way, but it is, I think, what he meant. It is what all of his work is ultimately about. He spoke at the close of *Lest Innocent Blood Be Shed* about "a community of ethical belief" of which he felt himself and his family and the Chambonnais to be a part. "It is not," he says, "a homogeneous community. It has atheists in it, devout Christians in it, and Jews."[14] They all believe in the preciousness of human life. But not only in an abstract sense. What *really* ties them together—and reaches out to any others of like mind—is that "imaginative perception" connecting good and evil in their own lives to that in the lives of others. What connects them, that is, what helps to give them a common *experience*, is the stories they share linking the preciousness of their own lives to other lives, stories that fire their imagination and inspire what they do, however imperfectly, from day to day. Philip Hallie's great contribution, in this book and the earlier ones, is to have added, in a powerful way, to our treasure of such community-creating stories.

There is much more to ethics, to be sure. We need continuing, careful ethical analysis of difficult situations. These days we are all too aware of the conflicts of good with good and of the inevitably tragic character of our attempts to respect the preciousness of human life in all we do. There is no easy solution to the question of abortion, for example, or of capital punishment, or to the question whether or in what way it might be right to help another person to die rather than to live. Ethical judgments in specific cases are often terribly complex and require more than exemplary stories to go on.

Hallie knew this very well, but he wanted to insist, nonetheless, that there *are* clear cases, there are *some* "plain facts" in ethics that we must not let ourselves be "bullied out of." That it's good for a person, any person, to be nurtured and helped when in need and bad to be tortured or starved are such facts. And, he thought, the stories of Chambon and Joshua James, as well as of Auschwitz, "can display as 'plain fact' the 'true north'—or the 'true south'—of ethics, the clear cases which might help us to take our bearings when we study more problematic cases." [15]

Not everyone accepts these ethical facts, of course. The religious zealots of Montaigne's sixteenth century did not. Nor do racists and Nazis today. They are not likely to be persuaded either—although some have been. The range of their ethical sensibility closes out certain people for ideological reasons that are almost impossible to overcome. To understand this, we have, again, to see what "ethical facts" are. In Hallie's view, they are not impersonal facts for some kind of pure reason or given in some inherited doctrine, disconnected from the feelings of particular people. Rather, they are personal and communal facts. They are the rock bottom experiences of communities of human beings, felt in their bodies and articulated in their shared stories, in the "imaginative perceptions" they have connecting themselves to others. It is not surprising that such perceptions differ, for people find themselves in differing circumstances and they share differing stories. Hallie, in his Montaignesque way, says:

> For those who believe in the absolute preciousness of life, there is no proof that the feelings and images involved in such a belief are correct or even plausible. They can only show their beliefs, the way a mother can show how precious her child is to her by rushing without hesitation into a fire to save it. [16]

But part of this "showing" is also telling the dramatic story of such mothers and children, and of other real victims and their rescuers, in the hope that one's hearers—even some of those who may have disagreed—will be moved to enlarge their "imaginative per-ceptions" and come to see the evil etched in the faces of those vic-tims and the goodness in the deeds of those rescuers. All one can do, in the end, is to give personal testimony to one's own experi-ence. In the stories in this book, Philip Hallie is doing just that.

Solidarity

When I think of Philip Hallie, I think of him vividly present—a warm and loving man, a dear friend from whom I always learned, a man who struggled with himself and to understand himself, and who had the twin gifts of ethical insight and the power to commu-nicate it. When I think of Philip Hallie the philosopher, I think of the compassionate skepticism of Bertrand Russell, the radical ethi-cal openness of Emmanuel Levinas, and the embodied mysticism of Gabriel Marcel. But chiefly, I think of Albert Camus—brooding, inward, striking out at humankind's history of violence and murder, refusing to yield to despair. They seem, in certain respects, so much alike. Philip felt it and admired him deeply.

Philip met Camus once early in Philip's life, and he described that meeting in one of the last pieces he wrote. They talked about the problems of writing and Philip discovered Camus's own admi-ration for Montaigne. After Philip had left the room at Gallimard's where they'd talked, Camus ran down the stairs after him with Philip's glasses that he had left behind. "*Je t'ai trouvé*," he said, "*t'ai trouvé*," and he hugged Philip. It was a bodily communion Philip never forgot.

As he tried to sum up what Camus meant to him, Philip put it this way:

Two French words summarize the mood (for it is a mood and not a philosophic system) that Camus expresses in his writings and in his life and death. The words are *solidaire* and *solitaire*. Only one conso-nant separates the two words from each other, but the difference between aloneness and union is immense. We are born into separate-ness; then, after a while, we die into it; and, in between our birth and our death, we are strangers and afraid in a world we never made. And yet we feel solidarity with others, love, from time to time. We live out our lives apart from others and as a part of others.[17]

I think it is this abyss of separateness that Philip was struggling with all his life. Happily, he found more, much more, to affirm than Camus had. He found solidarity as a husband and father and as a teacher and friend. And he was able to see, and to show others in his writing, the possibilities of life-giving solidarity in our lives together. As he felt it to be with Camus's hug, however, "The abyss of out-thereness is crossed, but it is not." As Philip shows us in the stories in this book, it is a kind of miracle when it is crossed; we need the examples of those who have crossed it; and each of us has to cross it anew.

Notes

1. Philip Hallie, *Maine de Biran: Reformer of Empiricism (1766–1824)* (Cambridge, Mass.: Harvard University Press, 1959).
2. Philip Hallie, *The Scar of Montaigne: An Essay in Personal Philosophy* (Middletown, Conn.: Wesleyan University Press, 1966), p. xvii.
3. Quoted in ibid.
4. Ibid., p. 151.
5. Philip Hallie, *The Paradox of Cruelty* (Middletown, Conn.: Wesleyan University Press, 1969), p. 7.
6. Ibid., pp. 139, 159, emphasis in the original.
7. Ibid., p. 6.
8. Philip Hallie, *Lest Innocent Blood Be Shed: The Story of the Village of Le Chambon and How Goodness Happened There* (New York: HarperPerennial, 1994 [1979, 1985]), p. 287.
9. Philip Hallie, "Scepticism, Narrative, and Holocaust Ethics," *Philosophical Forum* 16, nos. 1–2 (1984–85), p. 47.
10. Hallie, *Lest Innocent Blood Be Shed*, p. 277.
11. Ibid.
12. Hallie, "Scepticism, Narrative, and Holocaust Ethics," pp. 44–45.
13. Ibid., p. 46.
14. Hallie, *Lest Innocent Blood Be Shed*, p. 292.
15. Hallie, "Scepticism, Narrative, and Holocaust Ethics," p. 48.
16. Hallie, *Lest Innocent Blood Be Shed*, p. 274.
17. Philip Hallie, "Camus's Hug," *American Scholar* 64, no. 3 (Summer 1995), p. 434.

ACKNOWLEDGMENTS

I could never have realized my determined desire to publish my husband's posthumous book without the caring encouragement of loving friends and colleagues, eager to help with Philip's work.

I am overjoyed to be able to thank them here:

Bill Blakemore, former student, friend, and enthusiastic interpreter of Philip's philosophy, has been my steady ballast from the beginning, when I found and then read Philip's manuscript. He was always there with realistic words of encouragement, especially when I had self-doubts about my inexperience in this area of publishing.

Marjorie and John Compton listened to my many stories that were a part of the process, empathized with my tears as I read Philip's words, and worked hard themselves in preparing part of this book.

Richard Vann, respected colleague and longtime friend, read the manuscript and my afterword and without hesitation said "Send it to HarperCollins." Perfect advice.

Hugh Van Dusen, Philip's editor at HarperCollins, immediately brought me into the process of preparing the manuscript. His unquestioning acceptance of me in this publishing partnership gave me an uplifted feeling of confidence, which I badly needed. I am most grateful to him.

Copy and Production Editor Sue Llewellyn and Associate Editor Kate Ekrem at HarperCollins were always there for me with my questions of editing and protocol, and they were forever in good spirits with their responses.

Nancy Smith, a former editor, spent an entire day with me—as carpenters were noisily renovating her nineteenth-century house—

checking Philip's original single-spaced manuscript, covered with his handwritten editing, against the clean double-spaced one I had prepared.

I am also grateful to these colleagues, with the expertise in their specialties, at Wesleyan University who answered my various questions and who were so happy to help: Morton Briggs, Brian Fay, Rabbi Ilyse Kramer, Karl Scheibe, Jan Willis, Krishna Winston, and Jeremy Zwelling.

Walter Schmähling, from Munich, clarified some points about his father and the meanings and spellings of certain German words and expressions.

I thank the librarian at the reference desk at Russell Library in Middletown, who searched assiduously from the bookshelves to the Internet and found answers to my questions on remote subjects.

And I want to thank my children, Michelena and Louie, who perhaps were sometimes skeptical or amused at my intractable persistence in getting their father's book published, but who always gave me their love and understanding.

PART ONE

LIVING IN THE HURRICANE

1

STARS AND STORIES

1

One November night not long ago I looked out our kitchen window and I saw some of the stars of the constellation Orion mirrored in a puddle. In the winter huge, handsome Orion dominates our southern sky in Connecticut; around the state many calm bodies of water reflect it. In fact puddles, lakes, rivers, and oceans far away from Connecticut reflect the same stars. They have been mirroring them since long before that November night, just as they will reflect them long after my puddle and I are gone. Stars can twinkle in remote places as plainly as they can shine outside your kitchen window.

Our ideals, our most wholesome hopes for our species, are like those stars. They are beyond us, hard to live up to, but there they are. In fleeting people and passing events, like puddles of water they make their enduring demands here and there, gloriously and ingloriously, around our planet. One of these demands is that we help one another, or that at least we resist the temptation to harm one another.

After Cain killed Abel, Cain asked God, with some asperity, "Am I my brother's keeper?" And much of the rest of the Bible is an answer to that question. The prophet Isaiah reflected his answer in these words, "Correct oppression, defend the fatherless, plead for the widow," and many pages before and after the Book of Isaiah reflect the same reply.

But not only ink reflects it. Living human experience reflects it, and reflects it as clearly as living human experience reflects a cold no to Cain's question. For instance, the experience I know best is my own, and my experience is like the puddle outside our kitchen window, a tiny, temporary mirror of long demands. In the course of my life I have seen and felt many demands for help, and I have seen and felt many cold and hot refusals to meet that demand. I have been a son, a husband, a father, a grandfather, an inhabitant of the Cockroach Building in the slums of Chicago, a combat artilleryman in World War II, a teacher, and the president of a drug-and-alcohol rehabilitation group. I have helped strangers, I have hurt strangers, and I have not given a damn about them.

Strangers are different from beloved intimates: Helping is the nerve of intimacy, it is what intimacy is. Mutual love is mutual need satisfied. My love for my wife and children, and theirs for me, *is* the mutual satisfaction of our fleeting and enduring needs. Where there is no need there is no love. We are helping—even rescuing—one another in almost every moment of our intimacy. But strangers are something else. In French *étranger* means foreigner, outsider, "alien." Strangers are usually useless to us, irrelevant, separate from our lives. They satisfy no enduring need, nor do we satisfy an enduring need of theirs. Strangers do not need each other.

That is why helping strangers has always had an air of mystery about it for me. How do we sometimes manage to treat outsiders, useless aliens, as if they were our intimates? Our bodies—and to a very great extent our minds—are equipped to help ourselves. Our hands, our eyes, our mouths, our stomachs serve us; they do not serve irrelevant outsiders. My white corpuscles protect me from bacterial invaders by destroying them. They are not very hospitable to many outsiders. Their job, like the jobs of my nose and my mouth and all my internal organs, is me, me, me.

But strangers? Strangers, when you see them as the separate bodies they are, are alien skin-bags that enfold alien bones and alien organs. Toward the end of his last, ripest essay, "Of Experience," Montaigne wrote: "And on the loftiest throne in the world we are still sitting only on our own rump." When I look at my hairy self in a bathroom mirror I see a poor, bare, forked animal, a bag of bones and organs, standing alone. And when I look at strangers in shower rooms I see the same sort of skin-bags.

And yet, and yet—helping strangers happens. The creature that the poet e. e. cummings described as "this busy monster, manunkind" sometimes is a kind creature. The help it gives is as plain as a pikestaff and as real as the self-serving cruelty and indifference that make history a nightmare from which we have not yet awakened. How one bag of bones and organs can be moved by the needs inside another, separate bag of bones and organs is a lovely mystery to me, and it is a lucid mystery, one that happens—if we look and are a little lucky—before our very eyes. The plain fact is that the Belgian priest Father Damien helped the lepers on Molokai until he died with them.

And such a fact is important, because without it human lives would be nastier, more brutish. Like a piece of music or a painting that seizes our attention and then dominates our memory, a man like Father Damien catches us in a net of song. Busy monster, manunkind that I am, I have been joyfully moved by the sight—or even the thought—of people risking and giving their own lives to save those of strangers.

But excellent things are as difficult as they are rare. We are in fact visibly, palpably, bodily separate beings; we are far more indifferent to the needs happening within other beings than we are willing to admit. The fact of help happens, but it is also a fact that we read in our morning newspapers and in our history books with mild interest to the point of boredom about the sufferings and deaths of strangers.

And so helping strangers is not only a useful and pleasing reality, and not only a biological mystery, but also an ideal, something as excellent and as difficult as it is rare. This monster manunkind is so busy taking care of itself that the good physician, Saint Luke, had to put into his gospel Jesus' story of the Good Samaritan. If we were not a species of self-serving skin-bags, he would not have felt called upon to tell Jesus' story about a naked, half-dead victim of a mugging between Jerusalem and Jericho who was helped by a stranger. A world of Good Samaritans would have found nothing interesting or challenging in the story of a Good Samaritan. His story reflects a realizable ideal.

And the ideal is this: Treat those who need you as if they were intimates, as if you were living in a loving transaction of mutual help with them. In the Good Samaritan story this means treating all those who need you as "neighbors," and it means treating your neighbors as solicitously as you treat the stomachaches, infections, and constipations inside the precious bag of bones and organs that is you. In the nineteenth chapter of Leviticus this demand for intimacy is spelled out: "The stranger who sojourns with you shall be to you as the native among you, and you shall love him as yourself."

Because the intimate communion of strangers is a mystery for unattached sacks like us, helping strangers is like an untouchable but plainly visible star. We look up to it because it is there, because it is beautiful, and because it is useful. But because each of us is irretrievably separate—especially from strangers—we need all the help we can get from lucidly mysterious stories like that of the Good Samaritan.

2

For forty years now I have been studying and teaching ethics in and out of American college and high school classrooms, and I have found that ethics is nothing more or less than the sporadic human effort to see and to treat all human lives as equally precious. I have found that the soul, the *demand* of ethics, has very little to do with abstract words like "good" and "evil." General principles, like John Stuart Mill's greatest happiness (which makes an action good insofar as it tends to create more pleasure than pain) or Immanuel Kant's categorical imperative (which makes an action good if the idea behind it can be made into a universal law without conflicting with itself), do not make the goodness in helping as clear to me as do the stories of the Good Samaritan or Father Damien. At their best Kant's and Mill's philosophies are ingenious generalizations about particular people doing and feeling particular things. I can understand their principles only insofar as I can understand a story that embodies them. If there were no stories to illuminate their principles, I would not understand the principles at all. They would be words about words about words. Somehow, when my fellow philosophers put the rich, accessible details of stories into their somewhat artificial languages, the stories lose much of their arterial vitality and much of their meaning for me. Stories of help and harm lose much in the philosophers' telling.

And so for years I have asked myself: Why not go to the stories themselves? Why not go to the horse's mouth? Why not go to where the action and the beauty and the ugliness are?

It has been said that God dwells in detail; be that as it may, it is plain that good and evil and help and harm dwell in detail, or they dwell nowhere. Our useful and beautiful ideals are in danger of ecological impoverishment if they dwell only in abstract formulas or proofs and use a few "good examples" to explain those formulas or proofs. Good examples are like good boys and girls: They are seen but not heard from. They are severely disciplined to fit the preconceived abstractions of their parents.

And so what you will read here are not general proofs or definitions concerning goodness and evil, but stories of owned personal experience about a beautiful, useful, and utterly clear mystery that has to do with the enhancement of human life.

3

Montaigne tells a story about a woman who used to watch the great philosopher Thales walking along and gazing, star-struck, up at the heavens. One night, while his face was turned upward and his feet were going their own way, the woman threw something in front of him, and he stumbled. She wanted to remind him to look to the world around him before he gazed at other worlds. She and Montaigne knew that supercelestial ideas and subterranean conduct often go together. They both believed that we should look closely at our own and our neighbors' behavior lest we become word-struck and stumble through the only lives we have absent-mindedly, with minds absent from our lives.

And so this book is not about distant Orion after all. It is more terrestrial than celestial. It is only a matter of a few true stories that may be useful and beautiful to think about for a while. If you are a single-minded admirer of impersonal, abstract principles, you may find it better to leave this page unturned. I am the woman who would make you stumble. What do you need me for? I cannot help you.

2

THE COCKROACH
BUILDING

1

When I was about nine or ten years old, in the middle of the Great Depression in the early thirties, my family lived in a gray stone tenement in the near southwest side of Chicago. The building took up most of a city block on Roosevelt Road, across the street from Douglas Park. Almost every dark corner in our one-room apartment had cockroaches in it. Kill them as you would, they kept coming out of dark places or running toward them. An important part of life for my father, my mother, my younger brother, and me was smashing them. One night when it was snowing hard, I was lying in bed with my brother. We were looking out at the snow falling on Douglas Park, making everything look peaceful. Suddenly I noticed that a string of cockroaches had crawled up my right shin and onto my kneecap. They were a little army on the march, and they reminded me of the war we were always waging in that crowded little apartment.

Everybody I knew called our tenement the Cockroach Building, and when I remember our dark toothless-mouthed entrance to it on Roosevelt Road, I seem to see the words "The Cockroach Building" carved in stone over the door, though I am almost certain that my memory tricks me. Whenever I walked into that brown, dirt-strewn hallway I felt that I was walking into a battle. It wasn't only the cockroaches that I usually thought of; it was the bitter fights between my poverty-baffled mother and father.

The only chairs in our room were wooden chairs my mother kept painting a bilious yellow-green. A few years before she died she told me that she hated that shade of green but that it was the only color paint we owned. One of the main reasons we were poor, aside from the depression itself, which had made him lose his dairy farm outside of Medford, Wisconsin, was that my father had a violent temper, especially when he was bossed around. Mind and body he was a farmer, who had found all the excitement and peace he needed living in the slow rhythms of crops and cattle. But all this had been taken from him when he could not get enough money from his potatoes and butterfat to make his mortgage payments.

Now that the land was gone, all he had was his tied tongue and his hanging powerful arms, and all he wanted was to be left alone to keep his own pace. He had lost his self-respect when he lost his farm. And what had taken the place of that self-respect was occasional fury. He was fired from one job after another for refusing to follow orders, or for following orders too slowly, and then exploding with rage when his bosses threatened him, until jobs were very hard to come by, hard even for the Great Depression. At last he became a taxicab driver for the Checker Cab Company. I think he liked sitting alone up there in the driver's seat where nobody could boss him around because he knew Chicago better than any of his passengers did. And there were some thrills in it: For instance, he occasionally drove Al Capone a few blocks and got a kind word and a five-dollar tip. My father looked like Capone—dark and short and heavy, with a quiet anger burning behind the eyes.

My mother had auburn hair and gray-green eyes, and she was full of energy, full of stories and dreams. She had done some vaudeville singing before a goiter operation hurt her voice. After the operation her mother saw to it that she married somebody before my mother got too old. Love had nothing to do with the marriage. They were both forced to marry by their parents.

They used to fight terribly, she bitterly complaining at being trapped in this cockroach hole, and he silent or muttering absurd sentences like, "Do you think the rain'll hurt the rhubarb?" My mother often became enraged by his sluggishness and repetitiveness, and all his clumsy mouth could do in reply was snarl out a few harsh words at her. During their almost nightly battles my younger brother and I cowered in a corner. We were afraid that they might kill each other, or that he might leave us and we would starve to death. The feeling my brother and I shared was fear. We seemed to be part of a war to the death, a war whose purpose we did not understand.

The fights I remember were almost always in the evening, and so I was glad when my mother sent me out before supper to get a loaf of bread. The grocery store was only a block or so away, but even with that short distance to walk I was often attacked by some blond boy or other from the nearby Polish neighborhood. I always bought Silvercup Bread, with its red-and-white-striped wrapper and its doughy texture, and I remember one hot summer evening when I was coming back from the store, a boy of about eleven or twelve came out of a doorway of the Cockroach Building and jumped me. He threw me down on my back, sat on my belly, grabbed my shoulders, and started snapping my head against the pebbly sidewalk. He must have had a sense of rhythm, because while he was snapping the back of my head against the pavement he was yelling in a singsong way words I shall never forget: "You damned Jews! You damned Jews! You killed Jesus! You killed Jesus! You damned Jews!"

I tried to tell him that I didn't do it, but the words would not come out, and I began to feel a wetness at the back of my head. Perhaps my eyes were beginning to glaze over and he got frightened; whatever the reason, he gave me one slap on my left cheek and ran away.

I came back into our apartment with the Silvercup Bread turned into a ball of dough, and there was my mother talking to her younger brother Louie. They both had auburn hair and gray-green eyes, and they were sitting facing each other on those light green chairs and laughing when I came in. I closed the door, and my uncle turned to me with a smile, and then a frown. I worshiped him and he loved me. I felt blood running down the back of my neck, and because he was there I was trying not to cry. In that deep voice of his he almost whispered, "Pinky! What happened? Whose blood is that? Is it yours?" I told him it was, and then my mother took me to the sink to wash my face and neck and the back of my head.

He stayed for supper, and while my mother was washing the dishes he took me aside and told me to come to his basement apartment the first thing the next morning—to hell with school. He was going to teach me street fighting. He had done some professional boxing in Chicago, but he had given it up because it was addling his head and damaging his handsome face. I remember him as a man without fear. He was never at a loss.

The next morning the lessons began, and they were simple: Get the first blow in, usually with a knee in the groin. The trick was to keep the angle of your knee small, so that your leg could not be grabbed behind the knee while you shoved your knee hard under the groin. The "horse kick" had to be so well placed, and so hard, that it was the last blow. We practiced and practiced. My uncle was a relentless, even a cruel teacher. While we were practicing his face was hard and pale. I have never forgotten how shocked I was to see the cold hatred in his eyes, those eyes that had always looked upon me with love, while he was showing me what to do.

For the rest of our last year in the Cockroach Building I was the cock of the walk. I leaped up when my mother asked me to get a loaf of Silvercup Bread in the evening, and with or without the bread in my hand I walked *toward* any blond boy of about my age if I saw blood in his eye. It ended suddenly if he made one aggressive move, and it ended exactly the way my uncle had taught me to end it. After a while the blond boys left plenty of space around me, and when I walked down Roosevelt Road I felt freer and happier than I had ever felt before. I felt that I was the only one in my family who could carry his head high. My uncle had rescued me from the coercion of despair, and he had done it by empowering me.

A few years later—in 1934—I was throwing a ball with a friend in the street just around the corner from the Biograph Theater. Out of the silence of a windless hot night we heard some bursts of gunfire, and we got to the alley next to the Biograph just in time to see two plainclothesmen pushing John Dillinger's body into what we called a meat wagon, a black police ambulance. The toes of Public Enemy Number One were pointing up, and his feet were sticking out of the wagon when we arrived. A policeman took a foot in each hand and with one disdainful thrust shoved him far into the wagon.

As my friend and I were standing in the alley, I noticed a pool of blood on the bricks. Then a woman in a blue dress with big white polka dots walked up to the blood, looked around, and drew a handkerchief from her purse. She delicately turned her shoulders, bent her knees, and dipped the handkerchief in the pool of blood. Then she jammed the bloody handkerchief into her purse, snapped it shut, and minced away. Later I heard that people were selling handkerchiefs and paper that were supposed to have been dipped in Dillinger's blood. They charged a half a dollar for the handkerchiefs and a quarter for the paper. This was my Chicago in the thirties.

2

Except for two beautiful moments. One moment came just before nightfall every Friday. Our apartment had two narrow windows fronting on Roosevelt Road. Nobody on the outside could see into the windows because we were five stories up, and there were no buildings on the other side of Roosevelt Road, only Douglas Park, far below. Still, in the twilight of each Friday evening my mother pulled down the shades, "for privacy," she said. Then she put thumb-thick white candles in the two brass candlesticks her mother had brought from Romania before my mother was born. She waved my brother and me to the white, tin kitchen table that was the only table in the apartment, put a shawl over her bright hair, lit the candles, and then sang a few incomprehensible words over the flames, words that sounded like "Mebechibish, mebechibish, mebechibish." She did not know what the words meant—her mother had used them, and she was repeating her mother's Sabbath prayer.

Before she began to sing the words, she glanced at my brother, Milton, and me with a peaceful joy in every glint and line of her face, and my brother and I bowed our heads while she sang the familiar but incomprehensible words. The peace my brother and I felt so near to the candlelight and so absorbed in the darkness of the room still comes into my mind sixty years afterward, like a ghostly visit from her. The memory of this ceremony of innocence will be with me, I am sure, until my dying day.

A few times my brother and I asked her what the little ceremony meant, but her answer was never much help to us, especially because she never took us to a synagogue where we might hear an answer to it. Once when we asked her about the Sabbath prayer, she smiled and said the Shema: "Hear O Israel! The Lord our God, the Lord is One." But she never explained the Shema. She had learned this by rote too, in all innocence, in all ignorance.

But I had a feeling about what the candlelight and the darkness and the ceremony meant. I felt—as plainly as I felt my breathing in and out—that they meant that the world, the universe, was one universe, and that the universe was God. There was nothing mysterious about my feeling. It was just a feeling that there are no real boundaries, no real separations between the parts of this distracting, endlessly happening world, no ceilings, no floors, no walls. Just one vast, simple ocean of peaceful feeling. And I had this feeling on Friday evenings, when I closed my eyes, bent my head, and heard my mother singing her little incomprehensible prayer, "Mebechibish, mebechibish, mebechibish." When I closed my eyes, all separations, all combat, all fear, all bitterness were gone. And my oceanic feeling had such a quiet joy in it!

But it came only on Friday evenings then, and I seem to remember that when I was young I all but forgot the feeling from one Friday to the next. It was as irrelevant to my everyday life as last night's sleep. When do the young look back at a deep sleep and call it as real or as important as their waking hours?

My reality was my everyday experiences of hunger, of thirst, of fear, of occasional pride, of the struggle between my mother and my father, of my clumsy combat with would-be bullies. All I remember now, except for those Friday evenings, is need, need, need, and the fleeting satisfactions of need, need, need.

I remember another time when hurting dropped away, an occasion very different from prayer.

Before we moved into the Cockroach Building, we lived in the near southwest side of Chicago, near Sixteenth Street and Crawford Avenue. We lived in a basement apartment across the street from a big, clean, redbrick-and-granite building called Marcy Center. It was a Christian missionary house right in the middle of a Jewish neighborhood. But none of the blond, smiling people at Marcy Center ever tried to convert us to Christianity in any obvious way. They made Marcy Center a clean, unthreatening place for children who lived in a hard neighborhood. Milton and I played Ping-Pong, basketball, and baseball there.

But the games were usually turbulent. Then one June day a tall, heavily curved lady came across the street from the center to our dark apartment and asked my mother if she would allow me to go to a vacation camp in southern Michigan, a place called Council Camp. My mother had learned to trust the Marcy Center people for their gentleness and generosity, and the whole danger of conversion to Christianity never occurred to her. In those days she thought of herself mainly as a Chicagoan (she had been born and raised in Chicago), not as a Jew. We used to celebrate Christmas—stockings, gifts, and all. Only during the Friday evening ritual did our Jewishness seem important to her, and the ritual never mentioned any separations or distinctions or conflicts.

And so I remember her wiping her hands down her apron, shaking hands with the Marcy Center lady, and walking with her back to the front door, nodding her head and smiling. I was going to Council Camp! I had never set foot outside of Chicago.

The weeks I spent at camp were ecstatic. I still remember, after more than sixty years, the song we sang, to the tune of "School Days":

Camp days, camp days, good old Council Camp days.
Reading and writing and playing ball,
Watching the birds as they sing and call,
Drinking fresh milk three times a day,
Washing our hands after we play.
Council Camp, Hooray! Hooray!
Council Camp, Hooray!

Everybody seemed to love everybody else. In the morning we children sat down at wooden tables with big bowls of cereal before us, and we ate the fruit-laden cereal gleefully, because we were hungry, but also because there were lovely pictures and happy sayings at the bottom of every bowl. When we finished we showed them to each other.

The last day of camp all the children went out to the little lake near the barrackslike huts where we slept. We had put on our bathing suits, and we were told that the boys and girls should go into the water and kiss each other good-bye ("Very gently! Very gently!"). We were seven- and eight-year-olds, and I do not remember the faintest stirring of sexuality in all that running and splashing and kissing. All I remember is the noisy wet sprinkling pleasure of that hour. I remember how, before we left the lake to shower and dress, some boys started kissing each other, very shyly. One of my camp friends kissed the top of my hand, and I picked up his hand and kissed it.

But Council Camp was an event that was irrelevant to my daily living, just as the Friday evenings were irrelevant. At the beginning of "The Over-Soul" Ralph Waldo Emerson wrote: "There is a difference between one and another hour of life, in their authority and subsequent effect. Our faith comes in moments; our vice is habitual." He goes on to say that our brief moments of faith, extraordinary as they are, may have more reality for us than our everyday, habitual experiences. This was not so for me then. Everyday life was my reality.

Nowadays I often remember that week in Council Camp, and I am moved to the verge of tears; but *then*, in the throes of my childhood, after the week was over, it was almost nothing to me—almost nothing but gone. The ordinary, not the extraordinary, was where I mainly lived. The times when boundaries fell were like dream-times. Danger, loneliness, hunger, and thirst had far, far more reality for me than the isolated dream-times. Struggle ordered my days.

3

This was my Chicago in the thirties. And so the mid-forties were no shock for me when I went into combat against the Germans in World War II. Reality for me was battle. Combat was what life was really about, under the veneer of the social politeness and the dreamy words I found in books. A power struggle was waiting to burst out at any moment in the streets, at home, everywhere. For much of my youth my most frequent nightmare was feeling myself riding in the front seat of my father's Checker Cab and then suddenly feeling the cab burst into flames.

The day our Forty-fourth Infantry Division landed in Normandy, near Montebourg, I found myself talking lightheartedly with another enlisted man, whose name was Alvin Silverman. We had stepped out of our "prime movers," the tractors that pulled our big guns. The next morning we would be on our way to the front. I remember that behind my friend, in the west, the darkening sky had a layer of purple under a layer of orange. He and I had been trained in Iowa City to do intelligence work with the Resistance in France, and here we were in an infantry division going off to shoot hundred-pound artillery shells at the Germans! That was the army for you: It trained you to do one thing and then made you do something entirely different. We didn't mind the switch—the whole business was an incomprehensible blackish green dream, like the color of our vehicles and guns.

Silverman leaned back on a tractor tread, looked at my face under my outsize steel combat helmet, and burst out laughing. I asked him what he was laughing at, and he said, "That helmet looks ten sizes too big for you. Imagine! A Jew, loaded with fire power, with a 155-millimeter howitzer and the whole Forty-fourth Infantry Division behind him, moving *toward* the Germans!" In Iowa City, during our training for intelligence work, we had been taught a great deal more than most Americans then knew about the mass murders in Central Europe. We knew that the United States and the other Allies were not fighting the war to help the victims of the Nazis. The propaganda and the facts that we had been taught made it very clear to us that we were fighting for the survival of democracy, not in order to rescue Gypsies or Jews or other victims of Hitler. But we also knew that the faster we got into Central Europe, the faster the mass murders would end. And here we were, two would-be victims of Hitler, all dressed up and ready to go, right down those Germans' throats! Standing there alongside our prime mover in our too-big combat helmets it was all dark fun. Having all that power was almost like being the cock of the walk in front of the Cockroach Building.

A few months later we crossed the Rhine north of Mannheim, and we dug in our artillery pieces on a long ridge overlooking the city from the north. After we adjusted our fire so that we were hitting the key spots in the city, we started firing shells with white phosphorus warheads, instead of the usual high-explosive fragmentation warheads. The white phosphorus made stone buildings and people burst into flame. It was one of the few times we could see the effects of our artillery. Usually we fired our guns by using number coordinates, and we heard about our hits or misses on the telephone; now we actually saw what we were doing. I remember salivating while I carried shells to be rammed into the breech-block—salivating with a lust for burning that city down there, as if I were going to eat something delicious.

When the garrison to the north of the city surrendered and we passed through the remains of Mannheim, I saw burned legs and arms separated from their torsos, and once I looked down from my prime mover and saw the blond, beautifully symmetrical head of a young man, with its SS cadet cap still firmly on it, but with no body and hardly any neck. The eyes were open. They were light blue and seemed to be looking dreamily up at the sky. The skin on that face had never known a razor or a beard.

There was a stench, but there was mainly joy, the joy of winning and of being alive amid all that death. And right after we cleared out the snipers, there was the ecstasy of rumbling swiftly toward the open city of Heidelberg on our way to smashing the Germans once and for all. Harm stopping harm, power stopping power. That's all there was.

Since I had experienced months in combat, it was only natural that my first book on ethics was about power. In my book *The Paradox of Cruelty* I wrote about the kind of evil that involves the crushing and grinding of people by other people. The main idea of the book was that the slow smashing of a person—or of any other sentient being, for that matter—happens only when the victimizer is comparatively strong and the victim is comparatively weak.

Most of the stories I told in the book were about black slavery in the United States, where the overwhelming physical, economic, and political power of the white majority helped make the "peculiar institution" of slavery a way of life for hundreds of years. Of course the cruelties of slavery happened for many reasons, but it seemed clear to me that they could not have happened if the blacks had had as much power as the whites. If the blacks had had more economic or political power, instead of suffering the systematic humiliation and the unsystematic physical torture of slavery, they could have stopped the cruelty by challenging the whites toe to toe. Then there would have been combat between relative equals, not powerful, cruel victimizers and powerless victims. Or there might have been cooperation and peace, mutual respect. But with that power imbalance, cruelty persisted—like a spark jumping from a highly charged body to a less highly charged one. And it kept happening long after the institution of slavery died.

The big blond boy who sat on my belly and slammed my head down on that pebbly sidewalk in front of the Cockroach Building was bigger and stronger than I was. His power over me had made his cruelty possible, though the long history of Christian anti-Semitism, his upbringing, and his own personality helped make him use his power the way he did. Power ascendancy is not enough to make cruelty happen: It needs the help of hatred, fear, loathing, and many other elements. But without some ascendancy of force over weakness, cruelty does not happen.

When I wrote the book on cruelty I had in mind the way the word "power" is used in physics. Physical power is the ability to overcome resistance swiftly, and during slavery the whites could overcome the resistance of the blacks with dispatch, just as in the early thirties John Dillinger could speedily overcome the resistance of his victims and of society at large. But in 1934 the power of an organized society struck him down in a few minutes. By mid-1933 the Nazis of Germany had the power easily to overcome the resistance of their victims, and that power made it possible for them to perpetrate the cruelties of the Third Reich. Early in World War II the Allies had no real ascendancy over the Axis powers, and the war dragged on until the Allies could achieve that ascendancy. It was at this point—in 1945, when the industrial and military power of the Allies was at last fully mobilized—that Nazi Germany and its cruelties could be stopped with as much speed as that power permitted.

Having come to believe all this, I found it evident that the way to slow cruelty or to stop it is by narrowing the power gap between the victimizer and the victim. I stopped being a victim when I developed the skills and the brutality of a street fighter in Chicago, and the law enforcement officials of the United States stopped the murderous career of John Dillinger by outwitting and overpowering him. Even though World War II was not fought for the purpose of eliminating the cruelties of the concentration camps, only the military skills and firepower of the Allies stopped the many cruelties that Nazi Germany was perpetrating in Central Europe. Love did not do it. Life was a battle.

4

In the little dramas that were my life, mindless power had been the main actor, at the center of all the actions and passions I knew. The cockroaches in the Cockroach Building had the power to climb over my body at night and paralyze me with disgust; that heavy boy sitting on my belly and snapping my head against the pavement had the power to overcome my feeble resistance. The first time I struck back at one of those blond boys I felt that this was the way things were: You push or you get pushed; you have enough force to stop those who are trying to smash you, or you don't. Life was like two boys pushing and being pushed, until the weaker one backed down or was beaten down.

The stockyards of Chicago were only a couple of miles south of the Cockroach Building. One day one of my teachers brought my classmates and me to see them. The first room we walked into was the slaughterhouse. There was a soundproof sheet of glass between us and the animals, and since there were no sounds or smells to distract us, we looked at the slaughter with some detachment. A bull walked down a chute under a man who was standing on a platform with a sledgehammer raised above his head; the man slammed the blunt chunk of metal down just above the eyes of the bull, the bull fell, and then it was carried away on a moving strip of steel. One bull we saw seemed as stalwart as the Minotaur in his labyrinth; the sledgehammer only staggered it a little. After it was hit it shook its black head as if shaking off a fly, and it stepped onto the moving strip of metal with heavy grace; but a man standing on a platform above the moving strip finished it off with an ever more gigantic hammer. Again the greater power prevailed, as it has prevailed for thousands and thousands of years. The image of that bull finally dropping to its knees under the heavy hammer has remained clear in my mind for more than half a century.

Such memories were the elements of my deepest beliefs about the nature of life. The bruisers were the survivors, not the gentle ones. The creatures with the most concentrated and sustained ferocity stayed alive and thrived, just as I thrived during the last few months of our life in the Cockroach Building. My Uncle Louie had taught me two things: discipline and explosion. If you disciplined yourself in this world, and you knew when and how to explode in a burst of energy, you could overcome your opponents fast. Then—and only then—you could thrive.

All during the years after the war when I was learning to enjoy literature, the arts, and philosophical reasoning, I knew that these were escapes from reality, not reality itself. Ideas about good and evil that I read about in the history of philosophy and theology were ways of making people dream their way out of reality—for a while.

I kept recalling the killing of that great bull in the Chicago stockyards. I was one of those people Emerson called "perceivers of the terror of life." I came to see all living things as predators, prey, and propagators. I saw nature and civilization as a smoldering conflagration of violence, with nations being born and surviving in bloodshed, with cold salt seas swallowing ships full of people, and with leapers and eaters cracking the bones of the weak and eating their flesh. I saw a rude and surly world under the skins of civilization, and help in such a world had to be rude and surly in order to work. Anyone who had dared to claim that love conquers all would have had to sell me a long and dubious interpretation of the word "love."

3

MAGDA AND THE GREAT VIRTUES

1

One April evening, years after I wrote my book on cruelty, I had to get away from my family. I was feeling angry and frightened, and I was angering and frightening them. I have usually been able to walk right out of a mood, and I thought I would walk the mile to my office, even though there was nothing that had to be done there. For more than a month I had been feeling a mixture of fear, bitterness, and fury. I was not sleeping much, and sometimes when I was talking with students I found myself suddenly trembling with rage or bitterly silent over some trifle. I did not have much hope that I could walk out of this mood—it was more like insanity—but I was willing to try anything. Early in the walk it crossed my mind that if I killed myself, my wife, Doris, could pick up the pieces of our family life with her strong Italian peasant hands, and manage. The thought gave me a little peace.

When I got to my office I threw open the tall windows near my desk and looked down on the skimpy lights of Middletown and the darkness of the Connecticut River Valley. I was more miserable than when I left the house. I had walked *into* my mood, as if it were a sucking swamp with no moonlight on it. During my walk I had thought about a man in a white smock bending over a metal table with a Gypsy or a Jewish child on it, cutting off a toe or a finger or an ear without anesthesia. I wanted to tear the head off the man, and I wanted to pick up the child and run with him or her out of the killing camp. But I could do nothing. After all, these "medical experiments" on children were in the past, in the forties, and far away, in Central Europe. I could do nothing about them but think my murderous, useless thoughts. And shadowing even these shadowed thoughts was my fear that this busy monster, manunkind, would do such things again, now that we have learned how.

For months I had been studying the torturing and killing of children in certain of the Nazi concentration camps. Imagine an Aryan adult clothed in the professional authority of a doctor and supported by the terrible power of a triumphant Nazi Germany in the first years of the forties. Then imagine a bone-thin Jewish or Gypsy child lying naked on a metal table with a funnel built into it to drain off the blood. Finally, imagine the doctor bending over the child and cutting the child's body and soul to pieces. If an imbalance of power between the victimizer and the victim has a lot to do with cruelty, what greater power difference could there be than this between a Nazi doctor and a Gypsy or Jewish child? Many firsthand sources had helped me to see the so-called medical experiments on children in mind-shuddering detail, and my previous work on power and cruelty had made me feel duty-bound to study the Nazi doctors and their child-victims. Here was the ultimate cruelty, the ultimate evil, writ large in clinical detail and often illustrated with photographs.

But I had learned that you cannot go down into hell with impunity. You must pay an entrance fee, and an exit fee too. I had found myself consciously imitating the victimizers by yearning to victimize them, or I had found myself feeling like one of the victims on one of those bloody tables. Worse yet, I had found myself seeing my son or my daughter being dissected there. But the deepest torture I experienced was the shame I felt for my occasional objectivity. Sometimes as I studied the records, the reports, the photographs, the letters, I found myself consciously imitating those monsters who could watch all this without a qualm. I was looking at it all with a cold eye so that I could analyze it. If Wordsworth is right, and "we murder to dissect," we countenance murder when we analyze murderers with indifferent eyes. The bystanders, the spectators, the vast majority of manunkind have usually supported the handful of actual murderers by their refusal to feel and to act.

Only the stars are neutral. There were relatively few hands-on murderers among the Germans of the Third Reich; but they were
empowered by the vast, self-serving majority of the population,
who did not bother to see or to feel what was happening.

In the course of more than fifty years I had discovered that I
tended to become what I was fascinated by. If I looked long and
hard at something it became my mirror. I had become a street
fighter when I was fascinated by street fighters; I had become a
killer in combat when I was fascinated by soldiers in combat, American and German. Now I was staring into the face of cruelty and I
was becoming cruelty itself. I was becoming one participant after
another in the transaction of cruelty. Life was hellish, not only for
me but also for the people who needed me and wanted to love me.

That evening in April I sat down at my desk without a shred of
hope. I turned my chair around so that I was facing my books on
the history of France. I had believed for a long time that only sheer
force could prevail over the besetting need in manunkind to smash
the weak. I was certain that neither love nor persuasion but only
force could change the power imbalance that helps make cruelty
happen. The U.S. Army had taught me—before and during combat
in Europe—to understand many aspects of the French armed resistance against the German occupiers of France in the forties. Resistance leaders were my most admired heroes of all the fighters in
World War II. Limited to using only small arms, they still did much
to weaken the Germans and to shorten the reign of Hitler's cruel
empire. That evening, looking at the spines of my books about
them almost rescued me from despair. Despite all the temptations
to cowardice and indifference and comfort that the French endured
in those days, the Resistance had mustered what power they could,
and they *did* something to change the power imbalance between
the Germans and the French.

In the economy of brute force that is the natural world in which
we live and move and have our being, there is a vast difference
between combat and mere cruelty, though I have seen moments of
cruelty in the midst of combat. Usually combat involves at least
two relatively powerful combatants who are more or less equal in
power. Cruelty involves no combatants, only an active victimizer
and a more or less passive victim. Cruelty is a one-way street; the
crushing and grinding go only from the victimizer to the victim. In

the wild and in so-called civilized society the parties involved in combat trade blows, and they both share the dignity of being active, of taking the initiative from time to time. They both strike. The mere thought of the Resistance had always been a tonic to me.

And so I reached out toward the wall on that cool evening, and my hand fell on a book with some essays about the Resistance. The book happened to open on an essay called "Chambon-sur-Lignon." I had been trained by the army to know the centers of the French Resistance, and since the name of this town had never appeared in my information sheets, I was going to turn the page. The village could not have been important, or the story was a lie or an exaggeration. The army knew the centers of resistance in France. But by the time I had glanced at a few paragraphs I knew why I had not heard about the town: It was a center for *nonviolent* resistance against the Nazis, and the army had taught me only about violent resistance.

When I got to the bottom of the third page of the article my cheeks started itching, and when I reached up to scratch them I found that they were covered with tears. And not just a few tears—my cheeks were awash with them.

For a moment I thought that the tears came from my despair and my near insanity. Then I realized that the itching had started when I began to read a story about two boxy khaki-colored buses coming into the gray granite village square of a French mountain village on a Saturday afternoon in the summer of 1942. The buses had twenty policemen in them; they had come to this little village perched on a high plateau in order to pick up the Jews whom the Protestant villagers had been sheltering. The policemen were from Vichy, the center of the French puppet government that was trying to live cozily with the German conquerors and occupiers of France.

The two buses parked in the wide village square, and the police captain called on the head minister of the village and demanded that he give him a list of all the Jews in the village. The Huguenot pastor refused. Then the police captain ordered the minister to sign an official poster that told all the Jews in the village to turn themselves in to the police in order to avoid risking the lives of the families who had been sheltering them. According to the eighteenth article of the armistice between France and the conquering Germans, the French had to "surrender on demand" any foreign refugees. Again the minister refused. The police chief warned the pastor that if he did not sign the poster within twenty-four hours, he and his fellow minister would be arrested—by noon of the next day, Sunday.

The police slept in their buses all Saturday night, and on Sunday morning they raided the houses of the village looking for Jews. But during the night the Jews had been evacuated into the woods around Le Chambon, and the police could find only one Jew to put in their big buses. While he sat in the bus the villagers shoved gifts—mainly food—through the window by his seat. Soon there was a heap of gifts beside him. Later the buses left, with the one prisoner and his precious gifts.

On Monday morning he was released, because he had documents to prove that half of his grandparents were non-Jewish. At this time being only half Jewish could exempt people* from arrest. He reentered the village square, pulling a double wagon with the gifts on it. As soon as he entered the square the villagers appeared and stood around him greeting him with affection. He tried to give back the food the poverty-stricken villagers had given him, but they refused to accept it. They felt that he had earned it by his suffering. And they rejoiced in his return to the safest place in France for refugees. They sang him a song of greeting.

What was there in this story about a tiny village standing on a high plateau in the mountains of central France that made me weep? What had wrung these tears from me, body and soul, the way you squeeze a grape, seeds and all, to get its juice, though the seeds make the juice bitter? It was joy that did it, overwhelming joy, which can squeeze tears out of us as suddenly as misery can.

Much of my joy came from sheer surprise. All of a sudden I was witnessing help that was not lethal or even wounding. All of a sudden I was seeing in my mind's eye flesh-and-blood actions that did not involve force or threats of force, and yet these actions were preventing cruelty and murder. I was seeing spontaneous love that had nothing to do with sheer, brute power. I was seeing a new reality,

---

*Under the laws of Vichy France, persons with one-half Jewish ancestry could be exempted from arrest.

undergoing a revelation: Here was a place where help came from love, not from force!

For most of my life I had been a bitter opponent of the belief that love can conquer all. A loving smile on my face would not have stopped that blond boy from torturing me. Too often I had found nonviolent people to be too patient—patient with the murder of others. They would let their nonviolent resistance go on and on while thousands of victims of violence were being killed every day. I had long felt that the amative optimists were sentimental ideologues who would start off by being the accomplices of the strong by their refusal to fight and then would be crushed themselves. It was a fact that Hitler encouraged and even rewarded pacifism in countries he had conquered, while he destroyed the pacifists in Germany.

But surprise was not my main reason for weeping. I had found myself fascinated by this particular meek-looking Jew sitting in the big bus surrounded by people who cared for him enough to endanger their village. And because I had so often become what I was fascinated by, I had found myself sitting there in the bus looking out through his eyes and seeing those precious foodstuffs pile up beside him. I was, in a sense, Steckler (later I found out his name), and I was weeping tears of gratitude.

There was still another reason for those tears, a reason that had more to do with the villagers than with Steckler. It had to do with the rarity of pure goodness.

Most of the old ethical theories and commandments present ethics as a friend of life and an enemy of death. And so those theories and commandments praise help and condemn harm. They celebrate the spreading of life with two sorts of ethical rules or ideals: negative and positive. The negative rules are scattered throughout the Bible and other ethical documents, but Moses brought the most memorable ones down to the West from Mount Sinai: Thou shalt not murder, thou shalt not betray. . . . These rules say no to the deliberate extinction of life and joy. On the other hand, positive rules are also spread across many ethical documents. For instance, the Bible enjoins us to be our brother's keeper. These rules say yes to the protection and spreading of life.

The naysaying ethic forbids our doing certain harmful things, and the yeasaying one urges us to help those whose lives are diminished or threatened. To follow the negative ideals you must have clean hands; but to follow the positive ones you can be less hygienic—you can dirty your hands doing something helpful. If you would be your brother's keeper you must go out of your way. The negative ethic is the ethic of decency, of restraint. It is terrible to violate it—to be a murderer or a liar—but obey it and you could be a dead person. A corpse does not kill and does not betray. Moreover, you could obey the no ethic by being silent, and it was the silent majority in Germany and in the world who fed the torturers and the murderers with their silence. The murderers and the torturers drank the silence like wine, and it made them drunk with power.

On the other hand, the yes ethic demands action. You must be alive if you would meet its demands; sometimes you must even put your life on the line. You must go out of your way, sometimes very *far* out of your way. In combat I had to become a killer in order to help stop Germany in its tracks. I had to violate the no ethic in order to help stop the many tortures and murders that Nazi Germany was perpetrating in Central Europe.

For me Chicago was not neighborly. For me preventing the diminution of life *demanded* the diminution of life. It demanded that I make a choice: him or me, violating the ethic of decency or violating the ethic of help. The federal government and its state and municipal agencies had a similar choice: John Dillinger or us. They smashed Dillinger, and when they did so Americans celebrated the fact that defenseless American citizens would no longer be robbed and murdered by him. In situations like this, to be a friend of life is to be a killer. Harm is the price you have to pay for help, indecency the price you have to pay to preserve decency. You have to be willing to say no to clean hands. My experience had led me to believe that human beings are doomed either to be clean-handed and helpless or murderous and helpful. I knew no one who was both clean and noble.

But in that story about the village of Le Chambon I found people who were both. Here were people in this slaughterhouse of a world who avoided hating and hurting life and at the same time prevented murder. Imagine this happening in Europe at this time! In a wicked world, of which I was an integral part, they were, *tout simple*, good. It was the ethical purity of the villagers that drew my gratitude from me with my tears.

There was still another reason that I wept, and it is almost impossible for me to express with any clarity. The reason is the Friday evenings I used to spend with my mother. After sunset as my mother prayed over her mother's brass candlesticks, her prayers became part of me. When I was very young, she fascinated me when she prayed. After I learned to fight in the streets I stopped standing by the table while she prayed. Action was more exciting than prayer. But before I learned to fight I watched her bent over the lights with her own mother's black shawl on her head and pray to the vast darkness around us.

Before I became fascinated by people other than my mother, she drew me into a mystery that was not a problem to be solved, not the mere absence of understanding. Problematic mysteries usually irritate me; they puzzle and discomfit my will. But the shadowless mystery in which my mother prayed was something positive and comforting. It was full of peace, and it was as real as the candlelight. The peace we felt circulated in and around us like the air we breathed. That peace was God. To her and to me on those Friday evenings, God was a sweet, enfolding feeling. That feeling seemed to unite us with each other and with the rest of the universe.

I had never completely forgotten our need for that vast intimate moment over the candles. Sometimes after she prayed she recited the Shema. What the Shema meant to us both was that the whole universe was one law-abiding communion called God. All the walls and the ceilings were as nothing. We just stood there in those moments of peace feeling at one with each other and at one with the light and the darkness. But ever since I began to believe that life is really a life-or-death struggle, I had put all this behind me.

In the story about the villagers surrounding the khaki-colored bus with Steckler, I saw a lucid instance of human communion. Reading it I suddenly felt the kind of joyous comfort I had felt on those Friday nights. After those fights began on the sidewalks near the Cockroach Building, the world had been clear and exciting, but uncomfortable. Now, for a moment, and for a while after that moment, there was root-room in me for comfort and for peace.

2

But only for a while. I had to know more details about Le Chambon and its people during the war years. My motto was still the motto of the American physician-poet William Carlos Williams: "No ideas but in things." I had this little story about the village square, and some general ideas about the meaning of what happened in that square, but they were not enough. I knew that the word "good" is derived from some old German words whose base is *gath*, meaning "gathering" or "unifying." Goodness has something to do with bringing people together, with communion. And the story was certainly a story about human solidarity. Many Frenchmen and -women had been imprisoned or killed by the occupying Germans and their puppets for doing far less for Jewish refugees than the Chambonnais were doing. They had gathered these refugees into their homes, and they had decided to endanger their own lives, and to deplete their own very meager food supplies, in order to protect them. If this is not solidarity, there is none.

But such abstract ideas were not enough. And neither were the reasons for my weeping when I first read the story of the buses. I wanted to find out exactly how communion happened in Le Chambon. Reality and realistic hope do not reside in the vagueness of abstractions or in the dark boundlessness of sobs. Reality resides in detail or it is nowhere.

By chance on the day I first read about Le Chambon and experienced a momentary "conversion," or turning away from my past beliefs, my dear friend the philosopher John Compton was visiting at Wesleyan University, where I was teaching. And since he is so dear to me, I showed him the story and told him about my feelings about it. He heard me out patiently, and then he told me that he had worked in this obscure mountain village for a summer! The minister of the village who had defied the puppet police in the square of Le Chambon, André Trocmé, had founded an international school—Cévenol College—before World War II, and people from all over the world had come to build its buildings and to attend and teach its classes, as well as to brush up their French. John had been one of these people.

Compton drove me up to Massachusetts to meet two elderly Americans who had done much to establish and nourish Cévenol

College. They told me that Pastor Trocmé was long dead, but his widow, Magda Trocmé, was living in the south of France in a Protestant convalescent home, recovering from a serious operation. I wrote her, told her of my feelings about the story of the khaki-colored buses, and begged her to talk with me about the village and the whole rescue operation. She told me to come visit her. And so began my long love for Magda Trocmé and for the village she and her husband had turned into the most effective rescue operation to occur in France during World War II.

The afternoon we first met in her austere little room in the Protestant convalescent home called La Sympathie, she started to tell me the story of the village. She started from the beginning and told me about the first refugees who came to Le Chambon in the winter of 1940–41, and she told me that from 1940 through 1944 the village was a sanctuary for any refugee from any country, but mainly for those from Central Europe.

The weeks that had passed since I first read the story of Le Chambon had begun to distance me from my first reaction to the story. I found myself reverting to my long-held belief that life is fundamentally violent and self-serving. But as I listened to this endlessly energetic Italian (her maiden name is* Grilli), all I could hear were phrases like "the refugees" and "these frightened people." It was not Magda Grilli Trocmé she was talking about, it was the victims of the Holocaust. The more I listened, the more I found myself vacillating beween my Cockroach Building beliefs and my new ones—until she mentioned the fact that children were central to the rescue operation.

Almost casually she said that the rescue operation began with the idea of sheltering children whose parents had been deported to the concentration camps. An American Quaker, Burns Chalmers, gave Pastor Trocmé this idea, and Trocmé gave the idea a body and a soul by making Le Chambon a shelter for the foreign orphans.

What was plain was that life-giving had happened in the village. The children were the ones I had been studying in my work on the medical experiments; they were the ones on whom the most immense cruelties of all had been visited by the Nazis; they were the powerless ones who I had thought could be saved only by

* Magda Trocmé died in October 1996, at the age of ninety-four.

sheer, brute force. And here this somewhat gruff, matter-of-fact stout-hearted Italian was telling me how—for more than four years of danger and poverty—thousands of the most utterly helpless human beings in Europe had been saved from torture and death by a few mountain villagers.

I began to ask myself: Why fight spring? Why not simply face the vivacious facts instead of trying to explain them away? I remembered a few lines written by one of my "adorable geniuses," the Jesuit poet Gerard Manley Hopkins:

> My own heart let me more have pity on; let
> Me live to my sad self hereafter kind,
> Charitable; not live this tormented mind
> With this tormented mind tormenting yet.

Magda Trocmé's stories were about feeding and educating the children and about putting them into *équipes*, or teams, and spiriting them across the great rugged mountains and through the police and military units that patrolled the mountains between Le Chambon and Geneva, Switzerland. The children, not the Chambonnais, dominated her stories. I had come a long way away from the Cockroach Building and from the killing camps. There was not an ounce of self-vaunting or hatred in her stories, only adventures. They were not stories of the hate-filled death-in-life I had known in Chicago. They were facts about lives saved, about human solidarity being tested and proved.

That first afternoon, overwhelmed by these thoughts, I found myself whispering half to myself and half to Magda Trocmé words that came from the same deep levels of my being from which my tears had sprung: "But you are good people, good."

To anger an Italian is usually not hard to do (I know this because I have a wife with a vast Italian *famiglia*), but I was still surprised and a little daunted at Magda Trocmé's sudden and vehement reaction to my words. "What did you say? *What*? 'Good'? *Good*?"

I muttered something like, "Yes, I mean—"

She interrupted herself and me in a quiet, sympathetic voice: "I'm sorry, but you see, you have not understood what I have been saying. We have been talking about saving the children. We did not do what we did for goodness' sake. We did it for the children. Don't use words like 'good' with me. They are foolish words."

I put her words down in my diary immediately after I went back to my little room near Magda's in La Sympathie. I am glad I put them down. They have helped guide the rest of my thoughts about the village of Le Chambon and about the rescue of about five thousand refugees, most of them children. They have helped me to keep my eyes on the facts.

3

After about a week of conversations I finally noticed that I was tiring Magda Trocmé. Her operation had been very serious, and she was no longer the unendingly energetic thirty-year-old Florentine who had come to the village of Le Chambon before the war. And so I asked her how I could continue my study. I asked her if there was someone in Le Chambon I could go to, someone who could introduce me to villagers who had been part of the rescue activities she and her husband had led.

"Well," she said in her rapid, slightly hoarse voice, "there is only one person who could help you to get to know the people of Le Chambon in the shortest possible time. That person is Édouard Theis. Édouard was the pastor who worked with my husband almost from the very beginning. His wife, Mildred, is dead, and he spends much of his time visiting around Europe and America with his many daughters. I'll find him for you, and I'll tell him to meet you in the square of Le Chambon—in, say, a week."

I was astonished at her absolute certainty that she could command Theis to leave his daughters and come to Le Chambon on a few days' notice. When I asked her if she was quite sure that he would come, she looked at me with almost violently energetic eyes and said, "He will come." This was the first moment I confronted the unshakable will of Magda Grilli Trocmé. It was not to be the last.

And so it happened that a week and a half later, on a cold, gray, windy day, I arrived in the granite square of Le Chambon on a bus from Valence. As the bus pulled into the square, I saw one bent figure waiting in the cold. Instead of a winter coat against the winds on this high plateau he wore two worn, thin coats. (He later told me that the inner raincoat was a kind of insulation, but from what I observed the inner coat was as threadbare and as full of holes as the outer one.) When I stepped out of the bus he took my bag, without asking me my name. He did say "Ah!" and he smiled shyly at me. He was slender and very tall for a Frenchman, with a full aquiline nose that came to a point right over his upper lip, and his eyes were watering from the cold.

The first complete sentence he uttered was a suggestion that it might be a good idea for us to go up the Route de Lambert—just behind the square—and take a cup of tea with Gabrielle Barraud. We got into his old car. It looked as if it could not make its way from the square to the Route de Lambert, but it got us up, around, and behind the square and the little railroad station with no trouble at all.

He knocked on the door of a gray stuccoed house. The door opened, and for a split second I was shocked to see no one before me. But then I heard a rapid, lucid voice, and looked down at one of the smallest persons I had ever seen. She was in her late middle age, very quick in her movements, and as voluble as Theis was silent.

We sat in her brown living room overlooking Le Chambon and the Lignon River. We talked about my trip, and then the conversation seemed to end. Theis had not told her who I was or what I was doing, and I did not know where to begin. And though—I found out later—Magda Trocmé had given Theis some account of what I was looking for, he simply sat there sipping his tea and dreamily looking out of the window toward the river. Looking at his drooping spirit I remembered that his wife had died not long before.

After a long few moments I asked Madame Barraud what she did in Le Chambon during the war years. She told me that she kept boys in her house, fed and sheltered them, and helped them with their studies in Trocmé and Theis's Cévenol College. She told me that she was Alsatian and that her husband had been a Communist who did not especially like having these nonpaying guests in their house. She said that she managed to keep him from knowing that most of the boys living there were indeed nonpaying. Then, with a twinkle in her eyes, she said, "You see, I would not let my Communist left hand know what my Christian right hand was doing!"

She said that whenever she used to see Magda or André Trocmé down there on the square, she would ask them, "Well, what do you need me for today?" Magda always had an answer, a whole list of things for her to do for the children in the Barraud *pension* and elsewhere in the village. But Pastor Trocmé was a little less driven; he would bow to her as deeply as his bad back would permit and say, "Oh, you're right to ask that! I talk to you now only when I need you!" And once the tall man offered to hug her, but he said that he would have had to put her on a box to do it with that back of his, and there was no box nearby.

'While Theis and I were leaving her home, I turned to him and asked, "Pastor Theis, didn't you ever hate these Germans for what they were doing to the parents of these children?" As we climbed into his car he kept his head down, thinking. He could be silent longer than any man I have ever met. Finally he said, "No. Not really. No. You see, we weren't only trying to save the children; we were trying to keep the Germans from staining their lives with more evil."

For me this was the most surprising thing I had heard since I first read the story of Le Chambon. Years before, when I had been in southern India at a conference of Eastern and Western philosophers, one of the young Brahmins at the conference, Daya Krishna by name, had tried to explain *ahimsa* to me. He had told me that the word was basic to Hinduism, and it meant "having no desire to kill." Like most of the Western philosophers at the conference, I did not understand how such a doctrine could be followed in a world full of predators and prey. It was an empty doctrine for me, a privileged position for elite Brahmins to hold, and a mystical flight from the realities of natural and social life. But the absence of mortal hatred was part of the way of life in Le Chambon, and it had worked. The people of Le Chambon had saved many people by living without hatred, and the village had somehow survived for four long, murderous years. They and their story at last explained to me what Daya Krishna had meant.

4

In the course of about two years I lived in the village several times, and I gradually learned that the mere recitation of the facts about those four years was not *telling* enough. The little afternoon train that brought children and other refugees into the railroad station between the square and the Route de Lambert almost every day, the privacy of the whole operation—only Magda, Édouard Theis, and Pastor Trocmé knew its full extent—because a villager had to know only about the refugees in her own house, so that she could not be tortured into telling where the other refugees were, these and many other facts showed me much, but they left me unsatisfied. I felt as if I had not put my finger on the nerve—if nerve there was—of the rescue operation. I did not know what made the operation happen.

The most obvious answer was Pastor Trocmé himself. His powerful sermons in the boxy granite temple inspired the people of the village to follow in the footprints of Jesus, loving all humankind and willing to suffer, even to die, for others. He was part and parcel of the great tradition of imitating Jesus the Christ. Above the main entrance to the temple of Le Chambon there is carved a quotation from the Gospel according to Saint John: *Aimez-vous les uns les autres*, "Love one another." His sermons explained this command of Jesus, but, eloquent and lucid as they were, they were too close to the old abstractions of theology for me, too full of language that did not move me. His ringing and yet practical sermons helped me to put the actions of the village squarely in the center of the great traditions of Christian ethics, so that I could readily speak and write about them; but they did not help me to feel the force that nerved the hands and minds of the Chambonnais through four years of danger and hunger.

One story I heard did this for me—for a short while.

The first winter of the German occupation of France was a brutal one. The snows in the rugged Cévennes Mountains were deep, and the winds made them drift wildly, so that transportation of foodstuffs and other necessaries was sometimes impossible. This difficulty, and the Germans' rape of France during the first summer and fall of the occupation, left Le Chambon in desperate need of the necessities of life.

One day, very early in 1941, one of the refugees somehow made her way to a farmhouse on the outskirts of the village. She had heard about the so-called gray market, farmers who would sell you some of their products more cheaply than the black market and more plentifully than the rationed legal market did. The refugee was from somewhere in Central Europe, I still do not know where. Her head covered with snow that had the shape of her shawl, she pounded on the door of the farmhouse. The door opened, and the farm woman and the refugee looked at each other. The farm woman invited her in out of the cold without saying a word.

For a little while the refugee stood in front of the big fireplace with the snow melting from her shawl. She gathered her strength and asked, in broken French, "Eggs. Do you have eggs to sell for my children?"

Apparently she was the first refugee the Frenchwoman had seen; in any case, the farm woman looked deeply into her eyes as they stood in front of the fire and asked, "*Êtes-vous juive?*" "Are you Jewish?" As early in the history of the persecutions as this was, the refugee must nonetheless have been terrified at the question. Here she was, separated from her children, who were up in the village, and she was being asked the question that could take her back to the horrors from which she had come. But the question was direct, and she felt that she had to answer it. "*Oui,*" she said.

The farm woman ran to the staircase opposite the fireplace and called up the stairs, "Father, children. Come down! Come down!"

The terror of the refugee must have been great when she heard that shout, and she must have trembled even there in front of the big fire that supplied heat for the whole house. And there she stood, alone.

Then the farm woman added, still looking up the staircase, "Come down! Come down! We have in our home today a representative of the Chosen People!"

For many of the people of Protestant Le Chambon the Bible was a book of truths and commandments to be taken literally (*au pied de la lettre*). The word of God had to be taken that way or not at all. The felt allegiance of the Chambonnais to God's words convinced them in their heart of hearts that they were doing God's work by protecting the apple of God's eye, the Jews.

Well and good, but the more I thought about this story the less it told me. All *I* knew and felt about the Jews as the "Chosen People" was that we were chosen to suffer hatred century after century, especially when people were in need of some comparatively defenseless group on which to blame their troubles. All I knew was that we were a target of choice, a chosen mark.

And then something happened that was very telling for me. One bitter cold winter's day I was attending a service in the temple with Pastor Theis. It had been an exciting sermon by a young man who wanted to explain the Protestant Reformation not in terms of theological differences between Protestants and Catholics but in terms of different ways of loving God.

When the service was over, Theis and I rose and headed for the main doors to the temple with the words *Aimez-vous les uns les autres* carved in granite over them. Theis, wearing his two ragged coats, was leading the way. As we passed the alms box, he put his right hand through the hole in the inner coat and pulled a fistful of paper money out of his trouser pocket. Without looking at the money, he put it all in the box.

I was shocked. He was a poor minister. Mainly his tiny parish gave him food and wood for his fire. The little money he got was vital to his existence.

After services the Chambonnais gather in the gravel yard outside. Except when the mountain winds tear their nerves to shreds, they stand talking together a few feet from the main door to the temple. A few people were greeting Theis at the moment I caught up with him, and there was the usual silence that emanates from him. I broke the silence by blurting out, "But Monsieur Theis, all that money you gave—where is it going? How will you do without it?"

As soon as the words were out of my mouth, I regretted them. Theis and the people near him just stared at me. After what seemed a long silence, even for Theis, he almost whispered, so that I could barely hear him in the powerful mountain wind: "Oh! I don't know. Somebody needs it."

And that was the end of his answer, but not the end of my thoughts about his answer. While we were standing about in the gravel yard there came to my mind one of the phrases Gabrielle Barraud had half-whispered again and again when somebody thanked her for something: "*Toujours prête à servir,*" "Always ready to help." It occurred to me that I had heard the phrase in the village, usually with those exact words but also in many other forms. I remembered Magda Trocmé's greeting to new refugees whom she suddenly found standing in terror and in hunger outside the presbytery door. Usually she had only one thing to say: "*Eh bien, naturellement, entrez, entrez.*" And they came in, "naturally," "of course," and that was that. They remained with Magda's family sharing the beans that could never be cooked enough to soften, so that they *ping*-ed when they were dropped on the plates. They remained for a few hours, a few days, or sometimes for a few months, and even a few years. They had come into a world where people were always ready to help.

For centuries people have understood that habit can be second nature, as much a part of our feelings and behavior as the physical traits that we were born with. People have also known that habit can be made of invisible, intangible iron: It can be hard to break. The iron of the habit of helping was embedded in the soul of Magda Trocmé, as it was embedded in the soul of Gabrielle Barraud and others in Le Chambon. "*Toujours prête à servir*" is the iron axiom of villagers in Le Chambon. From this habitual readiness helping the refugees sprang "naturally," like sparks from struck iron.

For Magda and for many of the other villagers, helping was automatic. They weren't conscious of it, let alone proud of it. Are we conscious—or proud—of our breathing when we are in good health? Helping and receiving help were like breathing out and breathing in to Magda Grilli Trocmé. She expected the women of the village to help her as matter-of-factly as she expected herself to open a door and invite a refugee into the middle of her busy, dangerous life.

She was never a prayerfully religious person. For the most part she has left theology and preaching and prayer to her husband. He had the habit of seeking perfection by imitating the perfection of Jesus Christ; but she had the habit of helping those who came to her in need. She did not go out to seek refugees, as her husband had done in Marseilles with Burns Chalmers, when Trocmé got the idea of making Le Chambon a village of refuge for orphans of the Holocaust. But she helped anyone who came to her, "*naturellement.*"

Standing there facing Theis in that windblown churchyard high in the Cévennes Mountains, I realized that the habit of helping meant more to me than Pastor Trocmé's habit of perfection. I could not understand very well, being who and what I am, the glorious habit that had led him to guide the village in its perilous rescue operation, but I could, to a degree, understand the habit of helping. This I could understand, though I had almost forgotten to face it over the years, because fighting was more exciting than loving— and more useful in the worlds I inhabited.

Somewhere the American philosopher William James once wrote that habit is the flywheel of civilization; well, the habit of helping was the flywheel of the rescue machine of Le Chambon. Before I found Le Chambon I had thought of rescue—when I had thought of it at all—as the use of force to save somebody. I knew that for a long time, in the language of English and American law, rescue meant the forcible removal of somebody from legal custody. Not only in my own life, but in novels, in films, and in newspapers, strong-arm tactics have usually been the only means of rescuing somebody from harm. The hero or the cavalry arrives, and they save the victims by making the victimizers bite the dust. And so, though I was no stranger to compassionate help, I experienced one of the greatest shocks of my life when I realized that such an undramatic thing as the habit of helping was the living core of the rescue operation of Le Chambon.

This quiet habit of efficacious compassion is easy to recognize when it stands before you in the words and deeds of a parent or a lover, but we are reluctant to recognize it when we see it happening between strangers. Sometimes we suspect the helpers of having ulterior motives. Self-serving is everywhere, it seems. We think of parents and lovers as close, and so we see how they can feel the force of the other's needs. But between strangers it is more of a mystery. Imagine taking the suffering of a person dangerous to your welfare and the welfare of your loved ones, a person who barely speaks your language, whom you have never met before and expect never to meet again—imagine taking the suffering of such a person as a motive for your own action!

This was a mystery to the philosopher Arthur Schopenhauer, this feeling your way into the skin of a stranger. But though it was a mystery, he founded his grim and beautiful ethic on it. The reason he felt able to do this was that though it is a mystery, it is plainly visible when it happens. We can see unselfconscious, heartfelt help happen as plainly as we can see pain happening in a child who has been struck hard across the face. We can see active compassion happening if we are its beneficiary, but we can also see it clearly if we are only its spectator. And the story of Magda Trocmé and the other people of Le Chambon-sur-Lignon during the first four years of the forties is the lucid story of such help.

5

Habit is by definition not inborn. It takes upbringing to create it and to make it firm enough to resist the temptations of fear and greed and cynicism. Magda Trocmé raised her four children in the presbytery of Le Chambon in such a way that danger-provoking, food-consuming foreigners were accepted affectionately into the very center of their lives. She bade them enter the lucid mystery when she opened the heavy presbytery door to dangerous strangers with an "Of course. Come in, come in."

The Italian novelist and essayist Natalia Ginzburg has made a distinction beween *piccole virtù*, little virtues, like thrift and caution, and the great virtues, like compassion and generosity. She has urged us to stop drumming self-serving penny wisdom into the heads of our children—they will learn it, she says, with a little prodding and by using their own common sense. In fact the little virtues *are* commonsensical. They protect our hides—that is their main function. If all we do for our children is pound into their heads reasons for protecting their own hides, their second nature will be as wide as the confines of their own self-seeking skins. One's life is usually about as wide as one's love. But if we make the often-impractical great virtues part of their lives, their second nature will be as wide as their love.

I have found that such a distinction as the one between hide virtues and heart virtues is somewhat hard for Americans to take seriously. We seem to understand best such ideas as are found in Benjamin Franklin's *Autobiography* and *Poor Richard's Almanack*. Maxims like Franklin's make sense to us: "God helps them that help themselves." "Get what you can and what you get hold;/'Tis the stone that will turn all your lead into gold." Franklin's writings—many of which he drew from folk wisdom—are reasonable, practical. They are the ripe fruit of millennia, and of the eighteenth-century Enlightenment, when reason and common sense seemed to have replaced once and for all the dark mysteries of the Middle Ages and of the religious wars of the Reformation.

Consider thrift, one of the basic little virtues, and one that Franklin cherished. He enshrined it in many maxims, including this one: "Spare and have is better than spend and crave." For many parents thrift is one of the prime virtues they wish to see their children possess. Money is portable power, and people want to hold on to power, if only in order to preserve their lives and their comforts. The little virtues of caution and self-interest were the Cockroach Building virtues I saw all around me in my youth in Chicago.

Even though Magda Trocmé during World War II was as poor as we were in Chicago during the depression, she was not much interested in money. The Trocmés kept all their ready cash in a box, and once in a while Magda would complain with absent-minded surprise when she opened the box and found it empty. When there was money in the box she never knew how much it was. Only the orderly mind of Jispa*—a tiny spinster who came from a Protestant religious community in 1943 to help the Trocmés for a few months and stayed with them to the end of her life—concerned itself with penny wisdom. It was Jispa who kept the presbytery financially alive. Little virtues are necessary—they are our handgrips on palpable, lucid reality—but they were not enough for the Trocmés in the presbytery. In fact they were hardly noticed. Poor Richard's wisdom was not an important part of the spirit of the presbytery of Le Chambon.

It is easy to explain and to praise thrift and shrewd caution. Such explanations and praise are part of a long tradition that uses our heads to save our hides. This tradition—from far earlier than the Enlightenment—rests on the sound biological and psychological bedrock of self-preservation. Early to bed and early to rise does indeed help to make one healthy, wealthy, and wise.

But being motivated by another person's needs is not so easy to justify or describe in commonsensical terms; it is not always conducive to self-preservation or comfort or security to help desperate strangers. When you try to talk about the heart virtues, you are always in danger of lapsing into vague sentimentality and empty metaphor, or into mysteries that only faith can embrace wholeheartedly.

This is one of the main reasons why all the villagers I talked with in and away from Le Chambon avoided all talk about help and courage. They were too clear-headed, too commonsensical to use such talk. They had acquired the silent habitudes of the great

* A name she invented by taking letters from the French for "the joy of serving in peace and in love."

virtues, and these habits were like bedrock in a garden: the spade turned when you tried to penetrate them, and bring them up to the light of day. Deeds speak the language of the great virtues far better than words do. Shrewd Ben Franklin could write books about penny wisdom; Magda Trocmé and the other people of Le Chambon simply practiced the great virtues without ever trying to explain them. The diminutive Gabrielle Barraud never tried to explain to her thrifty Communist husband why they should have dangerous nonpaying guests in their house. Words limp outside the gates of the mystery of compassion for strangers.

During the first terrible winter after the fall of France, the first refugee came to the door of the presbytery of Le Chambon. Unaccustomed to receiving illegal refugees, Magda Trocmé went to the mayor of the village to ask him to give the woman identification papers. There were frequent surprise checkups, and a foreigner was always in danger of deportation if she could not show the right papers. When Magda asked the mayor to give her the necessary papers, he—quite rationally—said, "What? Do you dare to endanger this whole village for the sake of one foreigner? Will you save one woman and destroy us all? I am responsible for the welfare of this village. Get her out of Le Chambon tomorrow morning, no later."

The voluble and eloquent Magda was wise enough not to argue against the little virtues. Their logic was above reproach, as far as that logic went. From that winter's night on, she never tried to justify the saving of refugees to the custodians of the welfare of Le Chambon or of France. She worked closely only with people who had more in their hearts than protecting their hides.

Only the mysterious virtue of taking other people's needs to be the motive of her own actions was natural to her. Still, important as it was in her life, she hardly ever noticed it. It was part and parcel of her psychological anatomy.

Once, when I was finishing my research on the village of Le Chambon, Magda Trocmé came to spend a week with us on our small farm in Connecticut. It was a couple of weeks before Passover, and we were in the kitchen together. I was preparing horseradish that I had just dug up in our garden. Horseradish is called *moror* in the Passover service; bitter herbs remind the participants of the bitter enslavement of the Jews before the exodus from

Egypt. I had peeled the long roots and cut them into thick little chunks. I put them into our food processor and started the grinding, but I soon stopped: The fumes were blinding my eyes and making it difficult for me to breathe. My wife took over. She is a descendant of many generations of Italian peasants, who were accustomed to suffering, but she did not stay at the job much longer than I did. My daughter, Michelena, who fights her way through suffering with valor and even bitter happiness, tried. She did not last much longer than her mother had.

During all of this Magda was sitting at the kitchen table thinking about a question I had asked her. I think the question was about her youthful lonely years in a Catholic convent in Italy. When Michelena sat down beside her with her eyes blood red and full of tears, Magda noticed what had been going on. She touched Michelena's shoulder with her heavy hand, stood up, went to the grinder, and finished the job. When she finished, her face and eyes were a violent red, and she was on the verge of fainting.

After she recovered I asked her how she did it. She shook her shoulders hard, raised her hands as if to push away the questioner, and said, "What do you mean? It had to be done, that's all." That simple yet perpetually mysterious answer is the fullest description she would ever give of how she helped to save thousands of refugee children. We had reached bedrock, and the spade had turned.

6

Though the Chambonnais made it look easy, acquiring the lucid, mysterious virtues of compassion and generosity is far from easy. To raise children the way Magda Trocmé, Gabrielle Barraud, and others raised theirs in Le Chambon is not as easy as memorizing Benjamin Franklin's maxims would be for an American child. You do not have to do much to teach children how to be self-serving; it is part of their inherited biological apparatus. To raise children the way the Chambonnais did you must *be* what you are trying to teach. Words, however picturesque and passionate, are not enough. In the intimacy of a kitchen or a bedroom, the public face you prepare in order to meet the faces that you meet slips down a bit. At home you must teach by example, and the example you set must be flawless.

One day when my grandson Daniel had just turned three, I found myself alone with him in the kitchen at breakfast time. Such moments with him were among the most intense joys of my life. In the early morning his face was fresher and more beautiful to me than any morning glory blossom. I filled a bowl with milk and cereal for myself—his bowl was already full—and then put the milk carton back in the refrigerator.

There are six cats and a dog in Daniel's home, and he had spent most of his three years living almost at eye level with them. In his house people are very patient with animals—they have to be, I suppose, in order to keep their sanity.

When I turned back from the refrigerator, I saw one of the cats on the table with his right rear foot in my bowl. Without thinking I seized the cat, picked him up off the table, and let him drop to the kitchen floor with a little downward push of anger and disgust.

The next thing I knew I felt a pulling on my bathrobe, and when I looked down I saw my grandson looking up at me with confusion in his wide brown eyes and with his red lips opening and closing as if to catch his breath. From infancy he has called me "Poppie," and we have played together gleefully for hours and hours. But he was anguished by what he had just witnessed. He loved me and he loved the cat, and he was baffled by the disapproval he felt for me and the pity he felt for the abused cat. And so he stood there, all two and a half feet of him, pulling on my bathrobe, looking up at me, and sobbing, "Poppie! Poppie!" I had violated his way of life. He had lived eyeball to eyeball with them for all of his life; forbearance and tenderness toward them was part of his way of life. I had violated that way of life, and yet he loved me still. He was torn. There was nothing that I could say to help us in our misery. I had failed to embody a lucid mystery.

After a few moments he sought out the cat and took it in his arms—it was almost as big as he was—and he sat on the floor in the kitchen petting it, weeping a little, and not looking at me.

Such heart virtues as those that nerved the people of Le Chambon for four long years are taught—and exercised—by being, not simply by talking. And the one person in Le Chambon whose very being set the most visible example of unself-conscious love was Magda Grilli Trocmé, who was also one of the most abrupt, impatient, and demanding people in the village.

7

André Trocmé was a student in New York City in the fall of 1925, when he met Magda Grilli. He was on a scholarship at the Union Theological Seminary, and she was preparing to become a social worker. She had been raised a Catholic in Florence, Italy, but she had no allegiance to any organized religion. She had been placed in a Florentine convent early in her life and had felt imprisoned there, physically and mentally. In April 1926, when he proposed to her as they were standing near the 125th Street ferry, he said, "I shall be a Protestant pastor, and I want to live a life of poverty. I am a conscientious objector, and that can mean prison as well as all sorts of other difficulties." After she accepted him they walked on the cliffs of the Palisades while he uttered a prayer that sealed their commitment to each other.

She accepted him because she loved him, not because she believed in Protestantism, or poverty, or pacifism. In the fall of 1925 a little incident had occurred that showed that theirs would be a marriage of true minds, despite the differences beween a deeply religious and a deeply secular one. One windy day André Trocmé heard her say to one of her friends in her rather gruff, speedy way, "Go quickly and get your sweater. You need it." Those words crystallized his image of Magda Grilli: She cared for people on their own terms, not on hers. She helped them to take care of themselves. After all, you want people to cover themselves against the cold so that the heat of their own bodies can keep them warm, not so that you can parade your own virtue or intrude into their lives. You are not the center; the helped person is.

Beneath all their differences the bedrock was this conviction, and this conviction they expressed in their different ways when they made Le Chambon the safest refuge for terrified human beings in the whole of Europe. He was a man devoted to following the example of Jesus by helping his fellow human beings; she was a woman devoted simply to helping those who came to her for help. Her husband's belief drew its power from the life and death of Jesus; hers drew its power from no supernatural imperatives, only from the other's need.

There is a morally beautiful mystery in both of these beliefs. Still, the mystery closest to my own heart, being what I am, is her "Naturally. Come in, come in."

Once their son Jean-Pierre, a sensitive, artistically gifted child, said to his mother, "You know, Mama, father is really a good man. When he dies, I am going to have a wonderful funeral for him—you know? And he will be in a wonderful coffin all covered with precious stones. And I am going to have made a mechanical bird, which will stand on his tombstone, and this bird will say again and again, 'Here is the pastor of Le Chambon.'"

At another time he said to his mother, "Mama, I love you very much. I love you so much that I think I cannot get married because I cannot leave you. But if I do get married, why, I shall live in Tence [a few miles away]. And—I'll tell you what, Mama—when I have my first child, I shall give it to you."

He was not ranking his loves—not preferring one parent to the other—but expressing his loves, and he was expressing the boundless sensitivity of children to the great virtues.

4

THE EYE OF
THE HURRICANE

1

A few weeks after my book about Magda and the village of Le Chambon was published, I received my first fan letter. It came from a Massachusetts man who had not bothered to read the book; he had read a review of it in *Time* magazine. His first paragraph began with: "Nothing happened west of National Route 7 in southern France."

He went on to say that only great armies and great ideologies make a difference in history. Only a struggle between ideologies like Communism and fascism and capitalism goes down in history, because it changes institutions; it alters large patterns of life. A few eccentrics helping a few refugees changes no institutions. From the point of view of history, nothing happened in the little mountain village of Le Chambon.

At first I was shocked: Nothing happened west of National Route 7? Le Chambon is west of National Route 7. Saving thousands of people's lives is *nothing*? The courage and the will to shelter all those people, and the sacrifices of food and privacy for four years when France was imprisoned under the will of the German occupiers—all this is *nothing*? If these saved lives are *nothing*, then what is *something*? Abstract political systems? Armies and the killing of millions of human beings?

I have long believed that the greatest sin the human mind can commit is to try to explain away the obvious. There were about three thousand villagers in Le Chambon, and they saved some five thousand refugees in the course of four years; there were millions of uniformed soldiers and ununiformed Resistance people fighting in Europe during that time. Does this mean that the eight thousand or so people involved in the rescue operation of Le Chambon did not happen? What do big or small numbers have to do with the fact that people are saved, or die? What do big or small numbers have to do with the plain fact that each person counts, counts immensely for his or her own sake, and for the sake of all those who love him or her dearly?

Right after I read the letter, I felt the urge to send the Massachusetts man a stinging philosophical reply. But the more I thought about his letter the more I saw the truth in it. The first four years of the forties were a time of war, a time when people were fighting for their countries. The central question of the war was: Who will win, the Axis powers or the Allies? The rescue operation of Le Chambon had nothing to do with answering this momentous question. The village did nothing to stop Nazi Germany from establishing the thousand-year Reich that Hitler promised his people. Only vast arrays of combatants and immense industrial might have addressed the question. Saving a few thousand refugees avoided it.

Early in my conversations with Magda Trocmé I asked her if she had believed that what the village was doing helped the war effort in any way. She answered, "No. We were more interested in saving people than in fighting Vichy or the Nazis."

I simply recorded this as the matter of fact that it was. But during the rest of my study of Le Chambon, the fact became clearer and clearer: The village of Le Chambon did nothing to shorten the war. Some of my early criticisms against pacifism kept surfacing in my mind: Pacifists can be patient as far as ending a war is concerned. They can even contribute to the defeat of the side they are influencing. While they are patiently refusing to kill, the mass murder of war can go on and on, and—in the case of World War II—so can the concentration camps that are killing thousands upon thousands of human beings every day.

I knew the old arguments for nonviolence. For instance, if all the people of Europe had refused to fight, and had also refused to work the land and the machinery of their countries, then the Nazis would have been unable to rule. But this is a big "if": World War II was happening, and the peoples around Germany were not refusing to work their lands and their machines. The discipline of nonviolence was nonexistent in the all-important, murderous *now* of the war. People in occupied countries kept their countries going—and their lives—going. The massive and cruel punishments the Nazis were eager to use in fact terrified people into submission. No. The fact was that during the war there was no time to create the discipline required by successful nonviolence.

And so my correspondent was not simply a crank, or a liar, or insensitive to suffering and death. Only armies, and political movements like Nazism, Communism, and capitalism "count" in history. Only great armies and great systems of ideas "go down in history," because only these forces make and change the public institutions of mankind. The Allied soldiers changed the institutions of Nazi Germany. They destroyed them, and what they did quite rightly went down in history.

I remembered my old conviction that love does not conquer all and that sometimes to endure you must use sheer force. All during my study of the village these not-so-distant memories had nagged at me, and I sometimes felt a little ashamed for admiring a village whose way of life was so fundamentally alien to my own deepest convictions, so totally alien to my own warlike way of life in Chicago and in Europe.

But—again—Le Chambon counted too. A few thousand flesh-and-blood human beings counted too, even though they had nothing to do with cutting short the millions of killings in World War II. The rescue operation of Le Chambon happened. There is more than one way to be our brother's keeper.

2

One evening a few months after I received the letter from Massachusetts, I was lecturing in Minneapolis about the village of Le Chambon. When I finished my prepared remarks, a woman stood up in the back of the room and asked if the village of Le Chambon was in the Département of the Haute-Loire. Her accent was French, and she obviously knew France: There are various Le Chambons in various departments of France, however, and you have to be specific when you mention Le Chambon to a French person. I told her that the Le Chambon I was speaking of was indeed in the Haute-Loire—the rugged, mountainous region that contains the sources of the great Loire River.

She stared at me for a few moments, and then she said, "Ah. You have been speaking about the village that saved all three of my children."

Then she stopped and bowed her head. The metal chairs on the hard floor of the room had been noisy during my talk, but there was utter silence now. It was as if nobody in the room was even breathing.

Then she went on: "I want to thank you for publishing the story of Le Chambon. Now it is written down. But also I want to thank you because now I can speak with my American friends about that terrible war and that beautiful village, and they will be able to understand me better. You see, sometimes I think America is a big island and does not understand what happened in Europe."

Again, utter silence. Then she asked us to let her give us a brief talk. We were all too stunned to answer, and so she shrugged a little and walked to the front of the room. She was obviously accustomed to speaking before large groups, and so with a clear, matter-of-fact voice she said: "The Holocaust was storm, lightning, thunder, wind, rain, yes. And Le Chambon was the rainbow."

Everybody in that audience knew what the rainbow meant in the ninth chapter of the Book of Genesis: *hope.*

3

It was as if, like Goethe's Faust, I was two souls in one body, under one person's name, and each soul wanted to tear itself away from the other. The story of Le Chambon did not destroy or even dim my vision of nature and society as power struggles. During every moment of our lives on this planet strong teeth are crushing tender flesh and bones. Big fish continue to eat little fish, and all predators are more powerful than their prey. I could not forget the Cockroach Building, or those feet of John Dillinger pointing upward and jutting out of the police meat wagon near the Biograph Theater. Nor could I forget what I did willingly in World War II. I could not forget the so-called medical experiments with twins and other children, and I could not forget the murderous force that ended them when it ended Nazi Germany. I was still convinced that killing is part and parcel of living.

And yet, and yet—there were Magda, and her husband, and Pastor Édouard Theis, and Gabrielle Barraud, and the villagers of Le Chambon, and all those children they rescued from despair and death. I was beginning to meet many of these children—now middle-aged people—at annual meetings in New York City. It was plain during every moment of those meetings that the villagers had saved not only the lives of these people; they had saved their spiritual sanity, their capacity for realistic hope.

These two souls of mine, like Faust's souls, were not simply different from each other. Each wanted to be the only one in my body. When I thought of the village, I wanted only the great virtues of life-loving compassion and generosity and courage to prevail in the world; when I thought of the Cockroach Building or of the war I wanted only the little virtues of self-serving self-preservation to prevail. I knew, as William Allen White once put it, that "Consistency is a paste jewel that only cheap men cherish," and I have often been delighted to change my mind—for the better. But now I did not know which one of these two souls was the better, and I felt forced to choose between them.

There is truth in the old Spanish maxim: "No wind serves a ship that has no port." What was I heading for in my life? Which of these two ports was the better, and how could I live—with something like wholeness and peace—heading toward two competing goals, sheer force and love?

It is important to see that this was an emotional problem for me, not an abstract, philosophical one. I needed to know, or to feel, which of my "*zwei Seelen* [two souls]," to use Goethe's phrase, was mine. I was not looking for an abstract "solution" to any problem. I am too skeptical, too suspicious of abstractions to need that. I needed to know where my heart lay. I needed to know what I most cherished in life: force or benevolence.

4

Then one late afternoon in the fall Hurricane Gloria happened. My family and I were eating spaghetti alla marinara—mainly fresh fall tomatoes, garlic, and olive oil—in our kitchen. We had been following the course of the hurricane, and we knew that it was going to pass right through our part of Connecticut. As we were eating the last succulent, red mouthfuls of spaghetti, Gloria struck. Before we could get up from the table she lifted our big chestnut tree out of the ground and laid it down on its side a few dozen yards from our kitchen. Like idiots my children, my wife, and I ran to the glass sliding door while Gloria struck: The hurricane could have turned the door into a thousand glass bullets, but there we stood—hypnotized by its power. Our silver maples are more than a foot in diameter, but they swayed like willow branches. The sound was not unlike the sound I had often heard when I pulled the lanyard of our 155-millimeter howitzer during the war. It was not a mere sound, not just a matter of hearing something; it was a massive feeling of an overwhelming power drowning one's whole body and mind, not merely striking one's eardrums. And there we stood, side by side in a kind of detached terror.

Then, suddenly, there was peace. I looked up, and the sky was pale, pale blue over our farm. There were birds sailing far up in the blue. Even the leaves on the fallen chestnut tree barely fluttered. We were in the eye of the hurricane. The four of us kept holding each other's hands for a little while, but now there was a surprising gentleness in our feelings. Our feelings of terror had become feelings of tenderness toward one another and toward the world outside our kitchen.

Then and there I realized that the peace I had found in Le Chambon was like this. Peace sometimes stands like the eye of a hurricane in the very middle of power. The indifferent, destructive power of nature and of fellow human beings is always near; it surrounds the blue beauty of our tenderness, and it is always threatening to invade it, the way the winds of a hurricane surround its eye. Amid the killing and the letting-kill that are always happening on this planet, amid the deliberate cruelty, the hating, the eating and the dying of creatures in the air, on the land, and in the waters, amid all of this there can be room for peace and warmth.

In the midst of our struggle for survival that always ends in our death we creatures on earth have made room for thoughts and deeds of love. Some creatures have made more room than others. The people of Le Chambon in their kitchen-resistance to murder made room at great risk and with great sacrifice not only for about five thousand refugee children, but for a love that encompassed all mankind. The ethically pure Chambonnais, who did not hate and did not kill in order to help life thrive, pushed back the walls of the eye of the hurricane until the murderous winds seemed so far away as to be unreal. There was one murderous Gestapo raid on Le Chambon, but for most of the rest of the four years of the war in France there were peace and safety in Le Chambon, while torture and murder and betrayal were happening all over the rest of the continent of Europe.

Each of us needs to make some room in life for peaceful communion, but some of us make more room than others. In one of his articles in the French Resistance journal *Combat*, Albert Camus tells a story about Heinrich Himmler, who, under Hitler, was responsible for the humiliation, torture, and murder of millions of defenseless people. When Himmler was working near Munich and had to come home late at night, he would enter very quietly, from the rear, through the kitchen door. Before he stepped into the house he would remove his jackboots. He did not want to awaken his canary.

Here was the narrow, narrow eye of the hurricane for him. This was the range of his compassion. The peace, the silence in his home, in his kitchen make the murderous winds of destructive power outside deafening for me, just as a little candlelight can make darkness visible. But still, here was a little peace and a little caring, just as the candlelight in great darkness is still candlelight, not darkness.

Almost every one of this restless manunkind of ours has to take care of someone, if it is only oneself, only one's own hide. There are those who carve out a very narrow space for generosity and compassion and who consign all others to the indifferent, destructive forces in the world. And there are those who exclude no one from their love. Such are the people of Le Chambon, who were as intent on keeping the Germans from soiling their lives with more murders as they were on saving the children who came to their village.

The fact is that some people are morally better than others, if by morally better we mean that they hate and torture and kill less than others do. Equality is a glorious political and theological idea, but in ethics there is a hierarchy, or there is no ethics, and no lives—even our own—are precious.

I believe—as surely as I believe that I am now alive—that anyone who believes in his or her heart that the Chambonnais are not better than the sadistic guards in Auschwitz is part of the destructive powers in the world, part of the hurricane. I cannot prove this belief the way I can prove that I am alive; I can only tell you this belief and then ask you to see if you do not, in fact, discriminate hierarchically between a Mother Theresa or a Martin Luther King, Jr., and a John Dillinger or an Adolf Hitler.

If we cherish murderers as much as we do rescuers, then we have cut ourselves off from the drowned and the saved of history, and we have our reward in the cockroach-narrowness of our caring. The British philosopher G. J. Warnock once wrote: "That it is a bad thing to be tortured or starved, humiliated or hurt, is not an opinion: it is a fact. That it is better for people to be loved and attended to rather than hated or neglected, is again a plain fact, not a matter of opinion." And he urges us not to let ourselves be bullied out of that conviction by the cold creatures in our species who try to explain away the obvious caring in the world.

Notice that Warnock is writing from the point of view of victims and beneficiaries, not from that of those who do the torturing or the loving. Torturers have been known to blind and deafen themselves to their victims' pain, or even to enjoy it sadistically. The drowned ones and the saved ones—and we are all victims and beneficiaries in some circumstances—know what is better or worse for them. If you wish to find out how wide your eye of the hurricane is, you must consult the beneficiaries and the victims of your actions and passions. They know.

Once a little girl was standing in line with her mother in Belzec concentration camp. They were waiting to go into the gas chamber, and the girl, with her hand in her mother's, asked, "Mama. It is dark in there. I have been a good girl. Why are we going in there?" She and her mother knew something about what is evil, and soon afterward, if only for a moment, they knew more. Because the guards at Belzec did not care, they did not know as much about evil as those two knew.

5

There is an old Danish saying that goes: "If there is room in the heart, there is room in the house." The hospitality that was the most intimate gift the Chambonnais gave the refugees was a demonstration of the truth of the saying. For instance, one summer during the occupation the Trocmés housed and fed (along with their own four children) sixty Jewish refugees in their little presbytery.

Still, the Danish saying makes rescue look somewhat easier than it often is. Danger and fear and hunger were always there in the presbytery and elsewhere in Le Chambon. Hospitality is not always easy to give. That this is so is one of the main reasons why there were so few—so very few—rescue operations like that of Le Chambon in the first few years of the forties. That beautiful Danish saying suggests that rescue is no more problematic than opening your heart to people who are not in your family. Life is sometimes more dangerous and harder than the best of old sayings.

A wide, efficacious love is as difficult as it is rare. If it were not so difficult, there might be more of it in this fitful nightmare we gently label "history." But the world being what it is, caring does exist in the nests and other nooks of nature, and in the kitchens, the bedrooms, and sometimes even in the public places of our planet. And some people care far more than others for the lives of their fellow human beings. The caring that I have done and that I have seen convinces me that the efficacious lovers of mankind feel the breadth and the depth of being alive better than the winds of the hurricane do. Lives, le'hayim, are wider than my life alone.

5

DECENT KILLERS

1

A few months after Hurricane Gloria struck Connecticut, the neatness of this image of making room for love in the middle of brute force began to disturb me. One day a friend who knew much about birds told me that the birds I thought were gliding happily high up in the eye of the hurricane were actually in trouble, fighting to stay aloft in powerful downdrafts. Trapped in the eye, they were reeling from having slammed into the wall of wind surrounding it.

I found myself remembering the harm I had done in order to help. I found myself seeing again—with the same clarity I had in 1945—the head and part of the neck of a blond SS cadet lying on the road to the right of my artillery prime mover when we started our race from Mannheim to the open city of Heidelberg in the last months of the war in Europe. Our big tractor had stopped for a moment to keep from hitting the gun in front of us, and I found myself staring down at a slightly chubby, beardless face whose pale blue eyes were staring from their sockets. People like me—and possibly my number two gun—had decapitated the boy. I had certainly killed others in Mannheim: From our position above the city I had seen them burn.

When I remembered that head, I had a vision of all the people who had been blasted or burned in the whole sweep of history and prehistory. I could almost hear the last scream, feel the last agony of every creature, murderous or innocent, cruel or kind, strong or weak, that had ever died a violent death. At the moment when you are being blasted or burned to death, you are only an exploding knot of agony, not a Nazi or a Jew.

But there is more to a violent death than agony. Emerson taught only one doctrine, and he described it in a journal entry in the spring of 1840 as "the infinitude of the private man." He was convinced that each of us is the only cosmos we experience. Look at the "private man" walking toward you in the street, and what you see from the outside is a roughly cruciform body a few feet long and fewer feet wide; but notice your own awareness from inside your own self, and you are as boundless as the sky you imagine beyond the farthest stars you see. When a person is blasted or burned to death, a universe—his universe—the only one he has, dies in agony.

Still, I do not repent the killing I did in combat. I can repent having done something only when I change my mind about having done it, only when I would not do it again under similar circumstances. But I have not changed my mind about fighting against Nazi Germany. I would do it again.

I had to learn to savage boys like the sadist who pounded my head on the sidewalk in front of the Cockroach Building, and we had to stop Hitler with brute force. Love and patience would not have done those jobs. What I feel in myself is an ever-burning—though usually smoldering—rage. It is a kind of fury that the ethically pure creatures of our species do not seem to feel. I am painfully aware of the agonies of others; but I would be violent again under circumstances like those in Chicago or in World War II. Violence sometimes stops violence in its tracks. I repent my brutality as little as I do my compassion.

When I began to study the life of André Trocmé, I thought I found this same crouching rage in the pastor of Le Chambon. In his autobiographical notes, he wrote about his feelings toward Hitler in the summer of 1939, a short while before the war came to France. He saw Hitler as "diabolical," as a violent merchant of lies, and he asked himself: "Should I not make use of my knowledge of German to slip into Hitler's entourage and assassinate him before it is too late, before he plunges the world into a catastrophe without limits?"

But I was wrong about him. He was not like me. After posing the question, he went on: "I feared separating myself from Jesus Christ, who refused to use arms to prevent the crime that was being prepared for him, and because of a kind of stubborn perseverance in the growing darkness."

His love of a nonviolent Jesus was the bedrock of his mind, the hot center of his energy. Moreover, his situation in life—his ministry in a relatively isolated mountain village that was growing more and more to believe in his doctrine of nonviolence and in him personally—"was becoming more and more interesting" as the war in Europe approached. And so that was the end of that project, and, for all intents and purposes, the end of his fury.

None of this applied to me. I do not know what the bedrock of my mind is, but it is not a commitment to live a life of ethically pure love. In fact, if there *is* any bedrock for me, it is the rage in me that drives me to meet brute force with brute force.

2

The immensity of life and the enormity of death are the reasons at once for my violence and my compassion. Life is too valuable to be monopolized by murderers. This is the paradox people like me have to endure.

And so I will not—and perhaps I cannot—change what Herman Melville once called "the reactionary bite of that serpent," the retaliatory malice that is part and parcel of my personality. The world being what it is, and I being what I am, I cannot change my belief that sheer force must happen at some times and in some places. Such a time and place for me was Europe in the forties, and such a time and place for me was Chicago in the thirties. I do not think that the world is much safer now.

Because of all this, deep in my mind a collision is always happening between the compassion I have felt and the destruction I have perpetrated. As a matter of fact, there has been a high-pitched hum in my head ever since my first long fire mission with a 155-millimeter howitzer. Usually I am not aware of the hum because it is unchanging, but sometimes I stop and listen to it. When I do, the hum is saying something to me about destroying and defending life.

I am not a rational animal as much as I am a paradoxical one—a walking, breathing contradiction. When I realize that the lives of others are as precious to them as mine is to me, I hate killing; but when I realize that in this world the destruction of precious lives is the price you sometimes have to pay to protect precious lives, I feel not repentance but sorrow. I feel sorrow that both the world around me and I myself are not more single-mindedly compassionate than we in fact are. I feel sorrow that this world is one in which Le Chambon is an extraordinary, almost a miraculous story.

It is very likely that not a moment has passed in the long history of sentient life on this planet when some creature has not been dying in agony. But my awareness of this does not make my life miserable. I love living too much to spend every moment bootlessly feeling compassion for all the victims in the world. There are already enough victims, more than enough. They do not need me to add to their number by stereotyping my compassion. I have learned to live more or less happily in a world in which the death of one sentient being means the life of another.

I have come to live in what William James called in *The Varieties of Religious Experience* "a universe two stories deep." The deepest level is my awareness of the paradox of living: that this is a cruel, loving world, in which creatures like me care and kill, sometimes in one and the same deed.

But the second level, the above-ground story of my universe, is the belief that some people are better than others, that there can be a large eye in the hurricane of self-serving indifference, cruelty, and murder. When I think about what happened in Le Chambon I feel myself coming alive with a mixture of sorrow and joy. They did not kill anybody, while I was a dutiful killer, a decent murderer.

Nowadays the hot source of my energy, the driving push behind my words and actions and passions, is my second-story vision, the vision of myself and others as trying to push away the indifference, the greed, and the rage that surround the eye of the hurricane. It is that vision that makes me reach out to my students with affection laced with rigor, and makes me yearn to see them come alive. It is that vision that makes me cherish generous friendships, that makes me glad to help lead a large drug-and-alcohol rehabilitation group here in the middle of Connecticut, and that has made me write this book.

At other times, in other places, I may yet again be motivated by my first-story vision, so that I shall want to hurt and even to kill human beings as I wanted to hurt and to kill them in earlier times. But now that vision is muted, dimmed, peripheral. Now it does not practically come to much. But it is nonetheless real, nonetheless me. And this is so because I cannot take lightly the fact that killing ends a universe as surely as it can feed another.

3

These are the ideas that made me see that the story of the people of Le Chambon was not very much like mine. The praise that I had given—and will always give—the people of Le Chambon was a little like the praise an earthworm might give a star as it lifted its head toward the sky for a moment and then went back into the soil. I needed to understand a kind of decency closer to my own condition than the goodness of the villagers of Le Chambon.

And so, in order to find a story more similar to my own, I started to turn my attention away from the Trocmés and their villagers. In doing this I remembered a story I had read in the autobiographical notes of Pastor Trocmé. It was the story of a man as ambiguous and as paradoxical as I am. His name was Julius Schmähling.

Late in the fifties André and Magda Trocmé made a tour of Central Europe lecturing in favor of nonviolence. Pastor Trocmé was a leading figure in the cause of nonviolence, and being an eloquent speaker (as well as fluent in German) he received many invitations to speak to the German people. The great Bavarian city of Munich was part of that tour, and so on a warm summer afternoon the Trocmés decided to pay a visit to a German friend who lived there. The friend was Maj. Julius Schmähling, who had been the commander of the German occupying troops in the Département of the Haute-Loire toward the end of the war in France.

They arrived at 37 Auenstrasse and found themselves in front of a partially ruined apartment house. During the war it had suffered a direct hit from a bomb, and more than a decade later half of it was still rubble. Schmähling, they had been told, lived three stories up. The Trocmés laboriously climbed the shaky, uneven stairs. André Trocmé had a very bad back, which would kill him in a few years, and he was still rather corpulent from having eaten so many chestnuts while he was trying to hide from the Germans during the last year of the war.

They pressed the buzzer outside the Schmähling apartment. A heavy, bald man in his seventies opened the door, hesitated a moment as he looked at the pastor and his wife, and then suddenly burst out with, "*Ach! Herr Pfarrer Trocmé! Ja, natürlich, kommen Sie doch herein!*" The warmth of the greeting and the strong arm of the German drew the pastor and his wife into the apartment.

The floor of the apartment sloped toward the ruined part of the building, so that if a pencil had been put on the floor, it would have rolled the full width of the apartment. A bed visible from the living room had a canvas tent suspended over it to keep off the rain that seeped through the ruined roof. One woodstove in the kitchen heated the whole apartment.

Emma and Julius Schmähling had an appetizing *Kaffee-Trinken* already spread out on a little table in the bare living room, and they invited the Trocmés to share it with them. After a cup of coffee and a piece of cake, André Trocmé, always very impulsive, leaned toward Julius Schmähling. "I have come to ask you two questions," he said. The first was: "You knew that Le Chambon was a nest of resisters. There were Jews and there were Maquis there. Of course your police did us some harm, but why didn't you strike us the way you Germans struck others in other places?"

Schmähling answered that pressures were being exerted on him to strike Le Chambon, but he resisted them because he believed that the resistance in Le Chambon had nothing to do with violence. "And so," he went on, "I argued against a military strike with all my strength."

Trocmé then posed his second question: "Well, then, if that was so, why were you not able to save Le Forestier?"

Roger Le Forestier was one of the two doctors in Le Chambon, and he was as profoundly committed to nonviolence as anybody in the village. In his twenties in 1944, he was a brilliant surgeon, and before he came to Le Chambon he had worked with Albert Schweitzer in Africa. He was strikingly handsome, as boyishly humorous as he was serious in his commitment to Schweitzer's basic principle of "reverence for life." In Le Chambon he married a young woman who was as beautiful as he was handsome. When they walked down a street in the village, people stared at them, so sparkling were they, so full of life and so full of love for each other.

One day in 1944 he was driving his Red Cross ambulance from Le Chambon to the capital city of the Haute-Loire, Le Puy, when he decided to pick up two young hitchhikers who were going in his direction. Before he let them in he asked them if they were armed, because he knew that they were *maquisards*, and they all knew that any Frenchman carrying on his person or in his vehicle unauthorized firearms was subject to immediate execution. They told him that they had no firearms, and they entered the ambulance.

But they were lying, and when they arrived in the great Breuil Square in Le Puy they shoved their loaded revolvers behind the rear seat of the ambulance. While they were sitting in a nearby café, and while Le Forestier was pleading with the German authorities for the release from prison of two other *maquisards*, two German military policemen discovered the revolvers in Le Forestier's ambulance. When Le Forestier came back to his ambulance he mildly objected to the search of the Red Cross vehicle. Suddenly one of the Germans struck him down, knocking out two of his teeth. The military policemen then brought him across the square to the headquarters of the German military government, at 33 Marshal Fayolle Boulevard.

Maj. Julius Schmähling was no longer in command of the German occupying forces in the Haute-Loire; Col. Ernst Metzger was. He had taken Schmähling's place two weeks before the Allied landings on the beaches of Normandy in June 1944. He was more than twenty years younger than Schmähling, and he was a career officer who was being spoken of for promotion to general. A committed Nazi, he had recently kept Schmähling from being promoted to *Oberstleutnant** on the grounds that Schmähling was publicly antagonistic to national socialism. Metzger was thought to be "*hart wie Stahl*," as hard as steel, and Schmähling was his second in command.

Within an hour of Le Forestier's arrest, Metzger convened his staff in his office and opened the meeting by recommending the execution of Le Forestier without trial. The presence of unauthorized, loaded revolvers in a Red Cross ambulance was a palpable threat to law and order in the Haute-Loire, and the law demanded his execution.

Soon after the preliminary meeting of the officers, there was an informal hearing with Le Forestier. The young doctor asserted that he did not know about the guns, but this made no difference as far as the law was concerned. As the licensee and driver of the ambu-

* Lieutenant colonel.

lance, he was responsible for the presence of guns in his vehicle. Since Le Forestier did not mention the *maquisards* who had left the guns in his ambulance—he did not want to cause them to be shot—there were no mitigating circumstances in the case, and the informal hearing confirmed Metzger's recommendation that there be an immediate execution.

But the previous commander of the *Verbindungsstab*,* Major Schmähling, disagreed with the decision. The two met in private and discussed the matter for hours. Schmähling managed to convince Metzger that executing the young surgeon would be like putting German hands into a French hornets' nest: Le Forestier was well known as a nonviolent leader in the nonviolent village of Le Chambon, and to punish him without a formal trial would not chasten but rather infuriate the French.

And so Metzger ordered a court-martial to decide the case, with Maj. Julius Schmähling presiding. In the course of the trial it became clear to Schmähling that Le Forestier was deeply incriminated. The letter of the law and all the evidence added up to immediate execution. Schmähling saw that Le Forestier's only chance for survival lay in the force of his personality, and so he asked him to tell the court about his deepest convictions.

Le Forestier spoke about his work with Albert Schweitzer in Lambaréné, where the two doctors engaged in what Schweitzer called "the direct service of humanity." Schweitzer's "reverence for life" had drawn Le Forestier to Africa, and Pastor Trocmé's Christian nonviolence had drawn the young man from Africa to Le Chambon in 1939. Le Forestier summarized his testimony by saying that the people of Le Chambon "resist unjust laws, we hide Jews, we disobey your orders, but we do these things in the name of the Gospel of Jesus Christ."

The transparent purity of motive Le Forestier showed in the courtroom satisfied Schmähling that he was innocent, and so, in the course of his hours of discussion with the senior officers of the *Verbindungsstab*, he convinced them that Le Forestier was no threat. Still, they maintained, he had violated the law against possessing weapons, and so he could not be acquitted summarily. He had to be punished.

* Liaison staff.

In the middle of these discussions Schmähling thought of a way out. After the Allied landings in Normandy, Germany was in need of workers, especially of doctors. Schmähling persuaded the court to accept Le Forestier's voluntary work in Germany as an alternative to imprisonment. However, important as it was to have skilled workers in Germany, especially gifted surgeons like Le Forestier, the German government did not want criminals—or even suspected criminals—to enter the German work force. It was not an easy task for Schmähling: Punishment and voluntary labor were separate, even conflicting ideas before he tried to put them together for his fellow officers. But after hours of discussion— mainly with his Nazi superior Colonel Metzger—Schmähling was empowered to send Le Forestier to work in Germany. In Le Forestier's favor, his medical work with the Maquis had prepared him for practicing the healing arts in the middle of violence.

And so Le Forestier was put on a train on his way to Germany. But on August 19, 1944, the secret police of Lyon, the Gestapo, whose leading spirit was Klaus Barbie, "the butcher of Lyon," stopped the train as it entered the city limits. They took only one man from the train: Roger Le Forestier.

In his postwar conversation with the Trocmés, Schmähling could give only one explanation for the removal. Standing there with tears in his eyes, in his dilapidated Munich apartment, he shook his fists and said: "Those *Schweinhunde* in the Gestapo must surely have sent a message to their colleagues in Lyon." A representative of the Gestapo must have been present at the Le Puy trial. The Gestapo knew that Le Forestier's village was a refuge for Jews. They must have decided to carry out their own kind of justice on this Frenchman from "that nest of Jews in Huguenot country," as Le Chambon was widely described. And so they must have telephoned their counterparts in Lyon and told them where and when to seize Le Forestier.

In any case Le Forestier was imprisoned at Fort Montluc.* His wife later discovered that in that grim prison he had been as cheerful as a boy. He sang hymns, read the Bible, and gave courage and joy to his cellmates. On August 20, 1944, at eight-thirty in the

---

* An early-nineteenth-century fort whose prison was used by the Gestapo for Resistance fighters and "traitors" (to the Nazi cause).

morning, he and about 110 other people were brought to Saint-Genis-Laval, a suburb of Lyon. The prisoners were tied together in pairs, and the Gestapo, with the help of some German soldiers, pushed three pairs at a time into the dilapidated fort of Côte-Lorette. There was a burst of machine-gun fire, and three more pairs were pushed into the ruined building. When all the prisoners had been shot, they were soaked with gasoline and set afire—some of them still alive. Farmers working nearby heard them screaming. When silence came, the remains of the old fort were dynamited.

A few months after the war in France was over, Danielle Le Forestier found proof that her husband was in fact dead. She left Le Chambon with her two boys and went back to her native city of Cannes. Before she left she made it clear to the Trocmés that she considered Major Schmähling to be one of her husband's murderers.

In Munich, Schmähling told the Trocmés that now, long after the war, he still had nightmares and sleepless nights about the death of Le Forestier. He never forgot an interview with Danielle Le Forestier before her husband left Le Puy for Lyon, an interview in which "that beautiful, beautiful young woman and her two children . . . came to beg me for his life. . . . She had faith in me."

Then he looked at Andre Trocmé and said, "I promised her that he would come back. What must she think of me?"

Trocmé, whose nonviolence had as its keystone the forgiveness of sins, found himself having to say "to this poor major who was now only an old retired teacher, 'She has not been able to pardon you.'"

What the Trocmés did not know was that because of his nightmares, in which the beautiful Danielle and her children pleaded for Le Forestier's life, Schmähling's sleep was so fitful and unrefreshing that he was on the verge of nervous collapse.

In Zirndorf, outside Nuremberg, where Schmähling's daughter, Annelise, lived, she saw him in the last weeks of his life standing in her garden, leaning on a pole or against a chair, shaking his head in abrupt little arcs, face downward. When she opened the glass door to go out to him, she heard him saying, again and again, "*Ach, Schrecklich! Schrecklich! Arme Frau! Arme Frau!*" "Oh, horrible! Horrible! That poor woman! That poor woman!"

I have studied André Trocmé's autobiographical notes and his more formal writings in order to discover his attitude toward Major

Schmähling. The clearest expression of what he thought occurs in his notes a few pages before the account of his visit with the Schmählings in Munich. He believed that Schmähling obeyed his orders from the German command *"assez mollement,"* softly, without the harshness of a committed Nazi. And he also believed that Schmähling had taken upon himself the task of *"sauver bien des gens,"* saving the lives of a number of people. And he adds: "Many of the people he saved bore witness in his favor, and he was the guest of the people of Le Puy several years after the war. . . . His efforts on behalf of the people [of the Haute-Loire] were appreciated."

Here was a man like me: compassionate, and a party to murder.

4

Having found all this in Trocmé's autobiographical notes, I decided to visit the son and daughter of Julius Schmähling in Germany. Schmähling's son, Walter, is about my age and is a veteran of World War II who fought in the European theater of operations, as I did. In effect we were both doing our best to kill each other. He was living in Munich, and I went there to visit him.

Early in my visit he and I were sitting in a library when I decided to ask him a jarring question: "Do you think I should write about some of the good things your father has done?" Walter Schmähling is a heavily muscled man who speaks and acts swiftly. All of a sudden he leaned back in his chair, glanced across the room at the cold aluminum bas-relief on the library wall, looked up at the ceiling, and called out in a powerful voice, "Oh, they will say: 'What is that Philip Hallie doing writing about a damned German?'"

That was all he said. But when we got back to his apartment in Bismarckstrasse, he took me into his office—he is a retired *Gymnasium** teacher—and handed me a pile of papers. "Here is the diary my father kept during his last months in France. Sit down and read it. It may help you to decide whether to write about him."

Toward the end of August 1944, Adolf Hitler's Third Reich was about finished in France. It had lasted four years or so, and during those four years the Germans had humiliated, robbed, and raped *la*

* High school.

belle France. But by the end of August the Allies and the French Resistance had almost completed the job of liberating France from the Germans. Now was the time of judgment for the Germans who were trapped in France. For the French it was a time of disgust and purgation. The French were disgusted with their countrymen who had let themselves be puppets under German hands, and they were disgusted with the Germans who had brought them four years of death and misery. The French poet Louis Aragon had summarized the French view of the Germans:

> *The Nazis have entered our homes, and they kill.*
> *Force is their only virtue,*
> *Death their single science.*

Now, in the last week of August 1944, trials were happening in many parts of France. One of them was in the city of Le Puy in the mountains of south-central France, the mountainous region where the great Loire River has been born anew every moment for millions of years. It is a spectacular city in spectacular surroundings, standing in a green basin surrounded by mountains and extinct volcanoes. Toward the edge of the city a thin spur rises more than two hundred feet above cobblestoned streets. It is Saint Michael's Rock, a needle with an eleventh-century chapel on its tip. A few hundred yards away is a vast chunk of hardened lava, Corneille Rock, on which there rises a colossal red statue of the Virgin Mary holding Jesus Christ in her arms. She was cast from the metal of 213 cannons.

Not far from the needle and the Virgin is the Préfecture, the main governmental building of the Département. In that building a *séance*, a hearing, was taking place. In the hidden pathways and meadows of central France, many of the Maquis had trained and camped. They were the Germans' bitterest enemies in France. Now that they had liberated this part of France, their leaders were conducting the hearing.

At four o'clock in the afternoon of August 23, 1944, while Paris was being liberated, a stout man with an oval face under sparse gray hair walked down the main aisle of a hearing room in the Préfecture. His body was shaped like an egg, and so was his head. He was Maj. Julius Schmähling, and he was wearing the grayish green uniform of a Wehrmacht officer. For part of the two bloodiest years of the occupation of France he had been in command of the German troops in the mountainous Haute-Loire. He had been *le grand responsable*, the most obvious and the most legitimate target of French rage. Now he was in the hands of his most violent enemies.

As he walked up the aisle toward the presiding officer of the hearing, something strange started to happen. People in the room, including the tough Resistance leader who was chairing the session, rose to their feet. The German officer bowed his head slightly toward the Resistance chief, and the lean Frenchman bowed back. Then, still standing, the *maquisard* delivered himself of a quiet, restrained speech. He spoke of the German's services to the people of the Haute-Loire, of their gratitude to him, and of his affectionate personality.

Elsewhere in France Germans were being swiftly tried and executed. North of Le Puy fifty-five Germans were mutilated and thrown into a deep well in the suburbs of Saint-Étienne. In a more dangerous part of France than Saint-Étienne, however, the former leader of the Germans was receiving what he called in his diary *Huldigung*, homage.

The next day, August 24, was different. The French had just discovered that German troops in the region had shot off the faces of two Maquis, the much-admired Captain Seigle and his young driver. The presiding officer asked Schmähling if he knew who had given the order to kill the Maquis. He did not. They both knew that Schmähling had not been in command of the *Verbindungsstab* when this had happened, and so the chairman did not pursue the matter. Instead he asked Schmähling what they could do for him. Would he like better food? Would he like writing paper? He answered no, but perhaps some books would be nice. He was already embarrassed at the special food and the other exceptional treatment he was receiving.

In his prison diary he calls the chairman's laudatory words *"fast peinlich,"* almost painful. What he had done during his command was an inward, personal matter, a matter of conscience, of simple humanity (*"Menschlichkeit"*). It had nothing to do with praise or rewards from the world around him. Back in Munich, where he had long taught in a *Gymnasium*, he had told his students that words like "good" and "kind" were superfluous. He had told them that such words are payments, and decency has no price, no market value.

A few days later the French moved Julius Schmähling and his staff to a castle near the village of Le Chambon, about twenty miles east of Le Puy. Made out of coarse gray material resembling cinderblocks, the sham bore the imposing name the Castle of Mars. During the few weeks the defeated Germans lived there, French people came from Le Puy to visit the major, and they brought him food and watercolors. He did a watercolor of the castle, which his son Walter gave me. The brushstrokes in it are stronger, more aggressive, and more definite than watercolor brushstrokes usually are. In the foreground he painted the barbed-wire fence surrounding the castle.

Two of the leaders of the village of Le Chambon, the Protestant pastor André Trocmé and his wife, Magda, visited Schmähling and brought him a few delicacies. For four years their village and a few other tiny Protestant villages on that high plateau had protected and fed out of their meager food supplies the Nazis' prime target, Jews. Now the leaders of the village were visiting that man who had been *le grand responsable* for all the danger and suffering the village had undergone. In the course of Schmähling's administration of the Haute-Loire, Pastor Trocmé had watched the face of his wife, Magda, becoming more and more skeletal while the German's remained pink and plump. What he had not seen was Major Schmähling enjoying one of his favorite desserts in his comfortable Le Puy apartment—peaches pricked with a fork and soaked in champagne.

Given all this, what had Schmähling done to earn the respect of the people of Le Chambon and the leaders in Le Puy? I knew something of what he did not do: He did not unleash the brutal Crimean auxiliary troops who were in barracks near him in Le Puy, and he did not call down troops from outside the Haute-Loire to smash the nest of Jews in Huguenot country.

A hotelkeeper in Le Chambon during the war years, Roger Bonfils, has insisted that there was an informal agreement between Pastor Trocmé and Major Schmähling: If Trocmé would discourage the harming of German soldiers in the region, Schmähling would turn a blind eye to what was happening in Le Chambon and would do his best to keep the village from being raided. But various people in

Le Chambon contest Bonfils's claims, because he worked too closely with the Germans to give reliable testimony of this sort. His hotel had housed and fed German soldiers. Once he had received the classic threat from the French Resistance in the region: a little black coffin containing a tiny string shaped in a hangman's noose. Besides, people I have talked to in the region believe that the two leaders would never have dared to meet, because any such meeting in those bitter days would have compromised both men to the point of making them traitors to their countries.

And yet a Jewish Maquis doctor named Nicolas Schapira—a man whose testimony is unimpeachable—told me that during the last two dangerous years of the occupation Schmähling did his best "to keep the Nazis away from the region." Schapira was convinced that the Germans and the French must have arranged "signs and countersigns," "*consignés*," in order to keep from colliding with one another in the narrow mountain passes of the Haute-Loire. Still, Schapira could not be more precise about what Schmähling actually did to protect the French people and the Jews in the region. Even after forty years the subject was too thorny to be handled.

5

When Julius Schmähling died in 1973, his son found a letter in his wallet, a letter that had been written in 1966 by the mayor of Le Puy and other city officials. Schmähling had carried the letter—which had as much warmth in it as the traditions of formal French letter-writing permit—in his wallet to his dying day. It thanked him for rendering the conditions of war as supportable as they could be "within the limits of the freedom that you were granted," and it assured him that the French people remembered with affection the compassion he exhibited "during an epoch when it was not easy to be a good German among good Frenchmen."

You cannot understand the words of this letter or the story of this man without realizing that Schmähling was not in France on a goodwill mission. One of his primary functions as *Kommandant* of the Haute-Loire was to keep the peace in that dangerous region—to keep the French quiet while Germany raped the country and went about its business of trying to conquer the world. A major part of his job was to facilitate the victory of a nation dedicated to

the murder of millions. He was appointed commander of that difficult region because Berlin was convinced that he would keep the
French quiet, even cooperative. And Berlin had been right; he did
his job well. There were very few attacks on German soldiers during his administration.

If evil has to do with the twisting and diminution of human life,
then the government he ably served was evil. In a mountainous
part of France where there were many French guerrilla fighters, he
helped keep the French from stabbing his fellow Germans in the
back and hindering the cruel march of Nazism. He helped an evil
cause ably, and importantly.

But if goodness has to do with the spreading of human life, and
the prevention of hatred and cruelty and murder, then he was
surely good. Good and evil have much to do with perspectives,
points of view. If you want to know whether cruelty is happening
and just how painful it is, do not ask the torturer. Do not ask someone like Obergruppenführer* Otto Ohlendorff, the head of the
special troops assigned to kill unarmed civilians in Eastern Europe.
The victimizer does not feel the blows, the victim feels them. Do
not ask a sword about wounds; look to the person on whose flesh
the sword falls. Victimizers can be blinded by simple insensitivity,
by a great cause, by a great hatred, or by a hundred self-serving
"reasons." Victims too can be desensitized, but usually they are the
best witnesses to their pain. They feel it in their flesh and in their
deepest humiliations and horrors.

And if you want to know about goodness, do not ask only the
doers of good. They may be doing what they do out of habitual
helpfulness or for some abstract cause. They may not realize
exactly how they are helping the people they have helped: They
may not be looking deeply into the eyes and minds of the beneficiaries of their good deeds.

But usually the beneficiaries of those deeds know. Usually they
have this knowledge in their flesh and in their passions. And usually
if they do not have this knowledge, goodness is not happening, the
joy of living is not being enhanced and widened for them. Do-
gooders can in fact do great harm. The points of view of victims
and beneficiaries are vital to an understanding of evil and of good.

* Lieutenant general.

The French of the Haute-Loire were both the victims of the Germans and the beneficiaries of Schmähling's deeds and non-deeds. They knew what Schmähling meant in their lives when he refused to strike at them individually, and when he refused to strike down the rescue village of Le Chambon, that nest of Jews in Huguenot country. And they praised him for being a "good German."

But it is important to notice the whole phrase "good German." The French knew—certainly the Resistance chiefs knew—that he was no enemy of the German Army when he kept the peace in the Haute-Loire. He was a German soldier. They knew that he was serving the German Army—and the government that governed the army—well. They saw that he was a good man "within the limits of the freedom you have been allowed," as the letter from the mayor of Le Puy goes. The authorities for both good and evil in the Haute-Loire found goodness in this man, within limits.

What the French—especially the Resistance chiefs—knew was that protecting a few Frenchmen in the Haute-Loire was entirely consistent with the main task of Maj. Julius Schmähling: to keep the peace in a dangerous time and in a dangerous place. They knew that his kindnesses were at one and the same time in the service of goodness and in the service of evil. They knew that he served an evil government well, that he was a soft pad in the paw of the monster, a pad that served as a cushion in the harsh terrain of the Haute-Loire and a pad that helped advance the march of the monster.

A *Kommandant* who was a failure in German eyes would in all likelihood have been a failure as a friend of the weak. He would at least have been swiftly removed from his command. Schmähling's actions and his refusals to act were at their very center morally ambiguous: They saved people's lives in the region of Le Puy, and they advanced the military purposes of a regime dedicated to the mass murder and total domination of millions of human beings.

In one respect he violated his duty to Nazi Germany: He drew a line in his mind between waging war and waging persecution, and he refused to persecute the Jews. He protected them in the city of Le Puy, and they lived there in safety under his administration, some of them working with Germans in a refrigeration plant at the edge of the city, others living openly in the center of the city. And he was fully aware of what was happening in Le Chambon. He saw combat, the struggle between more or less equally matched combatants, as his military duty, but he would not smash the weak. He served a government that systematically persecuted defenseless people, but he would not persecute them himself.

6

Early in my research into the story of Le Chambon, Mme. Gabrielle Barraud, the short Alsatian, had told me that "*le Major*" had helped the village during the last two years of the occupation. What he had done was not clear to her, and so I had not pursued the subject. But sometimes I wondered exactly what he had done, and why he had done it. Now, after the story of Le Chambon was published, and after I had begun to face the contradictions in my own mind and in my own behavior, I spent three years learning about "*le Major*."

I learned that he was a Roman Catholic, and at first I thought he was a deeply religious man practicing Christian love within the limits of his freedom as *Kommandant* of the Haute-Loire. But when I spent some time in Bavaria with his family and his former students, I discovered that religion was of no great interest to him. When he was in his teens and until the death of his mother, he scandalized and pained her by refusing to go to church. The only thing he admired about churches was their architecture. He thought that church ritual and theology were mostly nonsense. Once a friend met Schmähling in the streets of the industrial city of Aschaffenburg, near Frankfurt, where he was teaching, and asked him why he never saw him in church. Schmähling answered, "You can see me better out here. There's more light."

One cool evening in Munich, late in Schmähling's life, he was walking in the English Garden with a priest. The two were old friends, and they did not feel compelled to talk much in the autumnal quietness of the place. The priest was telling his beads and reciting the rosary while Schmähling was enjoying the flowers. Suddenly Schmähling stopped and pointed excitedly to a small flower near their feet. "What is the name of that flower?" he asked, surprised at not knowing it (he was immensely knowledgeable about flowers).

"Well," the priest said distractedly. "I don't know their names. I know only that each one is the work of God."

When he got home that evening Schmähling told his wife, Emma, how irritated he had been with the priest's answer. He felt an obligation (*Auftrag*) to see the color and shape of each flower in its own special lavishness. A flower for him was not a mystery, not a cup filled with God's inscrutable grace; it was something more obvious. It was *here* for the senses and for the passions. And so it was for him with the rest of the world.

Since he taught history and literature, I thought he might have some theory, some principles that he followed in the Haute-Loire. But I was wrong again. When any of his students, colleagues, or friends asked him what he meant by calling something "decent" or "vicious," instead of presenting a neat theory of ethics, he almost invariably uttered one little phrase: "*Das Moralische versteht sich von selbst*," "What's right is obvious." He was as innocent of theory as an inarticulate child.

Beginning to despair of understanding this man, I asked myself if he saved the lives of people in the Haute-Loire out of patriotic expediency, because persecuting the Jews there would disturb the countryside and would hinder Nazi Germany by causing the fatherland to commit more troops to the area. Wrong again. He and Emma had fought Nazism since the early 1930s, when Hitler was rising to power. Emma Schmähling took care of the theorizing, but both of them campaigned and voted for the only effective German enemies of the Nazis, the Social Democrats.

Moreover, he was so little interested in the German Army itself that, according to his son, Walter, he did not even know its hierarchy of ranks. Walter believes that he did not know because he did not care. He was a teacher by profession, and a reservist who had been forced into service in September 1939, when Germany invaded Poland. It was not very likely that he did what he did in the Haute-Loire because he cared for the success of the army, let alone that of Nazism.

As a matter of fact his reentry into the army (he had been a young commissioned officer in World War I) amounted to a forced

migration from a violently revolutionized Nazi Germany into the
relatively conservative traditions of the German Army. Even
though the migration was forced on him, it pleased him because as
a soldier he was more or less sheltered from the fanatical, demanding Nazi Party that dominated every corner of civilian life. In the
army, especially among officers his own age, he could find conser-
vatives like himself, and they could sit down and grumble together
against the radical young upstarts who ran the national socialist
revolution. For him the army was the lesser of two evils. Both
fanatical Nazism and traditional military discipline took his freedom away, but the military left him more elbow room.

I was baffled. I could find no institution or system of beliefs that
could explain Schmähling's behavior in the Haute-Loire. Here was a
man whose particular deeds and motives were hidden from me by a
veil. But I could see through the veil that he somehow managed to
help protect lives, and in particular that he managed to help preserve the village of Le Chambon, which was itself a saver of lives.

Then one day, when I was visiting his daughter, Annelise, in a
suburb of Nuremberg, I came across a letter he wrote to his wife
while he was *Kommandant* in a very sensitive post near Dieppe in
the north of France, the post he held before he moved down to the
Haute-Loire. In his letter to Emma he described "my hot-blooded
passion." He described his rage at SS troops in his region who were
threatening and torturing defenseless civilians. It was a rage that did
not need principles or religious commitments or political goals.

Everything I had learned about him from both the French and
the Germans seemed to fall into place. He was an inhabitant of the
now. He did what he did neither for long-term goals nor for high
abstractions. He did what he did out of passion. His own and other
people's present needs drove him. He loved food and drink and
people from the depths of his abundantly sanguine nature. He was,
to use a word from the history of art, "baroque," unruly, exuberant.
He was not classically restrained or deliberate. He was the exact
opposite of the "orders are orders" personality that abounded in
Germany. He lived in bursts.

To be with him in the streets of a big city was a terrifying experience. Even after the war, as an old man, he swept through the
traffic of Aschaffenburg or Munich like a fire truck on the way to a
fire. Red lights meant nothing to him, and he pulled everybody

who was with him into the very middle of the densest traffic as if he were king of the road. As a passenger in a car he would demand that the driver ignore lights and no-passing signs, even when they were in no special hurry.

He loved museums, and he loved to visit churches (they were all museums to him), and his rumbling voice shattered their silences. When he came up to a church or a museum door and found it locked, it never occurred to him to turn away meekly. He would find a bell or a door buzzer nearby, or pound on the door or windows until somebody got him a key, or told him where he could go to get the key.

A German who indulges in such behavior is bizarre. Almost invariably when you walk down a Munich street you see total obedience to signs and to lights, and you witness apparently endless patience. If you violate these public commands you become the cynosure of glaring or bewildered eyes. It takes an immense amount of self-containment to ignore the astonished looks, or even the anger, of law-abiding Germans. But Schmähling managed to do it, from the time of the kaisers (he was born in 1884) through the Weimar Republic, through Hitler's Third Reich, and into the seventies. Through all those changes in Germany he remained his own baroque self.

And his students throughout many of these years loved him for it. When he was an old man, no home was big enough to contain his students on his birthdays. Students who had studied under him forty or fifty years earlier crossed Germany to be with him. He ate food voraciously; he drank all the wine and beer that came to hand; he flirted with pretty young women; and he told apparently interminable stories that had no point at all and that drove his wife from the room in a fury (because Emma had heard the silly stories so many times, and because she could not stop him). He was the center of any party, and he was always the wildest, happiest person in the room.

If during a quiet evening at home his wife asked him to change a light bulb, he would suggest that she call in somebody to do it (she usually got a ladder and did it herself); but he was always ready to go to the *Lokal** for a drink, and he was always ready to

* Bar or pub.

help his students when they needed him. He would pound on any doors, call on any officials, work on any number of applications or letters, give any money, and sign any agreements in order to help them. When the needs of others became visible to him (which was by no means always the case), those needs became his needs, and he served them with the energy of a self-indulgent person who was *kerngesund*, physically healthy to the core.

7

In a letter he wrote to Emma from the Haute-Loire late in June 1944 he said: "Many a time I say to myself, even now after sixty years you have not learned to subdue your hot blood." Still, once in his life he learned a little about subduing his hot blood, and he never forgot the lesson. Here is a story he told again and again, a story he put into his memoirs when he was a very old man.

He was a young teacher in northern Bavaria toward the beginning of the century, when one day he came into the classroom of his little wooden schoolhouse to give his students a lesson on lions. He had prepared a dramatic lecture about the king of beasts, and he was full of it, and full of himself. He started the lecture: "The lion is—" but before he could say more a little boy in the back of the room who had been sitting dumbly on his wooden bench during the whole term caught his eye. The boy was standing up and frantically waving his hand in the air. The burly young teacher set his jaw and kept talking about the great beasts. Suddenly the little boy yelled out, "Herr Professor, Herr—" Schmähling looked at him in anger. He could hardly believe that this little dunce was going to interrupt *his* discourse on lions.

Then the boy did something that struck the teacher like a blow. He called out, "Yesterday, yes, yesterday I saw a rabbit! Yes, Herr Professor, yesterday *I saw a rabbit!*"

Before the words were all out, Schmähling thundered, "Sit down, you little jackass!" The boy dropped back like a stone onto his bench and said not another word for the rest of the year.

Until the end of his long life Julius Schmähling looked back at that incident as the turning point of his life as a person and as a teacher. In the very act of crushing the boy with all of the power of

German authoritarianism, he had violated something in himself. He had violated his own deep need to be compassionate.

After trying for weeks to bring the boy out of his silence, he vowed that teaching and living for him would from that moment forward involve making room for each of his students and for each of the people he encountered outside of the classroom—making room for them to speak about the rabbits, the wonders they had seen. He vowed to tame the streak of arrogant cruelty in himself, and he vowed to make the needs of his students his own. Within the limits of his wild temperament he succeeded, according to the dozens of his students I have interviewed.

8

Later in his teaching career he found out that the classroom is not a world of its own. He became a member of a group that made cruelty a science and an art: the National Socialist Workers Party, whose philosopher, revolutionary chief, and absolute political leader was Adolf Hitler.

On a sunny spring day in 1937, four years after Hitler had taken absolute power in Germany, the director of the women's normal school (a teachers' college) in Aschaffenburg called Schmähling into his office. He asked him to sit down, drew a deep breath, and told him that he must join the Nazi Party at last; no more delays, no more evasions. *Gauleiter* Helmut, the Nazi chief of the *Gau* (district) of Franconia, had just targeted their school for *Gleich-schaltung*, forced absorption into the Nazi Party. Faculty members had to join the party or lose their jobs. And once you lost your job in Nazi Germany because you would not accept the honor of becoming a Nazi, your career was finished, especially if you were a teacher. A teacher who was not a Nazi, at least in the judgment of *Gauleiter* Helmut, was an enemy of the state—and a dangerous one, because he influenced the thinking of the young directly and often powerfully.

The director was a friend of Schmähling, who knew that he had refused to join the party for four years. He knew that Schmähling resented Nazism because it had smashed the democracy that Schmähling hoped would flourish in Germany after World War I.

He also knew that Schmähling himself did not think much about political matters.

Emma was the political thinker of the family, and she and her husband had led a few rallies on behalf of some of the enemies of Nazism. Emma urged him to attend these more and more dangerous rallies, and she wrote his very brief speeches. She was gifted in languages, and she knew much more about current events and political systems than Julius did. But the Nazis were more interested in males than they were in females, more interested in teachers than they were in housewives, and so they never pressed Emma to join the party.

At first the Schmählings had been with the Liberal Democrats, but in 1933 they voted with the Social Democrats, even though the Social Democrats were somewhat less traditional than the Schmählings about some matters. The Schmählings believed—as did many other Germans—that the Social Democrats held the only realistic hope for a democratic Germany because they were the only political party that had the ghost of a chance to defeat the wide coalition that Hitler had created. All this the director knew.

And he also knew that Julius Schmähling had escaped membership in the party for those four years because he was a reserve officer in the German Army. Even though the revolutionary Nazi Party and the basically conservative German Army were often at odds with each other, the Nazis, like most Germans, respected the military. During the four years from 1933 to 1937, most people were "realigned" (*gleichgeschaltet*) with the Nazi Party by being drawn into the many Nazi "clubs" that had sprung up in Germany after the 1933 elections like so many fungi after a forest rain. There were Nazi Catholic groups, Nazi Bavarian groups, Nazi teacher groups, and so on indefinitely. A German was safe from suspicion if he or she belonged to three or four of them, even though he or she had not asked to join the Nazi Party itself. Neither Julius nor Emma had joined any of these clubs, and they had managed to avoid being investigated or penalized because Julius was a reserve officer in the Wehrmacht.

By 1937 it was plain to every German that the nation was at war against privacy. A "private citizen" was to be a contradiction in terms. Sex, food, leisure, the home, all aspects of life had to be *gleichgeschaltet*—had to fit Nazism. Hitler and his party insisted that the struggle for survival was the basic condition of nature. That is why power was so important: One wins this struggle, one survives and thrives, only with power, and one achieves that power only through union, union with the will of the leader.

The central enemy in this *Kampf*, this battle, was the Jew, in his or her various—contradictory—forms: capitalists, Communists, powerful international conspirators, weak vermin. By 1937, as Hitler was moving swiftly in his preparations for war with other nations, it was necessary for all types of leaders inside Germany, especially the highly respected schoolteachers, to choose between the Führer and the Jew.

As they sat there in the director's office, he did not have to tell Schmähling these things. But he did have to tell him that he was heading for disaster if he dared to resist *Gleichschaltung* any longer. They both knew that the occupational system of Germany had existed long before Hitler's coming, and it was rigid. There was practically no lateral mobility in it, no way to change occupations after you passed through your apprenticeship, except by going into a war-related industry or entering active military service. They both knew that if the director discharged Schmähling, as he was instructed by the *Gauleiter* to do if Schmähling did not join the party, he would never teach again, and he was fifty-three, far too old to learn a new profession. He loved teaching. He loved the prestige and the comforts that teachers enjoyed in Germany. And he was loath to take up active service in the army under the government of the National Socialists. His was a choice between nightmares, and at the end of the interview with the director he decided to choose the less horrific nightmare: He allowed the director to put his name on the Nazi Party list.

As he rose from his chair, Schmähling told the director that he would consent to join the party, but he would write no *Gesuch*, no request for membership, and he would attend only meetings that were absolutely obligatory. The director agreed to this nominal party membership, but both of them knew that it would be noticed by the *Gauleiter* or his staff and that eventually Schmähling would have to go back into active service in the army in order to protect himself and his family from being accused of siding with the enemies of the state.

The next year, 1938, Schmähling quit his job in Aschaffenburg and took his family to Munich. Here, he and his wife thought, they could have the anonymity of a large, securely Nazi city. After his Munich students came to know him, he felt free to express his feelings against the Third Reich. In March 1939, after the Germans seized Czechoslovakia, he burst into class one day, and while the students were still standing for his entrance, yelled out that Germans were growing accustomed to taking actions that would bring only "universal murder and destruction" into the world. While they were standing there, stunned by his rage and his dangerous imprudence, he attacked all "those Germans who can say only yes and amen to the authorities." And—they were still standing—he wagged his finger at them and told them to follow his example and say no.

With that violent temper of his, he could not keep still. His time as a civilian was running out.

When Germany attacked Poland in September 1939, the army reactivated Schmähling's commission, and he became a captain in the postal division of the army in Munich. His daughter, Annelise, remembers the thunderstorm of his voice when he opened the letter containing his call-up. "See who my commander is now? See? *Hitler*! *Ach*!" And he sank into his chair with his head far down.

Schmähling was lucky. His neighborhood *Blockleiter* was beginning to ask questions about his loyalty, but now that he was reentering the army the questions would stop, and when he entered active service his party membership terminated.

But he was nonetheless part and parcel of Hitler's Germany. In July 1947, since he had been a member of the Nazi Party from 1937 to 1939, he came before an Allied denazification tribunal in Munich. The tribunal solicited testimony in France and in Germany, and many of its testimonials have come into my hands. These signed statements, written under oath, have been one of the main sources of my knowledge of Schmähling's activities in France. The decision of the tribunal was that he was at "most [a] nominal" (*höchstens nominell*) member of the party, having had as little to do with it as one could possibly have.

But the fact remains that he was a successfully functioning part of a state that murdered millions of defenseless human beings. In a world dominated by the Nazis, he would have enjoyed a full life by reason of his record. He served the Reich well. He did nothing to slow down—let alone stop—the triumphant march of Nazism.

And yet, and yet—he held life dear.

9

John Milton in his *Areopagitica* could have been writing about Schmähling: "Good and evill we know in the field of this World grow up together almost inseparably. . . . It was from out the rinde of one apple tasted, that the knowledge of good and evill as two twins cleaving together leapt forth into the world." Ethical ambivalence, the intertwining of good and evil, is not confined to the case of this decent servant of an indecent cause. All of us are practitioners of the art of living in friendship, and even in admiration, with people whose generosity and kindness are flawed, darkened by blind self-interest or some other moral shadow. So many of us— perhaps all of us—are moral mixtures, impure. And the art of living with such people is a precious art, an art that William Blake celebrated when he called friendship "the unending forgiveness of sins."

I see the faults in my wife, my daughter, my son, my close friends, and I see those faults as clearly as they see mine. But we have all practiced the art of living with, and loving, morally imperfect human beings. Those we most deeply love and admire are loved and admired by us not in spite of their faults, but because their faults are somehow a facet of their virtues, if only a dark facet. Love is not blind; usually we love each other with our eyes open. A mother can love her child and be morally blind to the needs of all other human beings, and the very intensity of that love can make her morally beautiful, even to strangers.

But not only in intimate human relationships is there ambivalence. Almost all nations are born and raised in bursts of blood, and the bloodshed is sometimes part of their nobility, part of what we feel to be their desire to enhance and expand human life. Americans like me, for example, see the American Revolution and World War II as good and evil. We see such events as having the faults of their virtues. Their faults and virtues are intertwined with each other, even identical. They are ambiguous events for people like me, full of real cruelty and at the same time full of a need to stop real cruelty.

The United States has done many things that are plainly evil. There is no such thing as evil in the world if torturing and betraying and killing Native Americans and blacks for hundreds of years is not evil. These are not good-and-evil deeds, and they are not aspects of American history that make my country morally beautiful. If I sometimes find my country morally beautiful, I do so in the very teeth of these blatant evils. Persecution is not an object of moral ambivalence to me. I despise it with all my heart. But there are deeds my country has done that I love and hate in the same breath. Fighting in World War II is one of them. John Milton was writing about such deeds, and Julius Schmähling was doing them during the twelve-year empire of Adolf Hitler.

Human life is not all that is morally ambivalent in this world. Nature is the widest drama of good and evil that we can know. When a lioness closes her jaws on a zebra's throat, she is feeding life and destroying life in one and the same action. What is food to the predator is death to the prey. Biologists see this more clearly than the rest of us do. Rachel Carson in her early book *Under the Sea-Wind* ends her description of the death of some snowy owl embryos with the following sentence: "The six little owls-to-be were dead in the snow, and by their death, perhaps, hundreds of unborn lemmings and ptarmigans and Arctic hares had the greater chance of escaping death from the feathered ones that strike from the sky."

We creatures live off the bodies of others. This is the system we are part of, whether we like it or not. If we cannot learn to live and love in such a bloody, ambiguous world as this, we starve to death emotionally and cognitively, for we live with truth as necessarily as we live with high hopes.

AN APOLOGY
TO MY MOTHER

May 20, 1989
Middletown,
Connecticut

Dear Mama,

When I helped them bury you in the rain we rushed through the graveside ceremony because we were more interested in keeping dry than we were in you. Now I am sitting here in our maple-enclosed acre you used to call "a Gan Eden," a Garden of Eden. I can see daffodils blooming and swaying by the barn, and in my mind I see your body in a coffin that is dark inside, very dark, black, blank. I can see me throwing the first earth on that coffin; then I see the earth piled on it, and on the earth I see a granite gravestone that has a photograph on it of you in your green-eyed, auburn-haired youth. Life and death are so different, Mama! You never told me how different they are. No one can console me for your death. Relatives and friends who have seen the rage in me have not even tried.

Your death has done some strange things to your son. And I feel what it has done more sharply now, here in Connecticut, than I felt it while I was burying you in Chicago. One of the things it has done is to make it impossible for me to lie to you anymore. Before May 11 I used to say to myself, "She is there, in Chicago. She'll never find out." I was thinking like this when I took Louie with me to Germany. No more. I once thought that death is only parting, but it is more strange than that. Now I feel that you were separate from me before you died. While you were alive you were there, outside of me, there in Chicago, or there across the table stroking your right eyebrow and dreaming. I could think my own thoughts, I could plan my own travels, and I could feel my own guilty disdain for your fears.

But now you are within me as you have never been before. Now there is nothing you cannot find out about my thoughts. Sometimes I am like an empty house that is full of your spirit, your fears, and your sense of humor. I remember that first letter you wrote me while I was in combat. You told me how you had been yelling to God begging him to keep me safe, when all of a sudden you heard the voice of God say to you, "Nettie, what you are yelling about? Don't you think I can hear?" It was only your body we buried in that hole on that rainy day in May, your body, which was always separate from me, ever since you gave birth to me. I feel your soul as I never felt it before you died. Life parted us, not death.

And so I cannot lie to you now, and I cannot argue with you. Your terror, your laughter, even your prayers to a tender, suffering God inhabit me.

While the cancer in your throat was choking you and you were gradually losing the power of speech, I was writing Doris smug, self-serving letters from Germany. I did not know about the cancer, but I did know that you were far from well, and I thought more about the Germans than I did about you. I remember the day—it was a spring day in Munich—when it dawned on me that you would have to be in any book I wrote about a German soldier under Hitler. That day I wrote in my diary:

Now here's a good way to do concrete ethics: Don't just tell stories interpreted in the old words of ethical theories. Show the intimate feelings of the storyteller, me!

After all, good and evil are as personal as love and hate. And that means bringing mama into it, her terror, the mortal fear that perhaps all Jews feel after what the Nazis did.

When I look at these words I am horrified at this monster, myself. If it were plain to me that since the day I wrote that entry I have been making copy out of your feelings, I would raise an image of a gravestone in the air above my head, and I would carry that image over my head to my dying day. I would feel myself decaying and stinking under it.

Here is a letter you wrote me on the tenth of December in 1979:

My beloved and precious child—

I'll never talk like this, unless it's to save your life. In all your life you never caused me heartache—my heart aches in every word I say— and with my last drops of strength I'll talk like this Baby.

Please don't go to Germany. I am asking God to make you understand that you aren't safe to go there. I'm glad you phoned. Phil, you remember Germany and how they killed people all over on the streets. Innocent blood was spilled there. God will never forget, and just because a hand-full of Christians helped some Jews, Jewish people are happy. Not so with God. A book will open God's misery.

Please never let my child write such books.

Believe me, Germany is no place to go ever, and the people you will interview, surely you don't think they will tell you all the truth— they will only tell you how good they are. Don't go. *Please*. Don't go. My fears are that you will go there—so my prayers will take place regularly. My prayers are regular to God to stop you from going there with Louie.

                          With all my strength love to you.
                                                  Mama

        Don't go.   Please
        Don't go.   Please
        Don't go.   Please
        Don't go.   Please
        Don't go.   Please

Still, I went to Germany, more than once, and I took my son, Louie, with me. I am *almost* certain that I have not been using you as a foil for my "concrete ethics." I have been trying to learn about my feelings and my thoughts concerning this man Julius Schmähling. Intense feelings and home truths are not neat. They are mixtures, full of contradictions. Schmähling was part of one of the great monstrosities of human history, but he did some good things out of impulsive innocence. I have to understand what I think and what I feel about him. I do not wish to bury what is so alive in me—my yearning for moral peace in a world that is what Gandhi called "a conflagration of *himsa*," a blaze of killing and dying.

And so to help the you in me to find a little well-earned peace, let me tell you a story about a man who was also part of the monster—a German who was not only an adult when Hitler was in power, but was a member of the Nazi party. He was a man you would not have feared, Mama.

The man's name is Kurt Huber. He was a professor of philosophy on the faculty of the University of Munich. He was a small man. An early illness had crippled his right foot, so that he limped deeply, and that same disease had afflicted him with a stammer and a rather weak voice.

At three o'clock one afternoon in October 1942, he was sitting in his little apartment in Grafelfing, a suburb southeast of Munich. There was a knock on the door. He pulled himself erect, limped to the door, and opened it. There stood a young man who had been a student of Huber's not long ago. Now he was a soldier coming back from the Russian front on a rest leave.

When the two of them settled into their chairs, the worn chairs of a college professor out of favor with the all-powerful Nazi regime, the young man told his teacher that the German Army had recently attacked the Russians at Stalingrad, and that the battle for Stalingrad was becoming the bloodiest in German history. He went on to say that he had broken his trip home in order to talk with his teacher about matters that were troubling him.

The apartment was darkening as he talked about the sterilization experiments that the Germans were carrying out on Polish Jews, and on Polish non-Jews as well. The student's voice was beginning to rise out of control, and Huber told him to speak more quietly. A zealously pro-Nazi family lived right under the Huber apartment, and they might hear some of his words. The student started talking in almost a whisper.

Suddenly, unable to control himself any longer, he burst out, "Professor Huber, I have something terrible to tell you, and it is not a rumor. I saw it myself. We are shooting Jews in the Crimea. Sir, we are shooting Jews there!"

Huber screamed. His scream was a long, wordless lamentation

that overrode the weakness in his vocal cords and filled the little apartment. His wife, Clara, rushed into the living room and begged them to be silent. The children were asleep, and there was that Nazi family downstairs. Huber sat silent in his chair, bent double, moaning, his eyes wide and staring at his student.

At three in the morning, after hours of talk and long periods of miserable silence, the student rose from his chair. There was an early morning train he must catch if he was going to be able to spend enough time home with his family before returning to the front.

Still sitting, Huber said, "I envy you for being able to go to the front. There at least you can rush into the fire and die."

The student asked, "But isn't that suicide?"

Huber answered, "When horror becomes unbearable, death makes sense."

"I don't know, sir. Suicide is never good. . . ."

The thin, stammering voice of the teacher came back: "There are situations that carry us beyond moral laws."

These were the last words the student would hear from the lips of his philosophy teacher.

In the course of the next year Kurt Huber became the only faculty member at the University of Munich to work with a group of students that called itself the White Rose. He differed from them about some matters. For instance, he believed that the traditional code of honor in the German Army could help the White Rose make a strong appeal to the German people against the Nazi government of Germany; but the other, younger members of the group had no respect for the military. Despite their differences, Huber helped them write some of their pamphlets.

The students would shove their pamphlets into mailboxes, and even into the pockets of coats hanging in university cloakrooms. These could hurt innocent people, because anybody caught with such a pamphlet was prey for the Gestapo, or for any other ardent party member. In time the pamphlets of the White Rose appeared not only all over the university, but in many Munich neighborhoods, and in more than a dozen other German cities.

Some of the pamphlets described the mass killings of Jews and Poles, but all of them tried to undercut Nazi slogans with three weapons: facts, cool arguments, and passionate calls to action. Their final aim was to show the German people that Hitler was the embodiment of evil in the world, and that he and his followers must be resisted by sabotage, and by a general strike, a refusal to serve the government. In the fourth pamphlet they wrote: "Has God not given you the strength, the will to fight? We *must* attack evil where it is strongest, and it is strongest in the power of Hitler."

In February 1943, while Schmähling was settling into his duties as military governor of the Haute-Loire, the Gestapo struck the White Rose. Huber and all its student members were arrested. Soon afterward its leading students were decapitated.

After the first executions Kurt Huber came to trial in Berlin. On April 19, 1943, he stood before the Berlin People's Court and pointed out that he had fought Nazism not with violence or the threat of violence, but with the naked word (*das schlichte Wort*), because he wanted to awaken Germany to the meaning of decency, and he wanted to help restore people's trust in one another. He wanted neighbors to trust one another, and parents to trust their children. He wanted to show Germany that the rule of Nazism was the rule of brute force over public justice and personal conscience.

He said these things standing in front of the fanatical Nazi judge Roland Freisler, who alternately drummed his fingers on his desk and screamed at the defendant. But Huber continued his carefully written speech with that thin voice of his. He did not stammer.

On July 13, 1943, they took him from his cell in the Gestapo prison at Stadelheim, near Munich. The priest who accompanied him, a Father Brinkmann, saw the small man smile when he lost his right slipper as he went through the last door to the guillotine. They delayed the execution because some SS officers who were standing in front of the guillotine were discussing the pain involved in decapitation compared with that involved in other kinds of killing.

When their conversation was over, and just before Huber's neck was placed under the blade, he took leave of Father Brinkmann with the words, "Until we meet again on the other side." Then he dragged his slipperless right foot up to the guillotine, and the government of Germany chopped off his head.

Kurt Huber was a member of the Nazi Party. His widow, Clara, told me that she enrolled her husband in the party late in the thirties when it became clear to her that their family could not survive on the pitiful salary he earned as a non-Nazi faculty member of the

Nazi-dominated University of Munich. He and Schmähling joined the party about the same time, and for the same reasons: to survive.

And the two Germans hated harmdoing. They were teachers who, unlike the vast majority of their colleagues, tried hard to avoid joining a party that stood for hatred, destruction, and enslavement.

But here the similarities between them end. Kurt Huber believed with all his heart in the goodness of God, even as you do, Mama. Julius Schmähling loved God's houses much more than he loved God. Huber believed in the power of the "naked word" to awaken Germany from its moral slumbers. Schmähling had little faith in the healing power of words. Decency for him came straight from his own hot blood, and he never tried to express that decency in the lucid "naked word."

Kurt Huber tried to save everyone; he tried to preserve decency itself. He refused to compromise with indecency. Julius Schmähling tried to save a few people who were near him and in need of help, and he was a leader and very comfortable in an army that was ultimately in Hitler's hands. That scream in Huber's darkening apartment came from deeper regions in him than his disease-damaged trachea. It came from the center of his being, where mind and body are one. It is written that the wages of sin are death, but what you get for being decent can be a living death.

Schmähling's last months with those horrific thoughts about Doctor Le Forestier, and Huber's scream in his Grafelfing apartment were not part of the brute force in the world, but they were very close to it. Something in them was free from it, as birds in the eye of a hurricane may feel free from the violent winds, for a moment. The "*schrecklich*" of Schmähling and the scream of Huber were not separate from the conflagration of *himsa*. The violence around them hurt them. Moral peace is fragile; it is not all there is in the world.

Mama, now that you are nearer to me than ever, please let me keep trying to find some kind of loving peace before the brute forces in nature crush me.

Your son,
Philip

A PAUSE

VICTIMS IN
WONDERLAND

1

Toward the beginning of *Through the Looking-Glass*, Alice finds herself in a very dark wood, and she wants to get out of it before night falls. Bewildered, and talking to herself, she makes a sharp turn, and very suddenly she is facing two fat little men standing under a tree, each with an arm around the other's neck. They are Tweedledum and Tweedledee. Despite her efforts to persuade them to tell her how to get out of the wood, they insist on reciting a poem, and a rather long one, called "The Walrus and the Carpenter."

The poem is about a strange world in which the sun shines brightly at night while the moon is shining resentfully, because it feels that the sun has no right to shine after the day is done. There are no birds in the sky, and no clouds. Walking on a sandy beach in this bleak world are a Walrus and a Carpenter. They are weeping because there is so much sand and because it is very difficult to clear it away. They are given to shedding useless tears.

They come across some oysters, and the Walrus invites them for

"*A pleasant walk, a pleasant talk,
Along the briny beach.*"

The eldest oyster, without saying a word, winks his eye and shakes his head, but four eager young oysters jump up from their frothy beds to join them on the shore, and many more groups of four follow them. They all walk for about a mile until they get to a rock that is "conveniently low." The eloquent Walrus stops at the rock and makes a little speech about it being time to talk

> "Of shoes—and ships—and sealing-wax—
> Of cabbages—and—kings—"

He calls for a loaf of bread, and some pepper and vinegar, and then announces to the oysters, "We can begin to feed."

The young oysters turn a little blue and cry out, "But not on us!" They point out that eating them, especially after that kind invitation and that pleasant walk, would be "A dismal thing to do!" The taciturn Carpenter is concerned with getting enough bread and with being sure that the butter is not spread too thick, but not so the Walrus. He is the weepier of the two. He has compassion. He says that it is a shame to eat the oysters after walking them so fast, and he makes a heartfelt little speech to the young oysters who are lined up in a row before him.

> "I weep for you," the Walrus said:
> "I deeply sympathize."
> With sobs and tears he sorted out
> Those of the largest size,
> Holding his pocket-handkerchief
> Before his streaming eyes.

After it is clear that all the oysters have been eaten, and that the poem is finished, Alice says, "I like the Walrus best . . . because he was a *little* sorry for the oysters."

Her reaction to the story is rather similar to the ideas of many students of good and evil from Aristotle through Kant right up until the present day. Many of the "virtue philosophers" feel that good and evil reside mainly in the "moral agent"; they are qualities in the soul of a person. They believe that decency or viciousness has little to do with what that person does to other persons. For them ethics is a matter of character. Kant once said that a good will is the only thing truly and purely good, and a person's will is good "not because of what it performs or effects," but because of what is going on inside the mind of that person. He does not believe that the road to hell is paved with good intentions—on the contrary, he believes that the road to heaven is paved with good intentions.

In our own time a philosopher named Jonathan Bennett has defended the idea that Heinrich Himmler, who was responsible for the deaths of millions of defenseless people during the Third Reich, was a more moral person than the American theologian Jonathan Edwards, who killed no one and who wanted to kill no one. Why? For Alice's reason: that Himmler was a little sorry for his victims, while Edwards felt no pity for the sinners who would be eternally crushed in the hands of an angry God. Never mind what Himmler actually did in the world. Never mind the millions of unarmed civilians Himmler tortured, maimed, and killed; and never mind the fact that Edwards had no blood on his hands. According to Bennett good and evil have much more to do with being good-hearted than with the actual saving or smashing of flesh-and-blood lives. For them ethics dwells inside the moral agent, not in the world that contains the moral agent and others.

It is a fact that Himmler felt occasional nausea and stomachaches on those rare occasions when he chose to witness the cold-blooded murders in a camp or in a field. Once, when he was near some prisoners who were kneeling on the lip of an open grave and receiving the *Genickschuss* (having their brains blown out from behind so that they would fall right into the grave), some brain matter and blood leaped up and struck Himmler in the face. He nearly fainted with disgust. Years later the aide who helped him stagger away from the sickening scene laughed at the memory and said that Himmler's steel nerves were getting a bit rusty.

In a speech he is reputed to have given to the SS leaders who carried out his orders, he urged them to overcome their personal sympathies for individual Jews and to keep murdering them. His stomachaches and his words to his SS convince Bennett that Himmler was a decent fellow, with a good heart. He just had bad principles, the principles of Nazism. A man like this, Bennett says, is better than a person who murders no one, because it is compassion that matters in ethics, not what your hands—or what the hands that are following your commands—are doing. The morally commendable person is the one who feels at least a *little* sorry for others. Ethics is too spiritual to dirty its hands with the world.

But Lewis Carroll, or Tweedledee, is a bit more commonsensical than Bennett. Right after Alice says that she likes the Walrus best because he felt sorry for the poor oysters, Tweedledee points out to her: "He ate more than the Carpenter, though. . . . You see, he held his handkerchief in front, so that the Carpenter couldn't count how many he took: contrariwise."

Tweedledee sees that you can be just as murderous behind a tear-damp handkerchief as you can be without a handkerchief—in fact, you can be more efficiently murderous behind a handkerchief, because the other oysters cannot see what you are doing, and they tend to stand around listening to your speeches until you pick them up and eat them.

The fact is that Himmler was having some trouble on the Eastern Front in 1943 when he told his SS leaders to overcome their sympathies for individual Jews, Poles, or Russians. Some SS officers and subordinates were having severe emotional reactions to their torture and killing of women and children. Some of them were going into deep depression, and some were even refusing to follow orders. (Incidentally, when they refused to follow the orders to kill women and children they were usually not punished severely; they were usually transferred to other duties or transferred out of the SS.) In his speech Himmler was trying to make his followers more efficient. He was not simply opening his heart to them; he was preparing them for dealing with the psychological problems that ordinary people can have when they are torturing and murdering children who remind them of their own children, and women who remind them of their own mothers and wives and sisters and daughters. He was holding a verbal handkerchief before his eyes so that he and his followers could murder more and more helpless human beings, just as the Walrus was holding up his handkerchief so that he could eat more and more helpless oysters. Tweedledee saw that actions speak louder than wet handkerchiefs; but philosophers are not always so perspicacious.

After Tweedledee points out to Alice that behind his handkerchief the Walrus was eating more oysters than the Carpenter, Alice comes to her senses, and says: "That was mean! . . . Then I like the Carpenter best—if he didn't eat so many as the Walrus."

She is beginning to notice that evil has something to do with victims. Then Tweedledum says, "But he ate as many as he could eat." Finally, Alice summarizes the whole moral truth in the poem by saying, "Well! They are both very unpleasant characters."

Right and wrong are not simply a matter of what Mark Twain once called "tears and flapdoodle." They have to do with facts like killing and dying. In this strangely beautiful part of Lewis Carroll's masterpiece, Alice finally comes to see the all-important details of decency and viciousness. The truth about the evil of Heinrich Himmler must contain the details of the sufferings and deaths of his victims as well as the details of his queasiness.

Ignoring the victims of evil has helped make it fashionable to avoid the old word "evil" and to use words like "sick" or "insane." The only victim of a physical or mental illness is the patient him- or herself. When you think of a person as sick you are concentrating on him or her, not on anybody else.

And who can blame or disapprove of or be angry at a sick person for being sick? The only appropriate thing to do is to understand and to join in the sick person's fight against a disease over which he or she has no control. How dare we criticize? That person did not choose to be sick.

Vague words like "sick" put murderous cruelty in the same sack with kleptomania and manic-depressive disorder. They turn our attention away from the fact that vicious people cause other human beings to be screaming, bleeding, pleading, writhing victims, and that there is something despicable about the torturers.

When we make victims irrelevant to morality the scene of evil becomes not a visible, audible world of screams and bloodshed and horror-struck humiliation, but a veiled, muted, private, invisible world inside somebody's skin. And this is exactly why another philosopher, one of the most distinguished philosophers of our time, Hannah Arendt, wrote a book about Adolf Eichmann that was subtitled *A Report on the Banality of Evil*. Evil was banal to her because the mind of Eichmann was banal, and the mind of Eichmann was all Arendt was looking at.

Adolf Eichmann was in charge of carrying out the Final Solution of the "Jewish problem": the capture, transportation, and extermination of the Jews. In her report on his trial in Jerusalem in 1961, Arendt shows us a man whose main trait was that he had no interesting traits, except a certain "remoteness from reality." His mind was banal because he never *realized* what he was doing to particu-

lar human beings. He was an unimaginative bureaucrat, concerned
mainly with his own career, and he thought in terms of the clichés
in which bureaucrats live and move and have their being. His mind
was as devoid of interest as the mind of any other dusty bureaucrat.
Himmler's mind with its Walrus-tears was fascinating compared to
Eichmann's.

There is no denying that Eichmann was a bore—if you look at
him as he sat in the dock in Jerusalem, if you see him isolated from
what he did. Make invisible and inaudible what he did to hundreds
of thousands of defenseless children, and make invisible and inaudible what he did to millions of baffled, hungry, grief-stricken adults
who died in his roundups, in his cattle cars, and in the killing
camps—make all this irrelevant, absent, nonexistent, and you do
indeed have before you only that pathetic creature sitting in the
dock. If the viciousness of the man was in his feelings and in his
words, then his viciousness was indeed banal, commonplace, trite. It
was as pitiable as illness.

But evil does not happen only inside moral agents. It is true that
an aspect or a part of evil did happen in Eichmann's head. By artic-
ulating Eichmann's way of thinking, Arendt has made a major contribution to our understanding of cruelty. But only if you see the
victims of this man and of the organization he led—Group IV B
4a—do you see the full evil of this man. It is true that part of Eichmann's turpitude happened in his head, in his motives, in his way
of thinking; but another part—a vital part—happened in the
streets, in the cattle cars, and in the killing camps of Central
Europe. Evil is the sum total of his unimaginative, "remote from
reality" mind *and* the unimaginable tortures and murders he perpetrated.

The "and" that connects these two aspects of evil makes a tight,
essential linkage. We dare not separate the two if we would face,
and hope to understand, evil. And if we do not choose to separate
the two, if we do not make the victim invisible, inaudible, unreal,
we encounter something that is not flat, not commonplace, not
banal. We encounter the details of evil, the details in which evil
lives and moves and has its being.

I am not accusing those who commit the fallacy of the isolated
victimizer of being indifferent to the miseries of victims. People
like Bennett and Arendt, and those who talk about "sick" murder-

ers, often are aware of the miseries of the victims of evildoing. What they do not see is the intimate linkage between the moral agents of evil and the sufferings and deaths those moral agents willingly perpetrate. They do not see that these sufferings and deaths have everything to do with evil.

In fact they do not see that without these sufferings and deaths the word "evil" is empty of most of its meaning and all of its horror. They do not see that without the observable, empirical details of cruelty, cruelty is not horrible. Talking about its perpetration is much like making an objective medical diagnosis. And if we are not horror struck by cruelty we are sedentary versions of the monsters who sit back comfortably and let it happen to others. When we lose our indignation about cruelty we have lost our poignant awareness of the preciousness of living.

Very early in her book *Eichmann in Jerusalem, A Report on the Banality of Evil*, Arendt wrote: "On trial are his deeds, not the sufferings of the Jews." She was aware of the horrors of the Final Solution, but she separated them from morality, from evil, just as Bennett did when he described the preacher Jonathan Edwards as being "worse than Himmler." It is this artificial separation of the mental worlds of victimizers from the total worlds of their pain-wracked victims that makes evil banal and that leads a reasonable, compassionate man like Bennett to compare Edwards to Himmler, and then to find Edwards the more evil.

Moralists must not be allowed to afflict us with ecological impoverishment. When they talk of good and evil they must see it all, or at least all that they can see, and they must face it all. Without the actual tortures and murders that Eichmann perpetrated, Eichmann was not evil. Without his having done what he did, his maunderings in the dock in Jerusalem were those of a pitiable, not a culpable, man. He was merely a bureaucrat living in an unimaginative, narrow, bureaucratic world. The totality, the reality in his evil lay in all the details of his mental life *and* in the details of the tortures and the deaths he perpetrated as head of Section IV B 4a during the Third Reich.

What Bennett should have said about Jonathan Edwards and Heinrich Himmler was what Alice said when she passed through the gates of ethical wisdom with the words: "Well! They were *both* very unpleasant characters."

2

But mass murderers, when they are not artificially separated from their victims, are more than unpleasant, and different from being banal. What follows are the words of a monster: He is Otto Ohlendorff, who was head of Group D of the *Einsatzgruppen* (action groups) assigned to exterminate Soviet leaders and Jews in Eastern Europe in the forties. Here is some of his testimony at the Nuremberg Trials of major war criminals. It is horrific because the victims are never forgotten by his interrogators, and his interrogators keep Ohlendorff concrete.

COLONEL POKROVSKY (FOR THE TRIBUNAL): Why did they [the execution squads] prefer execution by shooting to killing in the gas vans?

OHLENDORFF: Because . . . in the opinion of the leader of the Einsatzkommandos, the unloading of the corpses was an unnecessary mental strain.

COLONEL POKROVSKY: What do you mean by "an unnecessary mental strain"?

OHLENDORFF: As far as I can remember the conditions at the time—the picture presented by the corpses, and probably because certain functions of the body had taken place, leaving the corpses lying in filth.

COLONEL POKROVSKY: You mean to say that the sufferings endured prior to death were clearly visible on the victims? Did I understand you correctly?

OHLENDORFF: I don't understand the question; do you mean during the killing in the van?

COLONEL POKROVSKY: Yes.

OHLENDORFF: I can only repeat what the doctor told me, that the victims were not conscious of their death in the van.

COLONEL POKROVSKY: In that case your reply to my previous question, that the unloading of the bodies made a very terrible impression on the members of the execution squad, becomes entirely incomprehensible.

OHLENDORFF: And, as I said, the terrible impression created by the position of the corpses themselves, and by the state of the vans which had probably been dirtied and so on. . . .

COLONEL AMEN (FOR THE TRIBUNAL): Referring to the gas vans which you said you received in the spring of 1942, what order did you receive with respect to the use of these vans?

OHLENDORFF: These gas vans were in future to be used for the killing of women and children.

COLONEL AMEN: Will you explain to the tribunal the construction of these vans and their appearance?

OHLENDORFF: The vans were loaded with the victims and driven to the place of burial, which was usually the same as that used for the mass executions. The time needed for transportation was sufficient to insure the death of the victims.

COLONEL AMEN: How were the victims induced to enter the vans?

OHLENDORFF: They were told that they were to be transported to another locality.

COLONEL AMEN: How long did it take to kill the victims ordinarily?

OHLENDORFF: About 10 to 15 minutes; the victims were not conscious of what was happening to them.

HERR BABEL (FOR THE TRIBUNAL): But did you have no scruples in regard to the execution of these orders?

OHLENDORFF: Yes, of course.

HERR BABEL: And how is it that they were carried out regardless of these scruples?

OHLENDORFF: Because to me it is inconceivable that a subordinate leader should not carry out orders given by the leaders of the state.

You should read these passages more than once. They draw a picture of evil in its wholeness. If that picture is not disgusting to you, then neither the preciousness of human lives nor the viciousness of torturing and destroying them means much to you—yet.

PART TWO

THE HURRICANE
IN NATURE

7

VENUS AND AENEAS

1

It was supposed to have happened thousands of years ago, and the Roman poet Virgil wrote about it in his epic poem, *The Aeneid*.

Troy had fallen, and there were corpses everywhere. The Trojan Aeneas was standing alone among the burning ruins that were once a magnificent city. Suddenly he saw Helen of Troy crouching in the hollow of an altar. She had been the cause of it all. She had abandoned her royal Greek husband, and she had brought about the Trojan Wars. She was hiding from both the husband she had betrayed and the Trojans she had ruined. Aeneas, standing there among the flames, as if in hell, found himself full of rage. He longed "to avenge my dying land and take repayment for her crimes." He moved toward her cringing figure, when suddenly his mother, the goddess Venus, stood before him in utter clarity and seized him by the hand. "Do not blame her," she said through her sweet red lips. "The ruins you see around you have been made by greater forces than Helen's. The gods in their anger have struck down the walls of Troy and have destroyed its towers. Neptune with his great trident smashed those walls and their foundations."

Then she added, "My son, put an end to the struggle." He took her advice and turned his back on Helen. Life-giving Venus, the goddess of love, who alone in the pantheon could bring peace into the very heart of Mars, the god of war, had spoken. And her son obeyed. He turned his back on the hatreds, the murders, and the confusion of the Trojan Wars.

After I had studied the life of Julius Schmähling for a few years, I found myself yearning to get away from the hatreds, the murders, and the confusion of World War II. The millions of lives that were smashed in the half dozen years of the war were not its only casualties. The people who studied and studied and studied those half dozen years were often casualties too. Bitter resentment that such things happened, and fear that manunkind might make them happen again, made many students of this period—students who had any compassion in their hearts at all—miserable and confused. For decades I was one of those students.

As a student of concrete ethics, of flesh-and-blood good and evil, I had turned to this period in history in order to find clear, richly textured, and true instances of help and harm, good and evil. And I found them. But the vast and subtle harmdoing made me bitter—it was so immense, compared with the loving help a few people gave! The eye of the hurricane was narrow, amid the millions and millions of murders.

And the ambiguities I found were almost as painful to me as the plain, massive harmdoing. While I was studying the life of Major Schmähling I tried to keep detached from the fact that I found myself praising—ambiguously, to be sure—a person I would willingly have killed with my artillery piece during the war. I tried to keep detached from the fact that my mother was begging me—in letters and in telephone calls—not to go to Germany to learn about him. I tried to keep detached from the fact that I had lied to her while her voice was weakening from the throat cancer that would soon kill her. And I tried to keep detached from the fact that the horrors that happened in Central Europe in the late thirties and early forties were stopped not by people who felt remorse for their own actions, and not by outsiders who were eager to save the victims of Nazism, but by nations that had no great interest in the victims of Nazism—nations like the United States, Great Britain, and the Soviet Union, which were serving their own self-interest and their own political purposes.

As if all this was not enough, some of my friends in France were writing me confused or bitter letters that accused me of serving the "revisionists" by finding some decency in a German officer who served under Hitler. The revisionists were—and are still—claiming that the Nazis were more sinned against than sinning. According to them there had been no killing camps, and the Germans had fought World War II in order to protect the world from the godless, murdering, Jew-inspired Communists. The revisionists called the Holocaust a gigantic hoax perpetrated by international Jewry, and they saw Holocaust survivors as barefaced liars and conspirators. Some of my best friends in France told me that by praising a German officer under Hitler, especially a member of the National Socialist Party, I was giving aid and comfort to the revisionists.

When their letters started coming, I went back to my mother's letters, which pleaded with me (with sometimes the old stain of a teardrop on the letter) not to go to Germany and not to praise a German. I was being pushed and pulled in a chaos of feelings as cruel and as bottomless as the horrors I had experienced studying the "medical experiments" on children in the killing camps.

Then I remembered my favorite story in Virgil's pre-Christian epic poem—the story about Aeneas and his mother, the goddess of universe-moving love. It told how Aeneas obeyed his divine mother and turned his back on the hurricane of war and vengeance. I thought that perhaps I, too, should have obeyed my mother. I began to think that I should have turned my back on the whole period of the Holocaust, with all its murders and lies and hatreds and fears. Like the mother of Aeneas, the goddess of all-loving communion, my mother had wanted me to have joy, not a life like this, a life as narrow, as troubled, and as dirty as the life of a cockroach in the Cockroach Building on Roosevelt Road in Chicago. Not a life of war.

People who have not been in combat sometimes think of war as clear and heroic. They think that war exhibits only obvious enmities and uncomplicated allegiances. But the state of war I knew before, during, and after World War II was far from clear, and far from heroic. Actual combat for an artilleryman like me, and for many other soldiers, was full of chaos. In warm weather you dug your gun into mud that covered you from head to toe and that would not hold your gun firmly in place; in winter weather the frozen ground resisted your spade when you needed to dig a hole for the gun trails and a foxhole to protect yourself from shrapnel, *now*.

The English word "war" has roots in the German words *wirren* and *verwirren*, which mean "to confuse, to perplex." In the midst of artillery combat in France and Germany, in the midst of the bitter little battles in and near the Cockroach Building, and in the midst of my feelings after I turned my attention from tiny Le Chambon, I found mainly confusion and unending bitterness—bitterness made all the more so by my occasional memories of peace and clarity.

My philosopher-teacher Montaigne once wrote, "The surest sign of wisdom is unending joy." And the "*jouissance*," the joy he was speaking of, had tranquillity in it, serenity. Well, in the course of these last few decades I had not made much progress toward Montaigne's wisdom. On the contrary, I felt that I had wandered into the world of Matthew Arnold's poem "Dover Beach," where there is

> . . . *really neither joy, nor love, nor light,*
> *Nor certitude, nor peace, nor help for pain;*
> *And we are here as on a darkling plain*
> *Swept with confused alarms of struggle and flight,*
> *Where ignorant armies clash by night.*

I needed to shake off my near obsession with moral enmities. Everything I had studied—including the anguished cry of poor Kurt Huber in his darkened Grafelfing room when he heard that his fellow Germans were shooting unarmed Jews—had venom in it. Even the villagers of Le Chambon, who saved thousands of children from the killing camps, were pleasing to me only in contrast to the bitter hatreds in the world outside Le Chambon. Often the light in the village made the darkness around it dark indeed.

Before my book about the village was published, Elie Wiesel, a survivor of the concentration camps, read it in manuscript and told me that it was a book about horror as well as love. I remember him saying on the telephone, late the night he finished reading it: "Imagine what kind of a world this was that made the hospitality of the people of Le Chambon so necessary and so extraordinary!"

I had absorbed enough venom from those terrible times. Even though my mother was dead now, and I could not please her anymore, I wanted to do what she had begged me to do when she used to tell me with that strangled voice of hers: "Please don't go there." I wanted to turn my back on human hatreds in order to find an unvenomed joy. I had suffered enough of the miseries of moral blame. I was suffocating in the smoke of war. I needed fresh air.

2

One spring evening, years earlier, I had gone to the United States
Coast Guard Academy in New London, Connecticut, to give a lecture to the faculty and the cadets. The lecture was to be about the
ethical issues involved in helping strangers. I knew that a good number of the people in my audience were part of the Search and Rescue
Service of the Coast Guard, part of what had once been called "the
Life-Saving Service." Their job was to save lives and property on the
waters around and within the United States. I was eager to talk with
them, not only because they were doing something life preserving
but also because they were intimately involved with what was a terrifying and beautiful mystery to me—the wide salt sea. I was a pass-
ably good and ecstatically eager navigator of small sailboats on Long
Island Sound, and sailors, especially lifesaving sailors, seemed to me
to breathe a fresher, livelier air than landlubbers inhaled.

When I walked into Waesche Hall on a star-bright night, I suddenly
felt baffled. There was nobody at the door to greet me, and there was
nobody working at the long desk that faces the door. The place was
empty, it seemed. To my left I saw a door with the letters "Coast Guard
Museum" painted in black on the glass. I was almost a half hour early
for my lecture, and so I went into the museum to pass the time and
perhaps to learn a little more about what interested my audience.

The first thing I saw when I entered was a sign that read: JOSHUA
JAMES, THE GREATEST LIFESAVER OF THEM ALL. The whole one-room
museum was devoted to photographs, letters, newspaper articles,
and lifesaving equipment that had to do with a man named Joshua
James, who lived in Hull, Massachusetts, from his birth in 1826 to
his death in 1902. He had saved hundreds of lives off the coast of
Hull, and he had been, as far as worldly fame is concerned, the
Lindbergh of his day.

One newspaper article in the exhibition caught and held my
attention. It told of the fact that when he died, after saving the
lives of many people, and after saving hundreds of thousands of
dollars' worth of property, his widow and many daughters were
entirely destitute. Money had to be raised in Hull and in nearby
Boston to feed and clothe his family. Saving lives seemed to be for
him not a way of earning a living, but a way of living that was precious to him for its own sake.

I found myself staring at a photograph of him, with his full white beard and his intense dark eyes under bushy black eyebrows. Those eyes seemed to be saying to me, "Well, figure me out, Mister."

I started looking around the room for a way to begin to understand that face and the fact of his dying in poverty after having saved so many lives. Near one of the photographs of him there was a letter that surprised me, and that seemed to have something to do with understanding him. It was a handwritten note from the greatest philosopher of his time, William James, who was teaching at Harvard University, not more than a few dozen miles away from Joshua's Hull. He was the founder of pragmatism, which is a way of living that turns its back on abstract, artificial dogmas and turns its face toward human action. He wrote the note in his home at 95 Irving Street in Cambridge, on December 10, 1898, soon after the great hurricane of '98. Here is what it says:

Captain Joshua James
Dear Sir,

I am one of the many who were moved to admiration of the splendid behavior of your crew and volunteers during the recent storm. But what is the use of admiration in a "dry" and academic shape? One ought to *do* something with it; and as I can't well go and save lives myself, I take the liberty of sending you a small check which you will best know how to place where it will do most good to those concerned, yourself included. I wish it were bigger!

Believe me, with cordial regards to you all, truly yours
Wm James

I was so engrossed in reading and rereading this letter—which was full of meaning for a student of pragmatism like myself—that I did not notice the passage of time. Suddenly I heard a sigh of relief coming from behind me, and I turned to find the round-faced, worried library director and curator of the Coast Guard Museum, Paul Johnson. He was in charge of my lecture, and he had been looking for me with growing despair. He took me straight to the lecture podium, where I gave a rather distraught lecture and got the response from the audience that I deserved: loose chairs scraping on the library floor while I lectured, and grateful silence when I stopped.

Driving home from New London that lucid spring night, I could not take my mind off the exhibit. The photograph of Joshua James, with his profoundly calm black eyes, was as clear to me as it had been in the museum when I stood before it; and the letter from William James, which I had memorized, kept running through my head. Even while I was feeling sad about my failed lecture, I was feeling as if I had suddenly gotten a burst of fresh salt air against my face. What I kept thinking was that this Capt. Joshua James had saved lives, and he had had nothing to do with evil. He confronted storms that were beyond good and evil. Mast-high, bone-freezing cold seas were more powerful than hand-wringing moral indignation.

I had learned that he would stand on Stoney Beach or on Nantasket Beach there on the coast of Massachusetts during those wintry days and nights, looking out for ships in trouble. And when he saw them being done to death against rocks and shoals, he and his crew would row a big wooden boat through a rock-grinding surf and sky-hiding waves out to those ships. I had seen in his eyes a masterful calm, a peace that had something wild in it, a steady need to act, to go for the body, a need like that of a crouching lion. But his coiled calm had to do with saving life in the very teeth of nature, not taking life for the sake of his own hunger. It had nothing to do with killing, with moral bitterness, or with betrayal. And there was no ambiguity in it: It was utterly focused.

Even while I was studying the village of Le Chambon, and then later spending months in Germany trying to understand the ambiguous Julius Schmähling, I found myself thinking about Joshua James almost every day. Between trips to Europe I visited Hull a dozen times to talk to the descendants of Joshua James, in order to see and hear and smell the long white-sand beach that had wrecked so many ships, and in order to experience what the French call *envergure*: breadth, wingspread, wide, fresh air.

When I felt that my work in Europe was done, I decided to look more deeply into the story of Joshua James. He fascinated me because he faced nature in its awesome wildness, and he faced it squarely, wordlessly, and efficiently. It was that wordless, vigorous efficiency that must have enthralled the pragmatist William James.

3

In the Western world at least, ethics has been appalled at a wildness wider than words. Ethical thinkers have done their best to overcome the unruly passions inside human beings, and they have tried to ignore the wildness around us. The ferity with which two naked lovers seize each other and suddenly find themselves bathed in ecstasy; the crackle of bones between the bloody jaws of the leapers in the jungles and the fields; the skies and the seas—these have always been wider and deeper than ethics. When ethics has not been able to ignore the wildness in human beings, then it has done its best to overcome it, to shame it or to punish it into submission.

By refusing fearlessly to accept wildness, ethics has narrowed and impoverished its domain. It has turned its back on the juices and joys of nature, and it has turned its wrath against the wildness in human nature, hoping that the wildness will go away, or weaken, or die. It often calls the wildness of killing and eating and lusting "evil," and sees such actions as inimical to human beings.

But during the lifetime of Joshua James, and only a few miles from his little village of Hull, there were people who were more accepting of wildness in nature than ethicists and preachers usually are. In fact, contemporaries of Joshua James in Concord, especially Henry David Thoreau and Ralph Waldo Emerson, found purity of heart in experiencing nature with all their senses, intelligence, and passion, not in ignoring it or trying to whip it into submission. These people were reluctant to use the word "evil." They loved the natural world around and in Concord too much to use it. In fact, they saw no evil in nature; they saw a wildness that was—some-how—good, joyously acceptable.

In *Walden* Thoreau wrote, "I love the wild not less than the good." He actually loved the body-vigor of plants and animals more than he did the desperate tameness of civilized human beings. The wildness in nature and in himself was dear to him, and the smug philanthropy of the do-gooders of his day disgusted him.

On the cold winter's afternoon of December 1, 1856, Henry David Thoreau took a walk in the snow and then wrote in his journal: "I love and could embrace the shrub oak with its scanty garment of leaves rising above the snow, lowly whispering to me, akin to winter thoughts, and sunsets, and to all virtue . . . innocent and sweet as a maiden is the shrub oak. . . . I felt a positive yearning toward one bush this afternoon. There was a match found for me at last. I fell in love with a shrub oak." Wild things in nature go for the juicy body. They live for the sake of the body, and they feed themselves on the bodies of others, like herons gobbling up tadpoles, or snakes swallowing frogs. There is a vigor in this system, nature, that can make millions upon millions of creatures the prey and the food for millions upon millions of other creatures, who in turn become prey and food. This vigor invigorated Thoreau; it did not appall him. He drank it in through all his senses, and it gave him joy. Indeed, the only thing that appalled him was the tendency of human beings to ignore the glorious abundance of energy that is nature in order to languish in quiet desperation within a social world of mutual enslavement.

For Thoreau there was no poison in wild nature. Everything worked together in this vast organism; everything served the system. In *Walden* he wrote, "The impression made on a wise man is universal innocence."

And while Thoreau was thinking and writing these things, a few dozen miles away Joshua James was working in nature. Like Thoreau, James was not daunted by the sea. He did not call it evil and try to overcome or ignore it. He faced it, and, joining it, working closely with it, he helped turn its murderous innocence into a vehicle for saving lives.

When Venus told her son to turn away from vengeance, she also told him to face the "divine majesties" that are beyond human judgments of good or evil. The gods in *The Aeneid* were for Thoreau the woods, the fields, the ponds, and the rivers of Concord, and they were the winter seas off the coast of Hull for Joshua James.

I decided to learn more about the hero of the Search and Rescue Service of the U.S. Coast Guard because I believed that by coming close to him I might come closer to forces wider and more elemental than those I had been studying for most of my life. After all, was it not Venus, the goddess of universe-moving love, who told her son to turn away from hatred and retribution, and hadn't my mother begged me to turn my back on bitter moral recriminations? Weren't both mothers asking their sons to make room for joy?

THOREAU'S WALK ON THE WILD SIDE

1

On October 9, 1849, while a violent storm pounded the whole coast of Massachusetts, Henry David Thoreau—with his liquid gray-blue eyes, his big drooping nose, and his loping gait—set out from Concord for a walking tour of Cape Cod. He was not unlike a lone, hairy wolf who had somehow strayed into the genteel town of Concord. His foster mother was Concord; his real mother was the wild. He was stubbornly independent and quietly savage. He often acted as if he felt that human societies were like transitory clumps of toadstools standing for a while along the fringes of the great pathways of nature. His home was on the pathways, not in the clumps.

The West was being won; gold was being mined by the forty-niners in California; railroads were spreading across the continent; new wealth was accumulating in a few hands; the Industrial Revolution was mounting, at least in the North, and especially in his own state of Massachusetts; preachers and political leaders all over New England were attacking slavery with ever-deepening passion after the Mexican War had brought slave states into the Union; the Civil War was abuilding. But Thoreau was putting busy America behind him. Like a wolf, he loved nature more than man.

When he reached Boston that dark, windy fall morning, instead of finding the steamer to Provincetown he found himself standing near an empty dock reading a handbill: "Death! one hundred and forty-five lives lost at Cohasset!" The immense storm that had just struck the Cape had sunk a brig carrying Irish emigrants from Galway to Boston. He decided to go to Cohasset. In his book *Cape Cod*, he gives no reason for the decision, but one of the reasons must have been that the waters around the Cape were still violent, and Thoreau was in love with wildness. In any event, few if any boats were going to Provincetown.

In the railroad cars out of Boston he saw many Irish people going to Cohasset to identify bodies, to give comfort to the survivors, and to attend the funeral that was to take place that afternoon. When they all got off at Cohasset, they had to walk a mile through the sullen skirts of a great storm to the beach where the wreck of the *St. John* lay. He saw hunters with their guns and dogs heading for the beach, possibly because they were after waterfowl, but probably just out of curiosity. He passed a big freshly dug hole in a graveyard, and beyond the hole, on a gently winding, rocky road, he saw wagons moving from the shore toward the hole, each carrying three crude boxes made of soft pine.

When he got to the beach, the sea was still smashing against the black rocks of one of the most dangerous shores of America. Up and down the beach for a mile he saw people looking for bodies and examining chunks of the wreck—a woman's scarf, a straw bonnet, a broken mast. He saw eighteen or twenty of the deal coffins he had seen on the wagons; they were lying on a green hillside, and people were crowded around them. Some people were raising the lids and lifting the edges of the white sheets that loosely covered the bodies. They were looking for friends or relatives.

When somebody raised a sheet Thoreau saw bloodless skin and matted hair, and he saw the puffed, broken body of a girl, whose pale pink-and-white flesh had been bitten into by rocks and fishes so that her bones and muscles were exposed. Her eyes were wide open and staring, like the unbroken cabin windows of a wrecked boat filled with sand.

That afternoon walking there on the beach, Thoreau noticed no signs of grief. Both the Irish from Boston and the people of Cohasset seemed to be as matter-of-fact and as cold as the sea. In a little cove not far from the scene of the wreck, he saw an old man and his son picking up seaweed that had been tossed ashore by the storm. The man knew about the wreck, but what really interested him was the weeds, which he and his son were gathering for their barnyard. Kelp and rockweed were good fertilizer, and people near the sea also put them around the foundations of their wooden houses to keep out the winter winds.

As far as Thoreau could see, the shipwreck had not disturbed the people of Cohasset. For generations they had been gleaning what they could from the sea, and they showed no compassion for the victims of the wreck. The sea had not changed after it had swallowed and then spit up 145 people like so many grains of sand; and the behavior of the people of Cohasset hadn't changed either. As far as they were concerned, the bodies were less important than the seaweed.

After reporting all this, Thoreau added a brief essay on death, an essay that is at first as calm and unsentimental as the rest of his report. He thought about those 145 sea-killed people and found himself unmoved. If he had found one of them dead on a beach all alone, he wrote, he would have been moved; but all those dead people made him sympathize more with the immense power of nature than with the pains and deaths of human beings: "It is the individual and private that demands our sympathy."

And he wrote from experience. About seven years before Thoreau's first trip up the bent arm of Massachusetts, his brother, John, had died of lockjaw in soul-rending pain, and Thoreau had almost gone insane with grief. For a while after his brother's death, Thoreau himself showed most of the symptoms of lockjaw, and it took him a month in bed to recover from the psychosomatic attack.

But usually individuals did not get much sympathy from Thoreau. Usually he felt what he called "sympathy" for trees and rocks and brooks rather than for people. Shortly after the wreck of the *St. John*, he learned that the corpse of a young woman had come floating up to the coast in an upright position, with her white cap blown back by the wind. Her appearance, Thoreau believed, might spoil the neat, calm, mineral beauty of the beach for some people. Had he seen her, on the other hand, he would have felt that her death and the deaths of other drowned people enhanced the beauty of the beach. Her corpse, floating upright offshore with her white cap blown back from her head, gave the beach "a rarer and sublimer beauty" than it would have had without her.

2

When I first read this passage, I jerked my head back: What? I asked myself. How can this man find sublimity in a place where a dead woman has floated upright? I wondered what kind of man would think that a seashore that has wrecked many ships and has drowned many people has "a rarer and sublimer beauty" than a seashore where there is nothing to mar the peaceful contrasts and mysterious sympathies between the sea and the gulls and sky above it. How could all this destruction make a shore more sublime than it normally is? How could all this destruction improve on the rhyming, sympathetic whitenesses of puff clouds, sea foam, and gulls' breasts?

Toward the end of the section "Spring," in *Walden*, he had written, "We can never have enough of Nature. We must be refreshed by the sight of inexhaustible vigor, vast and Titanic features, the sea-coast with its wrecks, the wilderness with its living and its decaying trees, the thunder cloud. . . . We need to witness our own limits transgressed." The key words in the passage about the drowned woman and the wrecks were very carefully chosen. The destructive powers of nature were sublime for him because they thrillingly and irrefutably demonstrated the superhuman power of nature, "our own limits transgressed."

In the nineteenth century the word "sublime" was full of meaning. Whatever was sublime was vast, transcendently powerful, and forever energetic. The sublime elevates our feelings and our thoughts toward the divine. And long before the nineteenth century, people have felt that the superhuman powers in nature announce the supernatural power of God. In Psalm 107 the greatest forces in nature—especially the "wonders in the deep"—are "the works of the Lord." The psalm adjures us to "declare his works with rejoicing," and it picks out "they that go down to the sea in ships" as the ones who feel those wonders most poignantly. In the middle of a storm those who do business in the great waters feel the boundless power of God directly, immediately. To be in a storm at sea is to know much about what it is to be in the hands of God.

In the passage about the "vast and Titanic features" of a stormy seacoast, Thoreau was expressing a deep conviction, not simply a perverse whim. He was expressing the firm belief that limitless, overwhelming power was not only magnificent and inspiring but also a stubborn fact of nature. A few lines later Thoreau wrote about the terrible beauty of wild beings, the strong appetite of predators that "serenely squashed" their prey "out of existence like pulp." Untrammeled power is sublimely free from the tame impotence of civilized human beings.

Many times Thoreau had expressed his love for life-taking and life-giving wildness. With carefully honed, civilized sentences he proclaimed a wild, wordless appetite for a life that goes for the body the way a hungry wolf goes for a deer's body. In that way of life, the way of nature, he saw a reality deeper and more solid than the sniveling compassion and the enslaving institutions of society. He wrote about how tadpoles and herons gobble up their prey, and about how, wherever there is vigorous life, nature "has rained flesh and blood!"

He warned those who would look closely at the facts of nature that "compassion is a very untenable ground." Both the overwhelming power of the predators and the powerless suffering of their prey are *there* in nature. They are part of its vigor, its health, its appetite for living. And we are part of this system, whether we approve of it or not.

If we spend our lives suffering with all the sufferers, feeling compassion for all the victims in the world, then we spoil the only lives we have in the only system we have. If we do not see a special beauty in raw power then we are not at home with our own hungers, and we are not at home in our own universe. Strong appetites and strong bodies are a wondrous part of nature's ever-resurgent health, whether or not we have the stomach for them.

The timid inhabitants of snivelization would have us suffer with the weak and would have us ignore—or fruitlessly deplore—the real and magnificent power that great seas and great predators wield. But a queasy compassion makes us shrink from the fullness of life. It diminishes us; it adds one more victim to the victims in the world, and it blinds us to the life-giving fact that power prevails—that, in fact, in reality, in nature, living *is* power prevailing over weakness.

The main business of Thoreau's life was to develop the art of living through a day and a night. In all the vast range of literature and philosophy he had never found a page that told him how to do this. What he had learned from his own experience was that the business of life was living wakefully. From the point of view of the property owners of Concord, he was an idler—a somewhat shabby, somewhat queer duck they could occasionally send out to do an errand for them. But from his point of view, living itself—not accumulating money and not pleasing others—was the most basic, the most noble, the most challenging of his occupations. At the end of a day he did not ask himself, How much have I earned? or Whom have I pleased? The deepest and widest thrills of being alive were what he was after. At the end of a day if he asked himself anything, it was: Have I been awake?

And getting the most out of living, extracting the nectar from the flower of the world, involved mainly two things: walking and words. He had to "saunter," as he called it. He had to loaf, he had to look, he had to feel, he had to smell, he had to listen to the natural world around him. He had to live as an imaginatively and passionately *aware* inhabitant of nature, not merely as a guest looking coolly at deaf and dumb things that were not his. He felt one undying need: the need to feel himself coming alive, *now*. In order to honor that need he had to spend at least four hours every day—and usually more—strolling through woods and over fields. Sauntering to him was going to the "*Sainte Terre*," the holy land; but for him the holy land was not an ancient scene of supernatural glories; it was holy nature, *now*. The medieval Sainte-Terrers, or Holy-Landers, were trying to save their souls by moving out against the infidels; Thoreau the saunterer took off every day to save his soul by resonating with the vast, deep, mysterious, and ever-fresh energies in the air, on the land, and in the ponds of Concord.

He would not let himself be enslaved by other people's demands, or by his own fear and ambition. While he was sauntering, each here-and-now was for him virgin, vivacious, and lovely. Thoreau believed that there was nothing so totally opposed to the joy of living—even counting crime—as work, work, work. He believed that the land of redemptive, joyous living was wherever and whenever you sauntered, if only you wholeheartedly turned your back on the suicidal, quietly desperate, mutually enslaved slaves of human society. It was no accident that he moved into his still-unfinished hut on Walden Pond on July 4, Independence Day.

The United States had plenty of people who were willing to do the work of taming themselves, who were perfectly willing either to contract themselves into nutshells of politeness or to spread themselves out into mists of generosity or competition. There were enough ministers and businessmen. Let them go about their business. They have their reward. As for him, he felt himself coming alive only when he was free of social bondage. A tame dog lives to please its human masters; a wild animal does not. In fact, a wild animal is somewhat surly when you try to use it for your purposes. A badger or a fish or a bird will not go out of its way to please you. Their energies are vivaciously self-indulgent. Only when he was like them, demandingly moving through stubborn nature, could he satisfy his undying desire to feel himself, *himself*, mind and body, coming alive.

And yet his love for irresponsible wildness had art, the apparent opposite of wildness, at its very center. In order to spend a day walking in the "holy land," Thoreau needed to pay close attention to words. He was a practitioner of the hard work and the high art of mustering the subtlest tools of civilization, words. Only the combination of words and walking and nature satisfied his desire to come alive. A lover of paradox, he was himself one of the most paradoxical human beings who ever lived. He cherished a wildness innocent of all art, and yet he kept a carefully nuanced journal of millions of words.

On September 7, 1851, a couple of years after his first stroll along the coast of Massachusetts, he wrote about "The civilization that consists with wildness, the light that is in night." Spending a day living life at the top of his asocial bent meant to him expressing himself in sociable words, pressing out his thoughts and feelings into the inherited shapes and sounds that are the living core of society and civilization. To be more wild for him was to be less human, and yet he used that most human of tools, words that echoed the civilizations of ancient Greece and India, to intensify and capture the wakeful moment.

For him the way to spend a day was not to walk along in wordless ecstasy. He was very different from the muskrats, the foxes, the trees that he so admired. Idler that he was, he worked long and hard at transforming the nectar in the flower of the world into the honey of his own kind of experience. Getting the most out of life meant building with the sharp point of his pen a storehouse of forcefully expressed experiences, a squirrel's nest full of meaty nuts that he could savor and be thrilled by long after the original experiences were gone.

Like his older friend Ralph Waldo Emerson, he believed that nature was his "dowry and estate," his property, *his*, if only he had the words, the will, and the energy to vault into the throne and claim the kingdom for himself. Emerson believed that you can take up the world into yourself, make it your own, your proper property. This is so because, though you learn words from others, and though you use them to reach out to others, your wakefully used words are *yours*. With your words you can grandly relate yourself to nature; you can learn firmness from rocks, tranquillity from blue skies crossed by black clouds, and self-command from the healthy functioning of your own body. You build your own world out of your experiences and your words, even though your raw materials are public property.

But there was a certain gentleness, a certain sweetness of spirit in Emerson. Thoreau was different. He had a yearning for raw, bloody nature. Sometimes he wanted to seize an animal and eat it raw, not because he was hungry but because he wanted to taste its wildness wildly. He wanted the flowing, dangerous, rank contact with nature that a wolf has when it devours the deer it has just killed. Compared to him Emerson was courteous, almost tame. Thoreau needed to possess the ferocity in the world. He needed to appropriate it, the way the wolf appropriates a freshly killed doe. When he died, his last words were "moose" and "Indian." These words have raw wildness in them, the night that is in light.

When I read through the hundreds of thousands of words he wrote, one word—and its many, many synonyms—kept turning up in his strongest sentences: *sympathy*. And almost always when he used the word it had nothing to do with sympathy for human beings. In the "Solitude" section of *Walden* he wrote: "Sympathy with the fluttering alder and poplar leaves almost takes away my breath." In the same section he wrote: "Every little pine needle expanded and swelled with sympathy and befriended me." In a journal entry he says that no philosopher he has ever met has been able to show him conclusively *any* difference between a man and a fish. "We are so much alike! . . . they are to be understood, surely, as all things else, by no other method than that of sympathy." And when he is not talking about the "method" of sympathy, he is using the method in forceful expression: "This then, at least, is the office of the lungs—to drink the atmosphere with the planet dissolved in it."

Sympathy for him was not a social matter, not a matter that had to do with other people; it involved affinity (the Latin word *affinitas* means "connection by marriage"); mutuality; interaction; and fellow feeling with trees, animals, air, and everything that is not concocted by human beings. In January 1857, before he made his fourth and last walking tour of Cape Cod, he wrote in his journal: "The stones are happy, Concord River is happy, and I am happy too. . . . Do you think that Concord River would have continued to flow these millions of years . . . if it had not been happy—if it had been miserable in its channel, tired of existence?"

3

That is one of the reasons why he started his walking tour of Cape Cod on a day when a storm had just been destroying ships and human lives. He was going to put money-tamed and ambition-tamed America behind him, and he was going "to get a better view of the ocean" than inland Concord could give him. He was not going to do anything practical. He was not going there to "make a living," as we say, by catching and selling fish or by catching and selling anything else. While other forty-niners were digging for gold in the West, he was going sauntering. He was off on another leg of his lifelong honeymoon with his illimitably happening bride.

He was different from his friend Ralph Waldo Emerson. In "The Over-Soul" Emerson wrote: ". . . how often in my trivial conversation with my neighbours, that somewhat higher in each of us overlooks this by-play, and Jove nods to Jove from behind each of us." For Thoreau there was no such intimacy with other human beings. In the journal entry for September 1, 1850, Emerson mentioned that for Thoreau nature was more interesting than people. He went on to say that for him, Emerson, this was not the case: Both nature and people were equally interesting to him.

Toward the end of his chapter on ponds in *Walden*, Thoreau wrote, referring to Walden Pond and White Pond: "How much more beautiful than our lives, how much more transparent than our characters are they! We never learned meanness from them." On January 7, 1857, he wrote in his journal: "In the street and in society I am almost invariably cheap and dissipated, my life is unspeakably mean. . . . But alone in distant woods or fields . . . I come to myself, I once more feel myself grandly related . . . I thus dispose of the superfluous and see things as they are, grand and beautiful."

Emerson, one of the kindest and most generous of men, and perhaps the person in the world who knew Thoreau best, wrote in the summer of 1848, one year before Thoreau's walk on Cape Cod, that if you took Thoreau's arm you would get less human response from it than you would get if you took the arm of an elm tree.

Whatever else love is, it is the union of poverty and plenty, of the needy lover and the needed treasure, the beloved. Nature is never spent. Its fresh power is unending. On his first walking tour of the Cape, and on all three of his later walks there, needy Thoreau went off to be near a vaster force in nature than human society.

4

In the eighteenth century Edmund Burke wrote an essay on the sublime and the beautiful. The sublime, he wrote, is the tranquil experience of terror. It is a kind of delight radically different from the relaxing pleasure we feel while seeing a tender violet. The ocean, darkness, vast heights and vast depths, these are the objects of the sublime, and they do not please us; they astonish us.

At the very center of Burke's idea of the sublime is his notion of power. Cataclysms are manifestations of power, of great forces threatening and crushing the weak. Power is the ability to overcome resistance swiftly, the way a stormy sea smashes and sinks a ship full of people. It is in the vast difference between the power of the sea and the resistance of the ship and its people that power becomes plain, threatening, terrifying. For Burke our awareness of the disparity of power between a great force and a helpless human being is our awareness of the sublime.

In works of art and in nature this double awareness horrifies us when we concentrate our attention on the victim; we feel terribly threatened and miserably compassionate. But when we concentrate our thoughts, imaginings, and passions on the superior force our minds are uplifted. Instead of suffering and being crushed with the victim, we find our minds turning upward toward the superhuman, toward the boundless, toward the infinite. When we concentrate on the greater power we almost become it.

Of course, that "almost" is important. Between us and the scene before us, as mere spectators, there is a distance. In order to feel the delight of the sublime we must feel a detached awareness. The crushing of others produces delight in us "when it does not press too close," as Burke puts it. Because we are neither the storm nor its victims, we feel delight, not paralyzing horror or boundless empowerment. We must ourselves be safe from drowning if we are to experience the sublimity of a shipwreck.

The Roman poet Lucretius put our detachment in somewhat more sweeping language when he wrote, in *On the Nature of the Universe*, "What joy it is, when out at sea the stormwinds are lashing the waters, to gaze from the shore at the heavy stress some other man is enduring!" There is a certain tranquillity in standing and feeling aloof at the same time that you are aware of the sufferings of others under immense, destructive power. The delight of the sublime lies in our tranquil contemplation of great power crushing others, others for whom we feel only a fleeting compassion. The main element of our delight in the sublime is uplift, elevation, an almost religious awe resembling the fear of God. Its main element is not the downcast sufferer. There is nothing sublime about being the victim of a storm. The delights of sublimity reside in the mind of a spectator who is mainly concerned with untrammeled power. Sublimity is an experience of terror and exaltation rendered tranquil by *our* actual safety.

Something very much like this is what Thoreau meant when he said that the seashore where the wreck of the *St. John* had happened had "a rarer and sublimer beauty" than it would have if the murderous storm had not happened there. It was the murderous power of the ocean that had drowned the woman with the white cap that would forever make the seashore of Cohasset sublime for Thoreau.

In the nineteenth century, across the Atlantic, the art of the English painter J. M. W. Turner expressed that same need to be "refreshed by the sight of inexhaustible vigor, vast and Titanic features." Again and again his paintings present images of overwhelming power threatening or destroying human beings. In his mezzotint *Coast of Yorkshire near Whitby*, two small, broken fishing vessels and a few tiny figures are caught in the middle of a surging, whirling sea, massive cliffs, and a violent sky. The figures standing on the rock that has wrecked their lobster boats are waving helplessly at a few other tiny figures on the rocky shore; and between these two groups is the relentless sea.

In his watercolor *Ship in a Storm*, the ship is little, penciled in, and the waves around and on it are more than twice as high as the masts. The stormy sea is vastly more powerful than the slender, crippled ship. In a mezzotint called *A Shipwreck*, a vast, unending sea, dark and vague in the background and whirlingly bright in the foreground, is smashing three sailing vessels full of helpless sailors, the central vessel having been swept bare of its sails and masts.

Many of Turner's paintings express the sublimity of nature and the weakness of human beings. They show us massive destruction and hopeless terror within small areas of canvas or paper, and on flat surfaces. Seeing these paintings, we are moved by the power in them, and by the disparity of power in them, but we can be tranquil in our contemplation of that power, because we are not actually, physically threatened by it. We somehow contain it, even as its frame contains it; we encompass it, and we are exalted by our own vastness in containing it, as well as by the immense power that the picture frame contains.

In 1800 Turner exhibited an oil entitled *Dolbadern Castle*. In the foreground are three small human figures. Behind them and around them are somber, massive mountains, standing far above the heads of the figures. The mountains, like the figures, are not painted in detail. They are heavy and thick, and at the top of the central mountain there is a blasted tower, one of the many round towers to be found in Wales. This one has a heavy, wide foundation, and no roof. It has a single ruined window with some of the fitful light of the restless sky shining through it, suggesting that the far side of the tower is gone.

At the turn of that century painters sometimes put verses in the exhibition catalogs. Turner inserted the following verse below the title of the painting:

How awful is the silence of the waste,
Where nature lifts her mountains to the sky.
Majestic solitude, behold the tower
Where hopeless OWEN long imprison'd, pin'd,
And wrung his hands for Liberty, in vain.

He had composed the verse himself, and it summarized much of what he was trying to convey in the painting: the gloom of an alien, irresponsive nature; the noble aloneness of the tower; and the weakness—the trapped, hand-wringing weakness—of the thirteenth-century Welsh poet Owen, who had once been imprisoned in that tower. His weakness, his pining, and his bootless wringing of hands could do nothing against the powers that imprisoned him and that took away his liberty, just as the lobstermen were trapped in *The Coast of Yorkshire near Whitby*, and just as the sailors in *A Shipwreck* were overwhelmed by the power of the wind and the sea.

We do not see Owen in *Dolbadern Castle*; he is remembered only in the brooding scene we do see; the victim is *almost* absent from the scene; he is powerless to the point of extinction, except in the last pathetic lines of the verse Turner put in the catalog. There is this same "almost-absence" of the victim in *Ship in a Storm*, where all we see are the waves, those dynamic mountains, which are far, far higher than the ship's merely penciled-in mast. The almost unreal, doomed ship only suggests the human victims of the boundless, all-powerful storm, just as the chunks of wrecked ships being washed ashore in other Turner paintings and engravings only suggest the human victims of shipwreck. And the same diminution of the actual presence of a human being happens in the passage in Thoreau's *Cape Cod*, in which he describes the sublime beauty of the beach *after* the erect, floating corpse of the drowned woman has actually been seen.

Our delight in the sublime is possible because it is a fact of human life that we are fascinated with the destruction of anything, including a human life. We rejoice to see power mobilized, hammering on a single point. We hate and fear the destruction of a defenseless human being at the very same time that it allows us to experience a kind of wild joy in the presence of apparently unlimited power. We experience such awful joy in reading horror or Gothic tales like Charles Robert Maturin's *Melmoth the Wanderer* and Bram Stoker's *Dracula*. Our literature, our religions, our news media are replete with images of the torture and destruction of human beings, and those images are both attractive and repellent to us, provided that they do not press us too close. Because we love great power so much, we are ambivalent toward cruelty and murder. We hate the crushing and we love it, when we are somewhat detached from it. Children sitting in a theater, watching the screen while some innocent person is being approached by a murderer, cover their eyes with their hands and peek out between their spread fingers. Sublimity is one of the many thrilling forms of our ambivalence toward power, cruelty, and killing.

But it is also a fact of human life that we desire and praise the protection and preservation of human life. We admire those who do something to protect and preserve that life. We call them "good" or "brave" or even "heroic," because goodness or bravery or heroism is associated in our minds not with the total, blank smashing of life, but with its preservation and enhancement. We cherish people who fight against the powers of destruction—who in some way or another, to some degree or another, resist and withstand those powers and spread life. Such lifesavers are usually absent from Turner's sublime paintings. Mainly there is immense power and pathetic weakness—"hopeless OWEN," pining in that tower, wringing his hands "in vain." And sometimes there are not even hands to be wrung or people without hope; sometimes there are only passive, inanimate masts and the planks of wrecked ships.

We might call such art, in which the disparity between human weakness and natural power is almost infinitely great, the "aesthetic sublime." But whatever we call it, there is no place in it for a moral *agent*, for a doer who is able, to some degree or another, to preserve his or her life. We might call a scene in which there is a great disparity of power, but still a person resisting that power, the "Ethical Sublime," because ethics is centrally concerned with the power of human beings, and sometimes finds that power sublime, full of an invigorating delight that resists other kinds of power.

5

At about the time Thoreau was walking on a beach in Cape Cod and witnessing the aftereffects of the storm of 1849, Charles Dickens published *David Copperfield*. In the second volume of that novel there is a chapter entitled "Tempest," which contains an unforgettable description of the overwhelming power of a storm at Yarmouth.

But Charles Dickens was not content with the "aesthetic sublime."

He describes the agony—not the indifference—of the people on the beach. Shrieking, running wildly up and down, they are begging people to help the drowning sailors just offshore. He describes a figure clinging high on the mast of a ship that is breaking in two. The planks on the ship are bursting beneath him, but he takes off his red cap and waves it gaily. It is Steerforth, the brave, erring friend of David Copperfield. He is celebrating his love of life in the very teeth of all that power.

But these are not the only signs of moral vigor in this master-piece. At the height of the storm, Ham, who has been terribly wronged by Steerforth, ties a rope around his body, puts the running end in the hands of his friends on shore, and strikes out for the ship and for Steerforth. The immense waves throw him back on the beach with blood on his face. Then he adjusts the rope around his body: "And now he made for the wreck, rising with the hills, falling with the valleys, lost beneath the rugged foam, borne in towards the shore, borne on towards the ship, striving hard and valiantly. The distance was nothing, but the power of the sea and wind made the strife deadly." A vast green wave comes up to him, and he seems to leap up to meet it; but it swallows the ship and throws him back toward the shore. His friends pull him in, "but he had been beaten to death by the great wave, and his generous heart was stilled forever."

The "ethical sublime" does not need to conquer the immense physical power that is part of the sublime. No one, not even the bravest person, can subdue a sea storm. All the "ethical sublime" requires is that there be an undaunted will to resist, a will to do more and to do other than suffer and die under an inhuman power. Pining and wringing one's hands will not do for the "ethical sublime." There must be valor; there must be power pitted against power.

6

It is just this kind of sublimity that Thoreau denies in the rest of his account of his walk on Cape Cod after the wreck of the *St. John*.

Early in *Walden* he made this somewhat startling claim: "Probably I should not consciously and deliberately forsake my particular calling to do the good which society demands of me, to save the universe from annihilation." He was a loner, not a sociable do-gooder. He did not need to help others, just as he did not need to be helped by them. As far as feeding the hungry or rescuing the drowning was concerned, he wrote, "I can find you a Newfoundland dog that will do as much."

He saw around him in Concord and elsewhere preachers and teachers and political leaders telling people that they are completely involved in mankind and that their main duty in life is to do good. He saw people thinning themselves out or pulling themselves inward until they lived hidden inside little nutshells of timid obedience. On both ends of civility for Thoreau there is usually moral illness. The philanthropist out of self-congratulating sentiment drops a crumb from his well-laden table, and the recipient praises him out of his own selfishness. Wildness is our natural and joyous duty.

When he exclaimed at the end of his essay on the death of the Irish emigrants, "Infants by the score dashed on the rocks by the enraged Atlantic Ocean! No, no!" he was saying no to fruitless sympathy. And what he was saying yes to was a vigorous, unsentimental life of one's own as an inhabitant of nature, nature where death is as common as life, and sniveling sympathies are irrelevant. In the section called "Solitude" in *Walden*, he had written: "Nothing can rightly compel a simple and brave man to a vulgar sadness." Thoreau would not let himself be daunted by the spectacle of nature crushing other human beings, but neither would he countenance even the possibility of moral heroism. His version of the "aesthetic sublime" (like Turner's) has its victories and its joys, but these victories and these joys are in the minds of spectators. They have little to do with the power—or even the desire—of human beings to help others.

7

It is an interesting, and even a mysterious fact that what Thoreau describes in his account of the wreck of the *St. John* is mainly a world of unsentimental people like himself, people more concerned with their own lives than with helping others. Thoreau's description of that is as much a picture of his own mind as it is a picture of what happened on the rocky beach of Cohasset. It is a perfect instance of how his writing describes the world and expresses his own mind at one and the same time and in one and the same way. As far as what *he* saw is concerned, doing good makes little or no difference in a world where creatures do not live by compassion but live for themselves. The hunters coming to see the wreck of the *St. John*, the passionless faces of the friends and relatives of the victims, the townspeople gathering seaweed without any special interest in the victims of the wreck—all the scenes he saw with his own eyes are empty of pity, just as his own eyes were then empty of pity.

And when he writes about the only people on Cohasset Beach whose vocation was to help others, the lifesavers, he sees them as useless, irrelevant to the great forces of nature. While the *St. John* was breaking up on Grampus Rock just offshore, a British brig was cozily riding in Cohasset Harbor. Instead of drifting onto the rocks, it had slid smoothly into this protected harbor. Instead of going out to save the ship that was being wrecked by the storm, the lifesavers of Cohasset went out to the relief of the peacefully drifting British brig. They brought its unendangered crew ashore while the Irish emigrants were drowning around Grampus Rock! The only people they saved were the people who did not need saving. So much for the good that do-gooders do.

Thoreau makes it clear that the lifeboatmen were being neither cruel nor negligent. They did not see the *St. John* while they were bringing ashore the crew of the British brig. The waves were still too high. When they passed a boat from the *St. John* on its way to shore, they assumed that it held everybody who had been aboard. Thoreau does not blame them for failing to save the people who needed saving. He simply describes what happened.

The curious thing about this whole incident is that, again, Thoreau seems to be describing not only what happened but also his own expectations and his own attitudes toward helping others. He does not invent the story as an illustration of the futility of doing good; he simply tells the story of what actually happened offshore of Cohasset on that Tuesday. But he, being the person he was, noticed and recorded this futile act of "help." Thoreau brought with him a certain attitude toward helping others, and lo and behold! the actual events that he reported wore that attitude like a palpable garment. He received from the story of the Cohasset lifesavers exactly what he had brought to that story. Often "coincidence" is a facile name for "mystery," but whatever name one uses, in *Walden* he had recently written, "Do not stay to be an overseer of the poor," and behold! here was a story of lifeboatmen who did not stay to help the drowning.

And yet the lifeboat station at Cohasset was the first lifeboat station established in America. It was so effective that, in the first half of the nineteenth century, others started appearing up and down the coast of Cape Cod and along the whole Atlantic seaboard, as well as elsewhere in the United States. The volunteer lifesavers of Cohasset saved so many lives and so much property that all the lifesaving services in the history of the United States, including the present-day Search and Rescue Service of the Coast Guard, had much to do with that one team of lifesavers. But by the mystery of coincidence, Henry David Thoreau, who was no friend of do-gooders, happened to be at Cohasset when the most experienced lifesaving team in America, and one of the most successful, failed to do any good! By failing they confirmed his rugged individualism.

A short while after the wreck of the *St. John*, in the course of a rainy and rainbowed day on the beach just north of the elbow of the Cape, and after he had cooked and eaten a big juicy-sweet sea clam that the storm had cast ashore, he found himself standing before a "Charity-house." It was a shelter for shipwrecked sailors that the Massachusetts Humane Society had set up. The hut was eight feet long and eight feet wide, and it stood on piles sunk deep in the sand of a lonely hollow near the sea, but far enough up the beach to be beyond the high-water mark. It was supposed to have a sliding door kept shut with a thin nail bent through a staple, so that a freezing man could get in; and it was supposed to have a bench inside, some matches, some straw, and a fireplace. The particular shelter that Thoreau happened to find had no sliding door, no window, no straw, no matches, no bench, only some stones and some bits of rags on the floor. Even though his hands were not frozen, he could not turn the rusty nail to open the door, and he saw what was in the hut through a knothole in the door. As he put it, he "looked through the knot-hole into the Humane house, into the very bowels of mercy; and for bread . . . found a stone. . . ." Unable to get inside on that cold, damp day he crouched in the lee of the hut for a while and thought: "how cold is charity! how inhumane humanity!"

The hut was for Thoreau a symbol of "the wreck of all cosmical beauty." The reality behind artificial, civilized sentiment was a hut hidden in a hollow so that a shipwrecked sailor could not find it on a stormy night, a hut sealed with a nail that had rusted onto a staple, a box like one of those deal coffins with death inside. The hut, like philanthropy, was "but a stage to the grave." Help was as unavailing as pity in the presence of nature.

8

The Humane Society of Massachusetts had been building and maintaining shelters since 1787. From the time of its first meeting in Boston at the Bunch of Grapes Tavern at the corner of State and Kilby Streets in January 1786 through the time of Thoreau, its purpose was nothing more sentimental than this: "To restore to life such persons as were apparently dead from drowning, or any other sudden means of the extinction of life . . ." At first their main activities involved publishing pamphlets with instructions for rescuing and resuscitating people, paying rewards to lifesavers who had risked their lives in the process of saving people, and placing lifesaving apparatus along the waterfronts of Boston. For a while they adopted the policy of blowing smoke up through the anus of a victim in order to revive him, and one of their number confirmed the power of this method by asking, "If someone did that to you, wouldn't you sit up quick?"

Soon after their first meeting they started building shelters for people shipwrecked in the treacherous Outer Harbor of Boston and along the Cape. Very shortly after they started building these huts, they started financing and supervising lifeboat stations along much of the coast of Massachusetts. The rewards they paid lifesavers were not based on the number or social importance of the people saved but on "the risque and danger incurred" by the lifesaver.

In the archives of the Humane Society of the Commonwealth of Massachusetts there are so many detailed records—despite Boston's disastrous fire of 1872—of people saving the lives of others, and so many detailed testimonies from people whose lives were saved by "Charity-houses" that I found it difficult to choose one. The record I finally decided on involves a hut about as bare as the "Humane house" Thoreau found.

On December 15, 1803, the two-masted brigantine *Elizabeth* found itself anchored in near-hurricane winds a few miles from Cohasset, offshore of Hull. Suddenly the brig parted its anchor cable and struck very hard on the great sandbar off of Point Allerton. The immense waves of the bitter cold sea swept the length of the deck again and again during that night and throughout much of the next day. By four o'clock in the afternoon of December 16, it was clear that the *Elizabeth* was soon going to go to pieces on the sandbar. The wind and the waves were the vast hammer, and the sandbar was the anvil. To stay aboard until the boat splintered was certain death; and so, even though the crewmen were almost frozen to death, they decided to try to get to shore. Some of them were convinced that in their condition they would die in the attempt. The Boston Harbor pilot, one Thomas Knox Jr., who had come aboard the previous night, led the way by swimming to the beach with one end of a heavy rope, the other end having been bent to the bodies of the others. When he came ashore, he drew them after him.

When they were all ashore they slogged their way through wind and sands toward the Humane Society hut, which was marked by a large white ball atop a tall post. Covered with ice and almost dead from the cold, they pushed their way into the hut. Let me quote the account written a few days after the event:

But who can describe their extreme grief and disappointment, when, upon their arrival, they found no fire works, candles or straw, and but a small quantity of wood!—Capt. Gibson and Mr. Knox are, however, of opinion, that though they could not experience the salutary influence of a fire, they must have perished had it not been for the shelter afforded them by the house, from the violence of the wind and the extreme cold. Some of the inhabitants of *Hull* very humanely carried some fire works to the house, by which means a fire was kindled, their cloathes dried, and they recovered strength sufficient, by assistance, to get to *Hull* that night.

This is an image of a shelter hut not entirely different from the one Thoreau gave us: no matches, no straw, cold comfort. But there was comfort enough—with the help of some Hull people—to save their lives. Thoreau's "cold charity" meant the difference between life and death for the people from the *Elizabeth*, and for many people in the course of the nineteenth and twentieth centuries, even though they might have taken shelter in Humane Society huts that had been ransacked by vandals.

Thoreau saw the bare hut north of Nauset Beach as a symbol of failed sympathy, but the authors of the 1803 report took a different approach to the one on Point Allerton: They criticized the people who plundered it. Unlike Thoreau they did not dream of criticizing charity itself. As a 1795 report put it, the main enemy of humanity was not sentimental, unavailing charity; the main enemy was the "inhuman mouse in the shape of a man," who invaded and pillaged the huts. Instead of seeing the hut as a symbol of man's powerlessness in the face of nature, they saw the bare hut as a call to action. They demanded the arrest of the vandals who stole objects of such little monetary value and of such immense human value, and they recommended that men be hired to guard and to inspect the huts during the winter season. Then they recommended that the guards be held responsible for any pilfering that occurred.

All this was alien to Thoreau. For him the faces of those who lived out their days trapped in social networks were pale and livid. For him human society was always diseased, and the most diseased members of society were the helpers. For him the eye of the massive hurricane that is nature was the "aesthetic sublime," the detached ecstasy of a spectator.

THE PELICAN

1

The village of Hull is a few miles from Cohasset, where Thoreau witnessed to the power of the storm that wrecked the *St. John* early in October 1849. Hull is one of the tiniest villages in Massachusetts. It is at the top of a peninsula called Nantasket, which begins at Atlantic Hill in the east, near the place where the *St. John* was wrecked, goes west up Nantasket Beach, goes around a rocky bend called Point Allerton, and ends at Windmill Point. The whole peninsula is about seven miles long, and it is shaped like a pelican whose haunches are Atlantic Hill, whose head is Point Allerton, and whose pendulous beak ends at Windmill Point. Hull village is the pelican's beak, and the long back of the pelican, which runs down from Point Allerton to Atlantic Hill, is Nantasket Beach, one of the most awesome white barrier beaches in the world.

In the nineteenth century the peninsula was about as dangerous to shipping as anyplace on the Atlantic coast of the United States. Immense breakers, submerged rocks, shifting shoals and bars, and intricate, speedy currents destroyed many a ship, especially in the days before steamships when boats were at the mercy of the wind. A schooner or a brig with no power of its own, caught between a strong wind out of the northeast and the pelican in its lee, had to have a good master and plenty of luck, or it would be hammered to death on the beak or the head or the back of the pelican. In the age of sail, especially in the middle of the nineteenth century when the United States was becoming a great commercial power, and when

Boston Harbor was the second busiest port in the nation after New York, ship after ship, and person after person, died off Hull.

One evening in the spring of 1848, about a year before Thoreau visited nearby Cohasset, there was a protest meeting in Hull. The village had fewer than two hundred people in it, and only about thirty houses, but the upstairs room of the wooden Exchange on Spring Street was full. Unlike the villagers Thoreau was to see in Cohasset, the hard-fisted villagers of Hull were passionately concerned with the wrecks that were happening more and more frequently on their shores.

In the middle of more and more winter nights, when full gales and hurricanes and towering waves were coming out of the northeast, they would hear the old call "Wreck! Wreck! Wreck!" and those who lived close to the beaches could even hear the smashing of a vessel off the head of the pelican. "As men and Christians" (as they put it at the meeting), they had to drag themselves out of their warm beds, pull on their cold clothes, and then run out to the beaches to help save lives. Often they would have to run upwind toward the wrecks, so that they could not breathe with the wind jamming the breath down their throats. They would have to stop, turn their backs to the winds, and hunker down in order to catch their breath. The cold seemed to freeze their bones, even before they stepped into the surf to make living lifelines for the victims. But despite all this, the village of Hull was one of the safest places in the United States for shipwrecked sailors. Its wealthy neighbors—like Hingham—disdained its poverty but had to admire—grudgingly—its courage and hospitality.

That spring evening, upstairs in the rickety Exchange, the villagers of Hull were saying, "Enough! Enough!" They were protesting against the chiefs of Boston marine insurance companies and against the shipowners and captains who were letting those wrecks happen. The people of Hull had organized the meeting in order to prepare a statement for the Boston newspapers. They wanted to tell the city magnates to stop destroying lives by selling insurance to greedy shipowners, who in turn were hiring almost any captains they could find to command the ships that could bring in fast profits. A green young captain, hired by a money-hungry shipowner and insured by an equally hurried and greedy marine insurance company, would destroy lives and property on the rocks and shoals off

Hull. The captain was usually a well-to-do young man with lots of book learning, perhaps, and perhaps a Harvard degree as well, but with no knowledge of high winds, heavy seas, and hard knocks. The result of all this greed and ignorance was death.

In the course of the evening the most respected sailors in the village spoke up. One of the speakers, Captain Dill, was a descendant of the early English colonists who had settled Hull in the seventeenth century. He was not as fluent as some of the other speakers, or as humorous (the meeting had little pure bitterness in it—it was as much an evening's recreation as it was a protest), but Captain Dill was a sailor whose words weighed heavily with his fellow Hullonians. During his short speech he asked why Hull's own fishing vessels never piled up on the rocks or sand bars around the peninsula. We people of Hull, he said, take our boats out near bars and rocks, and we catch mackerel and perch and cod in heavy weather, often after long voyages, and we come home safely past our own shifting bars and shoals. Why? "Because *we feel our way,*" he thundered. "We use our hand-leads at the right times, and often, and we use our common sense always."

Captain Dill told of a New England captain of a fishing schooner, who sailed from New England to Cape Sable, by the Bay of Fundy, then down to Georges Bank and Cape May, and finally down along the whole eastern coast of the United States and around, into the Gulf of Mexico, to New Orleans, where he picked up a full cargo of fish. He got home safe and sound. And do you want to know what navigational equipment was aboard his vessel? A slate and a piece of chalk.

No, Dill went on, people and judgment are what we are talking about, not equipment or book learning. And if more men of judgment did not run insurance companies and ships, then death and destruction would continue to shake decent Hullonians out of their beds on winter nights, and the people of Hull would have to petition the Massachusetts Humane Society to send down more lifeboats. A Humane Society lifeboat that was standing ready at that very moment not far from the protesters had just saved about forty sailors. Hull would not stand by and let people die. And they would not stand by and let others let people die in a search for quick profit.

When Captain Dill sat down there were "thunders of applause," according to one journalist. The old captain had ended his talk not with a threat but with an appeal to the decency of the insurers, the owners, and the master mariners of Boston.

2

When I first read an account of this meeting in a little Hull Library publication called *Notes on the Seashore*, I was astonished. For coastal villages all around the world wrecks were heaven-sent gifts. The cargoes of the ships and the stuff of which the ships were constructed were immensely valuable, especially to poor, forsaken communities like Hull village—communities at the ends of the earth that made a precarious living out of the cold salt sea. Once I had heard a song sung on an English coastal island that went: "If there is going to be a wreck, dear Lord, let it be here!" I could hardly believe that one of the smallest and most desolate coastal communities in the United States would try to prevent shipwrecks from happening.

Robert Louis Stevenson wrote one of his most profound tales of terror about the joy and profit that human beings get from shipwrecks. "The Merry Men" in the eponymous story are a mass of murderous breakers on the coast of Scotland whose roar can be heard six miles away. The breakers are so called because the waters whirl fast in a dance of death on the great rocks off the coast, and they make sounds very much like gleeful shouting when the tide turns. Stevenson's story is about a man, Uncle Gordon, who *lusts* to see the Merry Men destroy ships and people. When the narrator of the tale accuses his uncle of being sinful for enjoying death and destruction, he answers, "If it was nae sin, I dinnae ken that I would care for't." For him there would have been no joy in lying on his belly on a rock and watching the Merry Men destroy human beings if he had not felt that his pleasure in watching this destruction was wrong. His joy in witnessing the misery of others made him come alive because he knew that that joy was evil.

The history of Western literature, from the earliest Greek tragedies to the most recent plays, novels, and short stories, displays in striking colors the sufferings of an Oedipus, an Othello, and an Anna Karenina. Our belles-lettres, our "beautiful letters," are full of pain that we find aesthetically pleasurable. The history of religion—

at essential moments—involves plagues and crucifixions and wars. We put the pain of others into many beautiful and even redemptive forms, but the pain does not mar the beauty—rather, it enhances it. It adds flavor and zest to that beauty, so that in art and religion, ecstasy and agony are often one and the same feeling. We hate cruelty in our ethically elevated moments, and we cherish it in our aesthetically and spiritually elevated moments. It draws us, at least in part, *because* it disgusts us. Our disgust makes cruelty interesting, engrossing. We human beings are walking paradoxes because some of our most intense feelings arise from paradox and conflict, and we love to feel strongly.

Nowadays on our modern highways, rubberneckers stop their cars and come as close as they can to a bloody wreck. Highway policemen for decades have insisted that rubberneckers seriously and sometimes fatally hinder their efforts to help the victims of car wrecks.

We human beings are fascinated by destruction, and when we are not fascinated by it we can be coolly indifferent to it or mildly stimulated by it, reading our papers over our morning coffee, or doing scholarly research on wars and persecutions. On the surface and in the depths of civilization—perhaps at its very heart—there are dark desires in us crying to be appeased by cruelty. In our everyday lives, as well as in our most significant works of civilization, we fashion the satisfactions for those dark desires into beautiful and "faith-full" objects that express at once our lust for cruelty and our hatred of it.

I remember the wild joy I felt in front of the Cockroach Building in Chicago while I thrust my knee into the groin of a surprised bully; and I remember how thrilled I was on a hill in Germany while I was firing white phosphorus warheads down on Mannheim, and saw the stone buildings and the people burning. It was a thrill mixed with loathing. I had the same feeling when I saw a slender uniformed arm and a boy's head lying next to each other in a ditch on the road going out of Mannheim toward Heidelberg. I felt the lust and the pride of power; I felt the thrill of wildness; I felt a joy deeper than compassion and more exciting. We live in nature and in civilization, and lusting after cruelty is part of both, a more important part than we are usually willing to admit. Christ's horrible passion on the cross is at least as important to Christian love as the plagues are important to Jewish redemption.

Perverseness—the deep desire in human beings to vex ourselves, to do and to enjoy what we think is wrong just because it is wrong—has played a large role in human life, as it did in Stevenson's story. But another kind of cruelty has played an even larger role: neat, reasonable, practical cruelty, the slow crushing and grinding of living creatures for some good purpose. The torture and killing of Native Americans had much self-vexing lust in it, but it was—perhaps—done mainly for the purpose of winning the West. The enslavement of the black people in the United States and elsewhere often had lustful perverseness in it, but the white majority did it mainly—perhaps—for self-serving economic purposes. And I enjoyed the killings we did mainly—perhaps—because they meant winning the war and getting home. And so history goes.

The more I thought about the usefulness of wrecks to a poor coastal village, the more incredible that protest meeting in Hull became. How could those villagers have wanted to stop that unending source of income and excitement: wrecked ships? How could they have resisted the temptation to indulge in the practical, self-serving acceptance of cruelty? Theirs was a poor village, laughed at, when it was thought of at all, by their well-to-do neighbors in Hingham, who described it as "Moon village at the ends of the earth." For such a village shipwrecks were an unending source of goods.

Beachcombers, who picked up the remains of ships above the waterline; and wreckers, who went out to stranded ships and unloaded and dismantled them; as well as anchor draggers, who salvaged the huge metal anchors of wrecked ships, not only helped many a poor fisherman's family get through the long, terrible winters on the coast of Massachusetts, but even helped make families prosperous. Along the beaches after a wreck, coastal villagers could find plenty of wood from the hulls and cabins and spars. Wood was the main fuel along that cold, deforested coast, long before coal became plentiful and cheap. And the hulls, spars, and superstructures of wrecked vessels had a hundred other uses as well.

But it was the cargoes of the wrecked ships that were the most dramatic blessings. Here is an incomplete list of the cargoes of ships that were wrecked off the beak, head, and back of the pelican during the years before the protest meeting of 1848: cigars and wine (*Lloyd*); lumber (*Emmeline*); iron and anvils (*Mohawk*); molasses

(*Tremont*); eggs and wood (*Surplus*); lime (*Nun*). All salvage from wrecked ships had to be brought to the wreckmaster and left with him for a while in order to see if any owner or insurance company would claim it; but there was no wreckmaster in Hull. And so for Hullonians it was always open season on wrecks. But even if there had been a wreckmaster, the wrecker or beachcomber or anchor dragger who brought him valuable cargoes and materials would still have received half their value.

Consider the Mooncussers. These coastal villagers waited for a moonless night and hung a lit lamp on a mule or a horse. Then they walked the animal along a dangerous part of the coast. On such a night a green or careless captain caught between a northeast wind and a lee shore would think that the light was swinging from a ship that was docked comfortably in a sheltered harbor. Immediately he would head his boat toward the light, only to lose his boat, and perhaps his own life and those of his crew, on the rocks or shoals. The Mooncussers (who cursed a full moon because its light would reveal hazards), according to the legends, then took the cargo of the ship and robbed the corpses of its crew and passengers. If any were alive after the wreck, they would be murdered, lest there be witnesses.

There are legends about Mooncussers on almost all of the seacoasts of the world, including Hull. But as far as Hull is concerned they are only legends. There is a story of a shipwrecked sailor who found himself hanging on to a spar floating toward another village on the coast of Massachusetts. When he came within hailing distance of the shore he asked a beachcombing villager what the name of the village was. The villager called out the name of the town, and the sailor promptly turned his spar around and headed back out to sea. He'd take his chances with a stormy sea.

There are times when the sight of the sufferings of others helps us to rejoice in our own safety and comfort. The sufferings of others are not always pleasurable in themselves, but they make our safety and comfort pleasurable by contrast. Ah! There but for the grace of God go I. Yet somehow the people of Hull found it commonsensical to resist the various subtle and gross temptations that beset human beings.

The ancient cry "Wreck! Wreck! Wreck!" did not cause them to nestle gratefully in their beds, nor did it cause them to rush out to the beach to enjoy the profits of the pains of others. It made them rush out and help. The women with homes near the beaches made big pots of soup for the survivors and prepared warm beds for them.

One woman of Hull was given a piece of broken china by a sailor she helped bring to life in her home. It was all he possessed at the time, except for his clothing. The woman cherished it for the rest of her life, and she passed it on to her daughter.

There were a few vandals in Hull, mice in the shape of human beings, as the Massachusetts Humane Society described them, who took candles, matches, and food from the shelter huts around Hull. And there were a few Hullonians who were so aggressive about salvaging that they were distrusted by everyone else inside and outside Hull. But the protest meeting of 1848 expressed a different attitude toward the miseries of strangers. It expressed the feelings of people who, to use Captain Dill's phrase, *"felt their way"* into the misfortunes and the lives of strangers. It expressed the refusal of most Hullonians to be tempted by blood lust or gain. And it expressed an attitude different from the comfortable detachment of the Roman poet Lucretius and the sublime attitude of that American lover of the "aesthetic sublime," Henry David Thoreau.

THE HANDS OF JOSHUA JAMES

1

On Sunday, November 25, 1888, a reporter for the *Boston Globe* was walking across Boston Common at about two o'clock in the morning, when he looked southward and saw a big cloud of dust whirling over Tremont Street. The dust sped toward him, getting thicker and thicker as it moved, until it hit the Public Gardens to the west of the Common. When it was at the center of the gardens it was as thick as a dense fog. Then he heard a roar "like the distant sounds of the sea," and a full gale struck. In what seemed like an instant it covered everything he could see with a crust of ice and snow. In a few minutes the blizzard was so thick that he could barely make out the storm-signal light high over Boston. The light had come on too late: One of the most ferocious storms to strike the New England coast in a hundred years had suddenly begun.

On Saturday the United States Weather Service in Washington, D.C., had announced the existence of two storm centers that might affect New England. One was over the Midwest, and the other was off the coast of Florida. The latter was the more active, but Gen. Adolphus Washington Greeley of the Weather Service chose to ignore it. He predicted either fair weather or light showers on the coast. But the Florida low-pressure area swept north along the Gulf Stream up the Florida, Georgia, and South Carolina coasts, gathering strength as it went. Hot air rises, and so the freshly heated air near the

Gulf Stream leaped up and left a hollow low-pressure area beneath it; into that low-pressure area the winds poured more and more violently, like water into an empty jar, while the whole jar raced up the Atlantic coast, struck Cape Hatteras, bounced east out to sea, swept north over hundreds of miles of unobstructed water, and hit the coast of New England, leaving behind it a thousand miles of disaster.

In the age of sail, when Boston wharves were forests of masts, a storm was the devil's brew. Whatever else the devil is, he is vast and murderous. And whatever else he is, the Prince of Air is a tempter. If you are in the middle of a storm at sea the pandemonium can tempt you into confusion and despair; and if you are safe on shore the pandemonium can tempt you to enjoy the comfortable thrill of witnessing the immense spectacle of overwhelming power destroying other human beings.

But the Boston Harbor wharfmen were not easily tempted into enjoying the "aesthetic sublime." They were running along the wharves and yelling wildly in order to wake up the crews aboard the ships moored near the wharves. Officers who had been biding their time until the tide was high enough to get under way reacted to the sudden storm by "swearing oaths enough to sink a Cunarder" (as the *Globe* reporter put it) at sleepy sailors under their command. The winds onshore were already strong enough to smash the ships against the wharves and bridges of Boston. In a little while boat crews were hauling all sorts of ropes, and channel pilots were moving their vessels out into the open water in order to avoid the anvil-shore.

But people like the reporter stood appalled and exalted by the tempest. The ancient interest of limited creatures in the mobilization of vast power caught him up as if his fascination itself was part of the storm. All he could do was feel—and express in words—a delightful horror at watching a vast force descending on little beings like himself. The reporter knew that his readers would be fascinated too. The storm was news.

2

Later that Sunday morning less than a dozen sea miles* south and east of Boston, a fourteen-year-old boy was standing beside his

---

* One nautical mile equals 1.5 statute miles.

father watching the same storm strike. They were on the beach at Point Allerton, the back of the head of the pelican called Hull. The boy's mother had a "delicate throat" and had not been able to leave the house that morning for fear of the cold wind. But his father was a sailor, and cold winds were his element. And so the boy and his father had gone alone to church, and then they had taken the train to the point in order to get a good view of the storm.

When the two of them had gotten off the little train the wind almost blew them off their feet, and they had to turn their backs to it in order to breathe. Behind the pelican's head there were thousands of miles of open ocean, a vast "fetch," on which the winds could pick up speed—and gather immense power—like a sled going downhill. The boy's father told him that he thought the winds were blowing about sixty miles an hour.

Through the snow and the spray and the fog the two of them could still make out more than a dozen ranks of breakers churning toward them from the east. The boy did not know it, but the waves around Harding Ledge, due east of Point Allerton, must have been about thirty feet high—mountains in motion. But he did see the spindrifts, the spray that great winds rip off the tops of waves. "Like a horrid nightmare," he said, they whirled toward them out of the snow and fog and fell with a crash at the high-water mark in front of them, or lashed their faces. The storm sent rolling and bouncing chunks of yellowish foam far up on the beach. The wind and waves had compacted the tiny bubbles into solid masses of dead foam, so that you could pick up the chunks without breaking them.

The boy and his father watched the water undermine the sand cliffs of Hull and tear gullies through the beaches. In the boy's mind the sounds of water striking the land were like the roar of battle between two armies of madmen, smashing up against each other again and again and again. He begged his father not to go closer to the water. It did not occur to him that any human beings would dare to go out on that sea in an open boat.

The two of them were crouching on a moor with some other people, and they heard someone say that Capt. Joshua James had just rescued nine people from a coastal schooner not far from where they now stood. Suddenly the people on the moor were in almost total darkness, and they could barely make out a three-masted schooner that had just struck the rocks about an eighth of a mile to their left.

An old sailor was standing with them on the moor, and he said, pointing up to Telegraph Hill toward the beak of the pelican, "Captain James is over on those cliffs. Who'll run and tell him about that wreck?" After a nod from his father, the boy ran up the cliffs, with the winds knocking him about. On the top of the hill, James and his lifesaving crew were huddled together; they had seen the wreck. The boy stared at the massive men gathered close around James in their glistening yellow sou'wester raingear with the white straps under their weatherbeaten faces. The men looked gigantic.

Years later, when he had become a Boston lawyer, he remembered James as a thick-bodied man standing in the middle of his crew, but detached, thoughtful, quiet, like a general before a battle. It was dark, but they could all see that the tide was up, and a great sea was running with the onshore winds. Great seas usually run with the wind, and wind and water could smash an immense vessel in minutes. They could barely see the orange-red flare that was burning on the wrecked schooner, which was too far out for the little cannon that lifesavers used to shoot the lines of the breeches buoy out to a wrecked ship. The only way to rescue the crew was by lifeboat through the wilderness of wind and rain and hail and moving mountains of water.

The boy heard the captain say, "It's only fair to tell you fellows now that we're not likely to come out of this. I don't want any man to come out this time, who—" Those were the last words he heard. After a little while all the quiet men walked down the hill toward their Humane Society boathouse. Not one held back.

The boy's father ran up Souther's Hill overlooking the schooner, and he and many of the other people of Hull tore up some picket fences near the crest of the hill and built a big fire that lit up the wreck and helped the lifesavers to avoid the flopping, slashing debris around the boat. The loose and broken spars of a ruined ship were one of the main dangers lifesavers had to face. But the sailors on the wrecked ship needed the firelight too. It showed them what the lifesavers were doing, and what they could do to help them. And it gave them hope: It showed them that they were not alone.

The boy saw the lifeboat moving toward the schooner with Captain James standing erect in the stern handling the long, thick steering oar. More than once the boat seemed to be standing on end in the troughs of the vast waves. Again and again it was on the verge of being pitchpoled.* The boy was sure that he would soon be seeing the bodies of the surfmen floating ashore at the foot of Souther's Hill. His father had told him that the surfboat was not a self-bailer,† and he could see two members of the crew frantically scooping water out of the boat with buckets. In the firelight he could barely make out Captain James, with his men crouched and rowing before him, moving into an immense darkness only dimly lit by the fire on Souther's Hill.

Then he heard the voice of a stranger, who was standing near him by the fire. A well-dressed man, he was shivering with the cold despite his nearness to the blaze. He said, "They'll never come back." And then he added, "I'll lay you two to one they don't make land, even if they reach the schooner."

Then he heard another voice, a familiar one; it belonged to a Hull farmer. "If they don't get back, we've lost the best man since Abraham Lincoln. James is a God-almighty man."

But about an hour later—at about nine-thirty—the boat reappeared a few hundred feet from shore, heading for the beach below Souther's Hill. It was overloaded with human beings, so that the crew was hard put to work the oars. The big sea running kept the tide from falling. The winds out of the east were driving the surfboat toward black rocks that jutted up between the boat and the shore.

Suddenly the boat struck a rock and rolled over with one side deep in the water. The boy heard Captain James call out: "Hang on to the boat! All at once the men in the boat climbed up the raised side of the boat and righted it. But it kept striking rock after rock, until only a few oars were left. Now it was hard to keep the boat headed toward shore, which was vital, because if it broached to‡ again it would turn over completely and spill all of them into the salt sea. In that tumultuous, cold water they could not live more than a few minutes.

And then the worst happened. Because of a strong "set," or current running along the shore, the bow of the boat swerved, and a great wave turned the boat upside down. All sixteen men were struggling in the sea. The boy buried his face in his father's coat.

---

* Being capsized end over end.
† A boat equipped with a device that allows water to run out through the sides.
‡ Yawing so severely as to lie parallel to the waves.

His father pushed him away and ran with all the other people down to the beach to make a human lifeline to pull the survivors to the shore. The people of Hull, who were now crowded along the shore, knew what they had to do to help: They had been doing it for years, for centuries. The boy lay in the dark by some bayberry bushes, listening to the shouting on the beach and trying not to think of all those people drowning in the wilderness of darkness, wind, and water, drowning so close to land, so close to help.

After a little while he learned that no one had drowned, and that only one crewman had been injured, with a broken arm. He felt that he had witnessed a miracle. But he had not witnessed the whole of the miracle. The storm of '88 had only begun, and so had the work of the lifesavers.

3

There was someone who saw it all from beginning to end, and from up close. That person was Joshua James, the captain of the volunteer crew of the Massachusetts Humane Society. A little more than a month after the storm that was to make him one of the most famous Americans of his time, he wrote out a summary of what he described as "work done by myself and others who joined me." Lt. O. C. Hamlet of the U.S. Life-Saving Service had requested him to do so. It is one of the very few available documents written and signed by Joshua James, and if we know enough about Hull and his life in that village, it gives us a picture of a man whose caring lay not on his tongue but in his nerves.

The document tells how in the first morning of the gale of November 25, 1888, James climbed Telegraph Hill in the wide beak of the pelican, looked down on the Lighthouse Channel, which ran between Hull and the Boston Light, and saw five schooners and a coal barge anchored there. While James stood on the hill he felt the gale rising out of the east, and since Hull was on the lee side of the anchored vessels, they were slowly moving toward Stoney Beach, on the top edge of the pelican's beak. They were dragging their anchors behind them. Once again, for the more-than-thousandth time in the long history of Hull, the top of the beak of the pelican was a lee, or protected, shore in a storm, the deadliest enemy of coastal sailors.

*   *   *

When I first read this report, I thought that I was in on the beginning of a suspenseful story, in which one dramatic action would follow close on the heels of another with not a moment of respite. But Joshua James, after he had studied those six endangered ships, walked down the hill to Spring Street and took his dinner.

He was not a man who acted impulsively. Persistence was his way, dogged attention to the facts at hand. But though he was as persistent as the tides, unlike the tides he knew how to rest. He knew enough to loaf with an absolutely clear conscience. When the facts required it he could go on the stretch and stay on the stretch. And he would show this constancy during the whole storm of '88, as he had been showing it for almost sixty years as a volunteer lifesaver with the Massachusetts Humane Society. But now the facts did not oblige him to exert himself and his crew. The anchored vessels were moving very slowly toward the beach. He calculated that by the time he and his crew were through eating, they could reach them. Moreover, he knew that in this immense gale, and with the heavy sea traffic into Boston Harbor, he and all the other lifesavers on the peninsula of Hull would soon be very busy, and for a long time.

He and his crew were hungry, and hungry men, weakened men, can lose their presence of mind as well as their physical vigor. And so they ate their main meal of the day in peace. I am not sure what it was they ate; James's report to Hamlet does not say; but one of the favorite dishes for the lifesavers of Hull, and a dish that could be kept hot for the lifesavers for hours without losing its savor, was fish chowder. It was a dish that the people of Hull loved. They made it in layers, usually in a big pot: the bottom layer was pork fat drippings mixed with water; the next layer was freshly caught cod spread over the bottom of the pot; the next was a layer of small potatoes; then they spread salt, pepper, and some more pork drippings over the potatoes; finally there was another layer of cod and potatoes. And all of it was set to boil for about a half hour, with a lid on the pot. While the chowder was still hot, they poured in a quart of sweet milk and boiled it all for five minutes more. This—with much bread—was the classic meal for hard winter work in nineteenth-century Hull.

James had already shown the people of Hull how he could loaf. One of his descendants, Gladys Means, has told me about the hours he would spend with friends by the flagpole on Spring Street. Around the flagstaff there was a crudely constructed wooden platform, and around the platform were spars and figureheads from vessels that had been wrecked on the beach a few hundred yards away. On that platform Joshua and some of his Humane Society crew would stand for hours in the summertime, laughing and talking, while other young men of Hull were off fishing or farming.

One day, Gladys Means said, the word got around Hull that there were lots of mackerel running offshore, so that you could practically scoop them up with a net and make good money selling them to the Boston dealers at Pemberton Wharf at the tip of the pelican's beak. And so men, young and old, took whatever boats they could muster and went out. But not Joshua. For some reason, or for no reason at all, he decided to sail a little boat out to Bumkin Island in Hingham Bay. He had his dog with him, and a gun. Almost all the little islands near Hull had birds on them, and Joshua was apparently going to shoot some birds. While his friends were busy making money he spent the day wandering around the island.

He shot one bird, but apparently he did not bother to search for it with any zeal. At the end of the day he came back to 104 Spring Street with nothing to show for his day of hunting. The next day a friend hunting on the island found the bird Joshua had shot and brought it to him.

When I asked Gladys Means why a poor man didn't go fishing that day, and instead just loafed, she told me, "Joshua was so wrapped up in saving lives he wasn't much concerned about whether his family had enough to eat or had enough money. It was summertime, and there weren't any wrecks. There was no other work that he was interested in but lifesaving." He was a man whose life was immovably centered, and when he was away from that center, even for a few hours at dinnertime, he could take it easy. It has been said that you can tell the strength of a horse not only by how fast it can run but also by how suddenly and how firmly it can stop.

At about two o'clock on that afternoon in November, after a meal that took at least two hours to finish, he and his crew took a surfboat out of the Stoney Beach Humane Society station and placed it on the beach at a spot where they expected one of the vessels to strike. The three-masted schooner *Cox and Green* struck nearby, just to the west, toward Windmill Point. But according to James the sea was much too rough to use the surfboat, with Toddy Rocks close by. And since the schooner was not too far offshore, James decided to use the ship-to-shore "bridge" called the breeches buoy to carry the shipwrecked sailors to safety. His report reads: "Many of the people in Hull assisted in placing and working the beach apparatus."

According to a letter written in the middle of the nineteenth century and published at about the time that Thoreau was taking his walks through Hull and on Cape Cod: "Almost every one laughs when the name of the town is mentioned. . . ." The writer surmises that the reason for this is that Hull was the tiniest village in Massachusetts. But he goes on: "Its bold and enterprising inhabitants have saved the lives of hundreds of shipwrecked sailors, and that of itself is enough to immortalize the place, and give its people a fame that will endure forever."

Again and again, through all the recorded storms that struck Hull, the people of that village were almost as important to the work of lifesaving as the famous heroes like Joshua James and his crews. They came to the shore not merely to look but to help. On the first day of the storm of '88 they helped push up and anchor the great wooden X that carried the heavy hemp hawser, the trolley line along which the breeches buoy ran from the vessel to the shore; they ran out into the surf and waves to pull the buoy along the line out to the ship and then to draw it back close enough to the shore to lift the exhausted, frozen shipwreck victims out of the canvas breeches of the breeches buoy; they carried them to their houses and gave them food and warmth out of their own meager supplies; and those who could not help with their hands stood on the beach and shouted encouragement to the shipwrecked victims freezing and screaming for help on the decks and in the rigging of their boats.

There is no understanding Joshua James, the patron saint, to this day, of the Search and Rescue Service of the U.S. Coast Guard, without understanding that he was a mere extension, a conspicuous part—but only a part—of the people of Hull. Especially in the nineteenth century, at the height of the age of sail in America, almost every able-bodied man and woman in the village was a saver of lives. As the record of the protest meeting of 1848 shows in its half-humorous, half-desperate way, Hull was perhaps the most hospitable village on the eastern seaboard of the United States, and Joshua James was one of them. He was not alone. Helpers often need help.

While the people of Hull were pulling the last crew member of the *Cox and Green* out of the stiff canvas trousers of the breeches buoy, Joshua James heard that another three-masted schooner was in trouble. About an eighth of a mile east of the wrecked *Cox and Green* the *Gertrude Abbott* was flying its flag upside down. It had struck the eastern edge of the Toddy Rocks.

It was getting very dark, the sleet was getting heavier, the wind and the tide were up, and the heaviest sea of the day was running. The water was too wild and the waves and breakers too high for the surfboat. James decided to pull the surfboat opposite the wrecked *Gertrude Abbott* and wait for low tide before launching it. Between eight and nine in the evening, they launched the surfboat with only the light of the great bonfire on Souther's Hill to guide them. Aside from the fire that the people of Hull had built out of their picket fences, there was the utter blackness of a moonless, starless night. The onshore wind and the waves and breakers were so violent that there was no low tide, only high seas.

Joshua James's version of the rest of the story of the *Gertrude Abbott* rescue is much the same as the boy's account: The great sea running, the eight crew members taken down from the big schooner into the small surfboat, the difficulty of keeping the boat head-in when it was so crowded that the oars were almost impossible to work, the capsized boat, the boat righted, the boat finally smashed, but everybody in it saved, all by about ten o'clock at night.

One of the things the boy did not know was how important to the rescue operation the hands and the eyes of Joshua James were. Only James could see where they were going, because he alone was facing the bow. His crew was crouched deep in the boat, facing the stern and looking up at their captain. He alone handled the big steering oar, and though the other oars propelled the boat, the main task of keeping the boat from broaching to was in his hands. It was he who had to keep the bow facing each oncoming wave

head-on, so that it could cut through the crest of the wave as soon
as possible without wavering on the crest. A moment too long on
the crest of an oncoming wave, when the bow and the steering oar
were in midair and the boat was out of control, could produce the
worst disaster of all, broaching to.

The boy did not know that James was a man of awesome physical power. His hands were four times the size of normal ones. It
seemed as if nature had made those hands to control the great
sweep oar in stormy seas. His shoulders were not wide, and at five
feet six and a half, he was not a tall man—slightly under the normal
height of Hull sailors in the nineteenth century. But his arms were
almost preternaturally long, and at their ends were those enormous
hands, powerful even compared to the hands of other sailors who
had spent their lives—and whose ancestors had spent their lives—
pulling thick oars. Lifesavers needed somewhat different physical
powers from those of sailors on coastal or deep-sea boats. Most
sailors did not spend much time rowing. Usually they did not have
to wrap their hands around broad oar handles and pull heavy oars
through turbulent waters. Mainly they handled flexible materials
like ropes and canvas. The long, heavily muscled arms and the vast
hands of Joshua James helped make him the perfect handler of a
sweep oar.

All of this the boy did not know, and he also did not know
about a certain point brought out by Lieutenant Hamlet's questioning of James a few weeks later. Hamlet asked the captain if during November 25 and 26 he ever felt that his life and the lives of
his crew were in great danger. James answered, "Yes, I did." And he
described the rescue of the crew of the schooner *Gertrude Abbott*
on the night of the twenty-fifth. He said, "The danger was in going
out and coming in through the breakers among the sunken rocks."
He said that the rescues after the *Abbott* rescue involved breakers
and sunken rocks too, but the other rescues were in daylight, and
the rescue of the crew of the *Abbott* took place in the dead of night
with only the distant light of the fire that the people of Hull had
built on Souther's Hill.

Seeing—*light*—was a matter of life or death in lifesaving. The
captain, the only one who could see ahead, and therefore the only
one in the boat who could decide what to do with split-second
speed, had to be able to see not only waves, and breakers and rocks,

but also the heavy debris that surrounded a wrecked ship. If he could not see an oncoming "slatch" (the smooth patch of water that often comes after the master wave, the third wave), or if he could not see the seventh wave (which is sometimes far larger than the preceding six), the surfboat could be broached to or pitchpoled in a moment. And if the captain could not see the heavy wooden spars of the wrecked ship leaping and falling all around it, his lifesaving efforts would be nothing but strenuous suicide.

On the night of November 25, the Humane Society surfboat *R. B. Forbes*, in sleet and rain and in mast-high seas that capsized the surfboat more than two hundred yards from shore, finally carried the whole crew of the *Gertrude Abbott* to safety under the light of the bonfire on Souther's Hill. If ever there was an instance of the "ethical sublime"—of unappeasable, limited human beings struggling to live and to help others live against overwhelming power— the rescue of the crew of the *Gertrude Abbott* was that instance.

4

But an event like this is not enough to make the doers of those deeds "good" people. In the first book of his *Nicomachean Ethics*, Aristotle writes, when he is discussing the good life: "One swallow or one fine day does not make a spring." A good deed must happen in "a complete life," as he put it. A good life takes time, more time than one fine action. Because this is so, there is more to tell about Joshua James and the people of Hull, Massachusetts, than what happened at the protest meeting in 1848 and what happened during the rescue of the crew of the *Gertrude Abbott*.

After ten o'clock on the night of the twenty-fifth, when the sailors from the *Gertrude Abbott* were all being warmed and fed and comforted in the homes of the people of Hull, James and his crew took turns keeping a lookout along the beach that forms the top of the pelican's beak. It was still very dark. The sleet had turned to rain, and the onshore winds were more ferocious than ever. A lookout close enough to the sea to be of any use was in great danger of being drowned in gullies that had been cut in the sand by the storm, or of being struck by wreckage that suddenly swept ashore.

At three o'clock in the morning of November 26 James learned that there was another vessel wrecked near the *Cox and Green*. In the black night James and his crew moved the surfboat *Robert G. Shaw* more than a mile to a good launching place opposite the wrecked schooner. This time there was no bonfire to help the life-savers, and so they had to wait until daybreak before launching. When morning came they saw sailors in the rigging of another three-masted schooner, the *Bertha Walker*, screaming for help. In all the noise of wind and water the winds carried their voices to the people on the shore as if they were shouting in a big room.

The winds were hurricane force, and the thickening rain was like a solid wet wall in the faces of James's crew. The sea was break-ing over the *Bertha Walker* fore and aft—it was deeply embedded in a shoal, being loaded with coal—and the heavy spars of the wrecked vessel were all around. And so it took a long time to get close enough to get the sailors to bend (fasten) ropes around them-selves, jump into the sea near the lifeboat, and have themselves pulled up. The captain and the first mate had been swept over-board and drowned in the night. When the lifesavers pulled the seventh and last living sailor into the boat and set off for shore, the people on the beach gave a great yell of triumph.

By nine o'clock in the morning, the crew of the coastal schooner was on its way to various homes on the north side of the thick beak of the pelican that is Hull.

The lifesaving crew had had no breakfast, but before they could leave the boat, James requested that a tugboat pull the *R. B. Forbes* out to another schooner anchored not far from the *Bertha Walker*. It was the *Puritan*, and though an upside-down flag was flying in her rigging, it turned out that the ship was in no danger; the captain wanted only to be towed in. James arranged with the tugboat cap-tain that this be done and headed for the shore near Toddy Rocks.

But the storm of '88 was far from over. Shortly after ten o'clock—that is, immediately after James and his crew had come back from the *Puritan*—they learned of another wrecked vessel in a dangerous situation off Nantasket Beach. This was the great white-sand barrier beach that constitutes the almost perfectly straight back of the pelican. It has the fetch of the whole Atlantic Ocean behind it to the northeast, and so it receives the most immense winds and waves of any place in the outer Boston Harbor. For this reason Captain James decided to use the large lifeboat *Nantasket*.

And so, a little more than an hour after they had saved the crew of the *Bertha Walker* on a sea more ferocious than any they had ever encountered, and after having spent much of the previous night on the lookout, James and his crew took the heaviest and biggest lifeboat in the United States down from the tip of the beak, south across Hingham Bay, down the Weir River under the feet of the pelican to the narrow strip of beach inland from the Hotel Nantasket. In order to cross the strip of beach to get to the sea, they had to make a landing from the inland side. In the process of making that landing, the big boat slammed against the rocks, and James and his crew had to put lead patches on the holes before hauling the boat across the strip of sand.

All this was happening while the storm was growing more and more powerful, and immediately after a morning of intense and dangerous boat handling. Ever since three in the morning of November 26, crises had arisen so swiftly, one after another, that the crew had not had a bite of food or sip of water. Now they were about to take the *Nantasket* out on the high seas to rescue the crew of a wrecked vessel at the height of the greatest storm of the century.

The boat they were using had never been used before in a rescue. An unfamiliar boat was an object of great suspicion for even the most fearless lifesavers. Experience had taught them that it is far more dangerous to go out in an untried boat—no matter how excellent it might be—than in a familiar, tested one that has its known faults. Especially in a storm like this, their lives depended on their knowledge of their boat. Nevertheless the whole crew of ten immediately agreed to take the boat out.

The *Nantasket* had been designed by Samuel James, Joshua's older brother, who had been helping for four decades to save lives off the coast of Hull. The James brothers had had great difficulty persuading the Massachusetts Humane Society that this twenty-nine-foot immensely heavy boat would be manageable in the breakers, shoals, and rocks off Hull. Edward Burgess, the designer of some of the most successful America's Cup defenders in the history of the race and the experienced boatbuilders who worked for him, believed that the boat could not succeed. But the two Hull lifesavers somehow prevailed, and the boat was built and put in the Stoney Beach Humane Society boathouse in April 1888, a half dozen months before the storm.

The *Nantasket*'s bow and stern were of the same profile; they were designed to keep the sea out of the boat during the launch and the landing. The wood on the bottom of the boat was fitted piece to piece so that the boat could turn in the water swiftly and with a minimum of effort. Most important, it was very light in the water, easily rowed toward the wind on a heavy sea, and easily maneuvered.

The ancient Syracusan Archimedes had shown that an object in water loses exactly the amount of weight of the water that the object displaces. The greater the volume of the object, the more water it displaces, and the lighter it becomes, the higher it floats. This is why a big raft, even when it is heavily loaded, floats high on the water with very little space below the waterline. The *Nantasket* was long and wide at the waterline, and so it floated like a gull's feather, able to respond to the will and the skill of the Hull lifesavers better than any other lifeboat ever built.

The fact that it rode high in the water and was responsive to pressures also meant that it could capsize quite easily, so the crew had to be immensely skillful and strong to keep it from broaching to or pitchpoling in the teeth of a storm. But the lifesavers of Hull had the skill and power to work the boat, and in their hands the *Nantasket* embodied the sea-wisdom of the two James brothers and the people of the village. It was to become the most successful lifeboat in American history.

It took four horses and fifty men to haul the big boat across the sands opposite the wreck, but at daybreak the brand-new dark green *Nantasket* stood opposite the wrecked ship, ready to launch.

Even with a boat as responsive as the *Nantasket*, it took a long time to get past the breakers and waves to the wreck, because of the heavy sea running, and because the most furious gale Captain James had seen in decades was running with it. I have mentioned that the heaviest seas almost always run with the wind. This means that rowing out to sea in a heavy surf demands speed, or all is lost, especially when a great onshore gale is blowing. There is no room for error in the steering of such a sea-responsive open boat as the *Nantasket*. The boat has to cut through the crests of the waves not only swiftly but head-on. The smallest swing from the perpendicular, the tiniest relaxation or overcompensation on the part of the captain or crew, can destroy them all.

But Joshua's "boys" (as he called them) kept the new lifeboat moving with enough speed to get over the crests of the waves handily, and the captain worked the immense new sweep oar truly, so that the surfboat reached the schooner without incident. Because he and his crew were what they were, the most dangerous part of the rescue operation came after the trip to the schooner. James's report to Lieutenant Hamlet is a masterpiece of understatement, describing most of the rescues in the storm of '88 as "work done by myself and others." But in describing the sea around the *H. C. Higgenson*, Joshua James became a different man: "The sea alongside of the vessel was terrible," he wrote. When I first read that sentence I rubbed my eyes and shook my head in unbelief: The seas must have been awesome to have made him say that.

In that sea, and having had no food or rest for almost twenty hours, James and his crew had to keep the surfboat clear of the wreckage around the schooner while staying close enough to it to pull the sailors out of the sea after they had jumped from the rigging. This they had to do speedily, even though the sailors had stout lines bent around their bodies. The waves towering over the masts, the bitter-cold water, and the whipping debris of the ship would have killed them in minutes. In his report to Hamlet, James wrote: "It is my opinion that no other boat, except the one we had, could have gotten up alongside of the vessel as far as the main rigging where the men were; no boat that I know of."

As in the case of the *Bertha Walker*, the Hull Humane Society crew saved everybody aboard—everybody, that is, who was alive when they launched their lifeboat. The master of the *Higginson* and his first mate had been swept off the boat and drowned during the night, and the steward had frozen to death that night hanging in the rigging. His ice-covered body had to be left hanging and swaying in the rigging offshore of the Nantasket Hotel for much of Sunday, November 26, while the storm continued.

A few hours later, at 5:00 P.M., Captain James's crew had to transport the *Nantasket*, with the help of four horses and fifty men, three miles across icy roads and shifting, crusty sands to Long Beach near Strawberry Hill on the back of the pelican. They launched their boat into a full gale of wind and monstrous seas, and they saved the men from the British brig *Alice*.

In about twenty-four hours they had saved the lives of twenty-nine people from five ships. Twenty men had done the "work," as James put it, but only four had been on all five missions. One was James, who at sixty-two was twice as old as the oldest man in his command, and another was his dark, handsome son, Osceola, who had been named after the dauntless, betrayed Seminole chief who had died earlier in the century. They were unpaid volunteers who received occasional medals or rewards for exceptional bravery and success. Saving lives was their avocation. They usually listed their vocations as "Fisherman."

5

In an interview with James after the captain had submitted his written report, Lt. O. C. Hamlet asked him if there was anybody in his command who during the storm of '88 conducted himself more bravely than the others did. James answered, "No. All of the men exhibited the same courage and determination, and no one did anything more than any other in the effort of rescuing the shipwrecked."

James was not being modest; he was—in a way—being factual. From the first trip out to the *Cox and Green* at two o'clock in the afternoon of Saturday, November 25, to the last trip out to the *Alice*, all the men were "in the same boat," as the phrase goes. From those who bailed water in buckets out of the surfboats to Joshua James himself at the great steering oar, these people of Hull worked together. There was not a "tub of butter," as James once described a new, incompetent crewman, among them. They worked for others together. And in this they were as much an extension of the tiny population of Hull as the captain was.

Still, the decisions to go out time after time, to haul the lifeboats for mile after mile, and to drive the boats forward so that they were close enough to the ships to receive the survivors—these and many lesser decisions were Joshua's only to make. No one could make them for him, though he always gave crewmen the opportunity to step aside and let somebody else take their place. He could not command them to risk their lives. And so the decisions to save those twenty-nine people were first made by him alone.

And not only the decisions: The actual conduct of the surfboats and the lifeboat *Nantasket* through those wild winds and waters and rocks and debris was dominated by his powers of body and mind. With those long arms and gigantic hands, that immense strength, and that inflexible will, he alone controlled the boat amid the shifting forces of wind and water. He alone decided and guided every move in each of the rescues, and almost every move was a major one. Almost every move could have destroyed them all.

6

There are those who think that citizenship is simply a possession, a legitimate right symbolized and legalized by a duly attested document that one puts in a strongbox, or something one receives as a birthright. For them being a citizen is primarily a public, legal matter, with no special obligations, except perhaps *not* to do certain things—not to kill, not to rob, not to cheat. Hull village had such persons in it, as, perhaps, do most political units. But this tiny community of two to three hundred families saw membership in the community of Hull as a life in common, a life in which people felt silently but firmly obliged to help strangers and one another.

One reason for this was that by the last quarter of the nineteenth century Hull was made up mostly of relatives. Almost everybody was related by marriage or by blood to almost everybody else. Once in a while a sailor or a soldier from the outer world, or an employee of one of the grand summer hotels on the pelican, would marry into the village. But others were in no rush to spend their lives in this poor, isolated, culturally barren village that the Industrial Revolution had bypassed without a glance. Hull remained a community of close relatives. A visitor to Hull would soon learn that he or she had better not speak ill to one Hullonian about another: The two were usually related, and they were as passionately defensive of each other before strangers as they were critical of each other among themselves.

Another reason for their intimacy was the size and location of the village. Since its founding in the seventeenth century it had stayed small. It had fewer than three hundred families in the last quarter of the nineteenth century. In fact it was the tiniest village in the state of Massachusetts. On the northernmost part of the peninsula called Hull, the village of Hull—the head and the beak of the pelican—lies between two long hills that run up from the south to

the west. The hills protect the village from the terrible northeast-
erly winds of winter, but they also help cut the village off from the
rest of the town. The only close neighbors of the villagers are one
another, and the salt sea.

Gladys Means, who has lived all of her long life in Hull and whose
parents and grandparents lived out their lives there, told me that one
of the reasons that the village was called "Moon village at the ends of
the earth" was that on clear nights when the moon was full, and the
weather was good, they would close a gate on what is now Nantasket
Avenue and shut out the rest of the world. Exactly what they did
behind that gate Gladys Means has chosen not to tell. She did tell me
once that what they did was "fun and games." And once she said, "The
reason you're upset about not knowing is that you're jealous."

But fun and games aside, before World War I, before power boats
and navigational instruments made the seas off Hull comparatively
safe in winter, and before land transportation took the place of
coastal navigation, every able-bodied man in Hull went down to
the sea to save lives as they had been for centuries. When I thought
about Hull in the winter, I found myself thinking of the famous
funeral oration of Pericles, in which he praises ancient Athens as
"the school of Greece," after having said, "It is only the Athenians
who, fearless of consequences, confer their benefits not from calcu-
lations of expediency, but in the confidence of liberality."

I sometimes smiled to myself when I found myself comparing
ancient Athens in all its glory to tiny, isolated, poor Hull village. But
I still find myself thinking about the two of them. One of the reasons Pericles called his great city the school of Greece was that he
found its people equal to emergencies. He saw them facing danger
squarely in the service of mankind, acting boldly, and trusting in
themselves. Of course, the Athenians got some of their glory by
conquest and threats, and the people of Hull did nothing notewor-
thy except save a few hundred lives. The Athenians gave the world
artistic, political, and philosophical gifts of such persuasive power
that—perhaps—no era in history did more than theirs to create civilization as we know it. All Hull village did was save human lives
and alleviate the terrible distress of shipwreck for centuries.

They resembled the village of Le Chambon, these few people
who saved a few strangers. They did nothing to stop or to alter the

course of the hurricanes they faced. But they meant much to those few, just as that French mountain village saved the lives and hopes of some children.

7

The last trip of the *Nantasket* during the storm of 1888 started from the long barrier beach by the Nantasket Hotel. Along much of the Atlantic seaboard the eighties and nineties were the decades of the great summer hotels, and the town of Hull was perhaps the most opulent resort of them all. The Nantasket Hotel was only one, and by no means the biggest, of many hotels that lay scattered along the top of the head of the pelican and clustered down its three miles of gently curving back. Other big hotels, like Atlantic House, Rockland House, Villa Napoli, and Hotel Pemberton, helped make Nantasket (as the town of Hull was usually called then) the queen of the Atlantic seaboard. Presidents of the United States, financial magnates, and internationally famous opera and theater stars spent summers in those immense wooden structures with their great ballrooms, their curving staircases, their foreign chefs (French, Italian, German, and Chinese, sometimes all in the same vast kitchen), and their roulette, poker, and blackjack tables.

The Nantasket Hotel, like the others, had a benign relationship with the sea off Hull. Like the others it was open only in the summer, when there were no storms and no dangers, when the living was easy. It was a place where nature seemed benevolent, peaceful, a pretty background, but only a background, for really important matters like human comfort, human display, and profit making. A veranda wrapped itself around the great wooden building, and the rich sat on that veranda and looked occasionally at the bland and harmless spectacle of a three-mile sweep of white sand and blue water. It was part of what Thoreau, after one of his walks there, called "the most perfect seashore" he had seen.

The hotel and the seashore that surrounded it allowed people to turn to one another for challenges. The hotel made it look as if humankind had total sovereignty over a harmless nature sprinkled with ribboned hats and peach-colored suits. For them Nantasket Beach posed no life-or-death problems. For them there was no need to band together against a wintry world that knew no pity.

But for the villagers of Hull that need was great, not only because the powers of a great sea threatened them but also because they felt an obligation to help shipwrecked strangers. They needed to band together in order to help them. All the rich and powerful needed to do was to impress and command others—during beautiful summer days—while they tasted the fruits of their ascendancy over everyone else. Social or economic ascendancy was of no avail on the cold salt sea during the winter. In the great summer hotels a person had the wherewithal to enjoy solitary splendor. In the village of Hull people could not survive narcissistic and alone, being where they were—and who they were.

During the last decades of the nineteenth century and the first decades of the twentieth, electric trolley cars, steam trains, and large, luxurious steam packets carried crowds of people into Hull from the Boston area and elsewhere in the United States. Occasionally Hull villagers would work at the hotels (Joshua James's five daughters sometimes played dance music there), and occasionally they sold lobsters to the hotelkeepers or to individual visitors from Boston. But somehow the village remained a poor, drab backwater that showed its powers to the world in the wintertime only, long after hotels were boarded up against winds and weather. At a time when not only great summer resorts were thriving in Hull, but great cities, high structural-iron-ribbed skyscrapers, immense corporations and corporation mergers, and vast "bonanza" farms were forming across the country, Hull remained a little place at the ends of the earth, where competition and self-aggrandizement were not as important as living out one's days in intimacy with one another and with the sea.

For years I have been asking my friends in Hull to help me to grasp in an image the differences between the wintry village and the great summer resort of Hull. And for years we failed to find that image. But one day I found it in a book written by a man born and raised in a little house in Hull, a wooden house his family banked around with seaweed to keep out the winds.

Dr. William Bergan lived from the late nineteenth century well into the twentieth, and in his book *Old Nantasket* he described in detail the great resorts of the gilded age in Hull. But he described even more forcefully the dark underside of that age.

There was once, he wrote, a forty-foot cabin boat lying ruined and high and dry on the beach near Pemberton Wharf, where the steamboats from Boston docked. Its large cabin had a padlock on it, and it had a broken glass porthole. When the town authorities decided, after four years, to break up this eyesore and take it away, they had to break down the door of the main cabin. When they entered they saw before them an immense pile of empty wallets and pocketbooks that reached to the roof of the cabin and filled the room.

It was one of the places in Hull the police had told pickpockets to use as dumping grounds for stolen items. Since the boat was close to busy Pemberton Wharf, at the tip of the pelican's beak, it was convenient for thieves; it allowed them to get rid of useless burdens and hide them from any passersby, so that new "suckers" would not be alerted. Were a tourist to see a pile of stripped purses and wallets when he or she stepped off the boat, he or she might well become careful. This would mean less money for the thieves and less money for the police, who were working with them. And so for years thieves dropped the purses and wallets of thousands of people through the open porthole.

The people of all ages and conditions who came to Hull to revivify the pleasure of being alive were forced to enjoy the hospitality of pickpockets—and of their accomplices, the corrupt police. For me the image of that wrecked boat loaded with the detritus of many small and great losses shows what summertime was—for many people—during the gilded age in Hull.

In the wintertime, the time of hurricanes, the village did its best to alleviate human suffering and save human lives. In the summertime the town of Hull created that twisted pile. Like people, some places are better than others, and if you think "better" is an empty word, imagine asking the sailors who were rescued from the *Gertrude Abbott* how they felt about Hull; then imagine asking a victim of the pickpockets the same question.

8

Thoreau was no friend of do-gooders. Usually when he wrote about human decency he despised doers of good deeds. His life task was to "set about doing good." When he helped people it was "aside

from my main path, and for the most part wholly unintended."
Being good for him mainly meant being independent and self-
reliant, not society-reliant. He was one of a long history of people
who believed that goodness was mainly a matter of inward mental
or spiritual power, not outward deeds.

Thoreau had tried to be philanthropic, but he gave it up
because it distracted him from living and loafing by his own lights.
He felt that a person should be like the sun, which does not exist
only in order to give warmth and life, and does not exist in order to
wake us up in the morning through our bedroom window. It exists
in itself. He believed that people do not exist in order mainly to do
good or bad deeds. They exist mainly to burn brightly in inward
power—so brightly that you cannot look upon them.

But the life of Joshua James was a concentrated, unswerving life
committed to helping others. Somehow he managed to help others,
to devote himself to lifesaving, and at the same time to achieve an
integrity: a powerful, immovable centeredness that Thoreau might
have admired, had he gotten to know James in those walks on the
Massachusetts shore.

9

Joshua James was tough and short-legged, with those great hands of
his that hung below his knees. Under his yellow sou'wester hat, and
behind his full, gray beard, you could barely make out his gray-
hazel eyes. He looked like a machine made to do what he was
going to do. And in a way he *was* a machine, made for doing the job
he did.

He was sixty-two years old, almost to the day, when he stood
atop Telegraph Hill that November morning in 1888 and watched
the vessels around the village being driven toward a lee shore. For
almost fifty years—ever since he was fifteen—he had been an
unpaid, unpensioned volunteer lifesaver using the equipment of
the Massachusetts Humane Society. Because of the fire that
destroyed the archives of the Massachusetts Humane Society in
1872, we shall never know how many people he saved in the first
decades of his service, but a Humane Society award he received in
1886 praised him for saving lives from the age of fifteen onward.

On a clear day in early April 1837, the schooner *Hepzibah*, which was owned by Joshua James's older brother Reinier, was crossing Hull Gut from Peddock's Island to Windmill Point at the tip of the pelican's beak. The two-masted fore-and-aft-rigged boat made a living for Reinier by carrying paving stones to Boston. But that shining spring day it had no steadying ballast in its hold. All it had were passengers, and very few of them: Joshua's mother and baby sister.

Hull Gut was a dangerous place, even for Hull sailors like the Jameses. Strong currents from three directions flow through it as if through a funnel, and a fourth current, or set, flows fast along the Hull shore at the top of the tip of the pelican's beak. Joshua, who was then eleven years old, was standing near the Tudor saltworks on the rise near the windmill that gives Windmill Point its name, when it happened. Out of the blue a great gust of wind suddenly burst out of Hingham Bay to the south, stirred up the conflicting currents in the gut, and in a split second turned the schooner on its beam ends. The boat was shipping water through every hatchway. Joshua's mother, Esther Dill James, was above decks when it happened, but instead of moving to the lifeboat, she rushed below through the forward hatchway. Her baby daughter was sleeping down there. While she was below the boat sank, under Joshua's eyes.

Joshua's older sister, Catherine, was fifteen when their mother and sister died. For the rest of Joshua's young manhood she mothered him in Esther's stead. Long after the wreck of the *Hepzibah*, she said that Joshua never wept for his mother and his baby sister. She said: "Ever after that he seemed to be scanning the sea in quest of imperiled lives." His only visible reaction was to devote his life to saving lives off the coast of Hull.

There was one thing besides lifesaving to which he was committed, body and soul. It was Louisa Lucihe, his fourth cousin. He first encountered "Little Louisa" when she was an infant and he was sixteen. In 1858, when she was sixteen and he was thirty-two, they married. When Sumner Kimball, then the superintendent of the federal Life Saving Service and the only biographer of Joshua James, asked Louisa in her old age why she married Joshua when he was twice her own age, she smiled and said that he had had his eye on her since the moment he first saw her. She told Kimball that his strength of will explained it all.

But she was oversimplifying. She had a will of her own. When she was very young she put her life in danger off Nantasket Beach in order to save a visitor from drowning. She was educated and beautiful enough to pick and choose, and she chose Joshua as stubbornly as he chose her. She had a small straight Roman nose that came down from between her eyes in a short diagonal line. It was not tipped up sweetly; it had three lines: a diagonal, a short vertical that was its tip, and a horizontal. She was as sturdy as Joshua, and an excellent boat handler.

The year after they were married they moved into the house at 104 Spring Street where they spent the rest of their lives together. Their house was full of music in the evenings, and Louisa and Joshua spent much of the little money they had teaching all five of their daughters how to play musical instruments. The girls formed a small band, and sometimes—very seldom, because they were not very accomplished musicians—they played at the big hotels. In the evenings in that otherwise quiet village you could hear the music coming out of 104 Spring Street, and anybody who wanted to came in without knocking.

There are not many stories that show much about James's home life or his personality. The stories are mainly about his work as a lifesaver for the Humane Society and later for the U.S. Life Saving Service. But there is one story about him that is personally telling.

He was a silent man. Even when he was young and used to stand on the platform around the flag at the corner of Nantasket Avenue and Spring Street, he seldom talked unless he was addressed. After the storm of '88, when he had been to Boston a few times to get awards and praise (and had managed to give the shortest speeches on record), a young woman reporter from the *Boston Globe* appeared at the front door of the house on Spring Street. She was a little timid, and she was not sure how she would interview him, famous and quiet as he was. James opened the door to her, and before she could utter a word, he took both of her hands into his vast ones, his dark eyes shining with the pleasure of seeing her, and said: "You are welcome here!" She never forgot that short, loving greeting for a stranger, and it was more important to her understanding of the man than any of the stories he told her.

Lifesaving was the only work of Joshua James. Others in the village were fishermen, wreckers, skippers of commercial vessels of various sorts, but for Joshua alone saving the lives of strangers was his only occupation. He loved family, music, and loafing as much as anyone in Hull, but for the last three decades of the nineteenth century nobody in Hull went in harm's way as persistently as he did; nobody in Hull saved the lives of as many human beings as he did. He was a being immovably centered, and the storm that struck Hull on the days and nights of late November 1888 showed how immovably, how stubbornly centered he was. It was his will, and his will alone, that drove his crew into the terrible sea again and again and again, and by the time he died he had spent fifty-seven winters of his life working only at this.

One morning I was talking about him with Joe Ottino, a burly old man, tall and weathered. Ottino was one of the last surviving lifesavers of Hull who could remember the days when lifeboats were rowed, not powered. He had a deep, ragged voice, and he was a little disdainful of my somewhat adoring attitude toward Joshua. And so in the middle of our conversation he reached his heavy hand out and put it on my knee. Then he said, "You know, Hallie, I've heard rumors about how Joshua's crew reacted to his death. One of 'em said, 'Good for the old bastard. It's about time.'" And then with a wry smile Ottino added, "But it's only a rumor. Anyway, I can tell you for sure that Joshua made his boys practice and practice and practice in between storms."

10

Often Thoreau leads us to think that we must choose beween allegiance to nature and allegiance to human society. He wants a freedom that is not just civic, but that is absolute. As he put it at the beginning of his essay *Walking*, he wanted "to regard man as an inhabitant, or a part and parcel of Nature, rather than a member of society."

For Joshua James that choice, that "rather than," was nonsense. He lived and moved and had his being in both nature and human society. During the long summer days and nights in the lifesaving stations, he read for hours and hours on end (an old drawing of him has him surrounded by books). The books were mainly about nature—astronomy, weather, and physics. As children he and his brothers and sisters had been forbidden by their intense, dutiful mother to read novels or fiction of any kind. Once she destroyed a beautiful, expensive copy of a novel she found in the hands of one of her daughters.

She helped turn him to studying nature, not human imagination. But of course books were not his main links with nature. Experience was, experience and his own powers of observation. One night when he was in his teens he was sleeping belowdecks on a voyage into waters far from Hull, and the captain of the boat, a fellow Hullonian, suddenly realized that he was lost. Someone suggested that he wake Joshua and ask him to help. When they did, Joshua looked up at the sky through sleepy, heavy-lidded eyes, recommended a new bearing, and casually said that in about two hours they would make a certain lighthouse. About an hour and fifty-five minutes later they made the light. James's father used to tell this story, but had no idea how his son had been able to examine the stars and draw such accurate conclusions in unfamiliar waters.

Once when he was sailing a boat into the Inner Harbor of Boston, he lost his bearings for a little while in an opaque fog. After a few moments somebody asked him where they were. Without hesitating he answered, "Off Long Island Head," and when he was asked how he knew it, he answered, "I can hear the land talk." A few minutes later when the fog lifted they were exactly where Joshua had said they were. He was a man in touch with nature—his eyes, his ears, his cast of mind, and the experiences of a lifetime at the ends of the earth had made him, to use Thoreau's words, "part and parcel of Nature."

From the age of fifteen until he was seventy-two years old he laid his big hands on nature, and he never lost his grip. He did not live with nature as a solitary being like Thoreau, but as part and parcel of Hull Village, and as part and parcel of the lives of the people he did so much to save from terror and death. His fifty-seven years of service as a lifesaver are unique in the history of the Massachusetts Humane Society, the U.S. Life Saving Service, and the Search and Rescue arm of the U.S. Coast Guard. He was both a do-gooder and a man of unshakable self-will. Thoreau could have been describing him when he wrote, "Let us first be as simple and well as Nature ourselves, dispel the clouds which hang over our own brows, and take up a little life into our pores."

11

On March 17, 1902, one of the worst disasters in the history of lifesaving occurred off the southern end of Monomoy Island, a strip of land hanging down from the elbow of Cape Cod. During a great storm, the Monomoy Point lifesaving station sent out a boat to pick up some men stranded on a wrecked barge. The seas and the winds were very high, but the five crewmen dropped into the lifeboat, and the Monomoy crew started rowing them back to shore. Then a great wave struck them, and the boat was suddenly full of water. The rescued men jumped up from their seats in a panic, even though Captain Eldredge of the Monomoy station had ordered them to stay low. They threw their arms around the necks and shoulders of the surfmen and kept them from heading the boat to the shore. The boat broached to, turned bottom up, and everybody on the boat, except a surfman named Seth Ellis, drowned.

All along the coast of Massachusetts the story of the Monomoy disaster was in the air. Within hours of the drownings, every surfman and most of the inhabitants knew the details. Capt. Joshua James was now head of the U.S. Life Saving Service around Hull. The Monomoy disaster reminded him of the immense dangers in his profession, and he needed that reminder, because for almost sixty years he had been saving lives without losing a crewman and without failing to rescue a single shipwrecked person who had been alive at the moment when Joshua and his crew set out to pick him up.

There is no record of his having said anything to express his feelings about the Monomoy disaster, but there is a very clear record of what he did. On March 19, two days after the disaster, a great northeast gale struck the shores of the pelican. There were no wrecked ships and no ships in danger. Captain James did an almost unprecedented thing: He called his crew to a boat drill at seven o'clock in the morning at the height of the storm. He wanted to reinforce the discipline of his men, and he wanted to reassure them and himself that they could handle the lifeboat safely in very heavy weather.

And so they launched the dark green *Nantasket*, with James, as usual, at the great steering oar. He was seventy-six years old, three decades older than the regulations permitted for a captain. He was the only lifesaver who was ever allowed by the U.S. Life Saving Service to keep his post so long after the legal age limit. A few months before the drill he had passed a physical examination with grades higher than any of his "boys." His eyes and lungs were normal; his pulse rate 84; he had no rheumatic symptoms and no varicose veins. And he was stronger than any of the men in his command.

For one hour he had his "boys" maneuver the lifeboat in the immense sea off Stoney Beach. These were steering maneuvers, and he alone was at the big sweep oar. At the end of the hour he was satisfied with the behavior of his crew and delighted that the lifeboat freed itself so swiftly of the water it had shipped.

He gave the command to head for shore. At the moment when the bow of the boat touched the sand of Stoney Beach, he leaped from the boat, took a few steps, turned, looked at the sea, and said to his men, "The tide is ebbing." And he fell on the sand, dead.

There is a legend in coastal communities: People here do not die when the tide is at the flood; they die only when the tide is going out. The legend goes on: If a person lives until the flood starts, that person will live at least until the tide starts ebbing. If this legend does not describe a fact, at least it expresses a spiritual truth. People along the coast are intimately acquainted with a superhuman force, the sea, which—like every cell in our bodies—is awash with water. They are in communion with something vastly larger and vastly more powerful than themselves. They are creatures of human society *and* creatures of superhuman nature. Such a one was Joshua James.

12

After I had been studying the life of Joshua James for a few years, I found myself asking whether I had managed to answer the invitation he had seemed to give me in the Coast Guard Museum the first night I heard about him: "See if you can understand me, Mister."

My first answer was that I had not done so. I had so few words from his hand and mouth, so few firsthand accounts of his feelings and ideas. Sometimes his actions had seemed to me to be opaque, as far as letting me see what was in his mind and heart. He was almost like an inscrutable though magnificent athlete who could do wondrous things with that powerful body of his. I could admire his actions, I felt, but I did not know his mind.

Then I realized that I was interested in him not because I was trying to guess or infer what was happening deep inside of him, but because of what he was *in the world*. I was interested in him because he had relationships with other human beings that I felt were beautiful and good. I was fascinated by him from the beginning because of the story he lived.

How much can we know for sure of the innermost mind of even a person much given to words, like Henry David Thoreau? Thoreau's hundreds of thousands of words were a little like Joshua James's many actions—they showed you Thoreau, but only up to a point. They brought you just so far into his mind, and then suddenly a line was drawn, a limit touched. What, for instance, did Thoreau mean when he wrote toward the end of the chapter "Economy" in *Walden*: "I never dreamed of any enormity greater than I have committed. I never knew, and never shall know, a worse man than myself"?

No, what interested me in Joshua James was his story, as far as I, a curious outsider, could hope to discover it. And after I had spent a few years seeking out that story, I knew all that I needed to know. I knew that the story of his life was the story of a helpful, lifesaving human being committed to helping other human beings, and strangers at that. Benevolence, hospitality, helpfulness were embodied in the plot of his story, and I had done my best to get the story straight. His goodness was not some secret, hidden feeling or thought inside his head or heart. It was not something you have to guess about or draw elaborate psychological inferences about. It was the visible, the very *form* of his life, and anybody who looked long and hard at his life could discover that form.

His power to spread life did not lie in one of his deeds, like what he did in the storm of '88. It was his whole persistent, centered, life-giving life that was the very form and essence of the decency I was after. There it was in the story of that life, like the light of the sun that Thoreau wanted to emulate. It was visible; it was there; it was luminous.

And it had beauty in it. Whatever else beauty is, it is a confluence of joys, a unity of different jubilations. Beauty is happening when one entity makes you feel yourself coming alive in a wide joy, the way the contrasts and harmonies between sounds and silences in any Haydn trio make me feel myself coming alive. It is a diversity of joys unified into a single joy, almost overwhelming.

And moral beauty happens when someone carves out a place for compassion in a largely ruthless universe. It happened in the French village of Le Chambon during the war, and it happened in and near the American village of Hull during the long lifetime of Joshua James.

It happens, and it fails to happen, in almost every event of people's lives together—in streets, in kitchens, in bedrooms, in workplaces, in wars. But sometimes it happens in a way that engrosses the mind and captivates memory. Sometimes it happens in such a way that the people who make it happen seem to unify the universe around themselves like powerful magnets. Somehow they seem to redeem us all from deathlike indifference. They carve a place for caring in the very middle of the quiet and loud storms of uncaring that surround—and eventually kill—us all.

11

KÄTCHEN IN
MIDDLETOWN

1

It was a clear afternoon in May 1991, and I could not shake off the feeling that I was going to fall backward right down into the Connecticut River. My little audience and I were perched on a ragged green hill that plunged steeply to the river and downtown Middletown. The green-and-white tent we were under was temporary, and people were sitting on folding chairs that scraped on the gravel of the driveway when they shifted their weight. A few hundred yards away was the Meadow Meat Market, with chunks of fresh, blood-red meat hanging from its hooks or stacked in its refrigerators. And up the hill in front of me the redbrick buildings of the Connecticut Valley Hospital lay scattered. The criminally insane, the homeless, and others who were lost in our wide, meandering valley had temporary homes in those buildings. The sun was very hot even under the tent.

While I was making my speech, in the front of my mind—I could almost feel it written across my forehead—were the words the German philosopher Schopenhauer used to use when he encountered a work of art: "Look here! This is life." Heat, insanity, addiction, bloody meat, those scraping chairs under the tent, and right in the middle of it all a tight-throated college teacher praising and opening a home for pregnant addicted women. This is life.

The reason we were all there was that the organization whose president I was, The Connection, was opening its seventh program for the lost, the Women and Children's Center. I was there to talk about why the center was a good thing. Millions of the babies in the United States are born to women whose minds and bodies are being shattered by drugs and alcohol, and the babies are the most deeply wounded victims of all. The center was there to help pregnant women purge themselves of drugs and alcohol and learn the redemptive art of mothering. Our architect, Jeff Bianco, had turned a shabby two-story wooden skeleton into fifteen bright little homes under one roof, with a wide patio-porch at the rear of the building that opened on an immense western sky and the Connecticut River Valley. The center was already filled, and it had a long waiting list of pregnant women. It was a tiny eye in the hurricane of indifference and pain around us, but still, there it was.

Before I started telling the stories of my soul's adventures among people who helped desperate people, I tried to explain my beliefs about ethics. I said that I did not know exactly where the pressures of ethics come from. Maybe—ultimately—they came from God; maybe they came from the biological needs of thin-skinned forked animals; maybe they came from a whole array of forces ranging from the divine down through the biological—I did not know. But I did know that the ethical "oughts" of life had to do with spreading the joys of living.

I told them that sometimes the constraining force to spread vivacity takes the form of No! Don't murder, don't betray, don't hate, don't hurt. And I told them that sometimes the demand takes the form of Yes! Be your brother's keeper, love your neighbor, help strangers. But whether the demands are don'ts or dos, they are innocent of legislatures, judges, and police; they are intimate, personal, naked of public pomp. You find their force in the feelings, thoughts, and actions of particular human beings with their particular stories, or you find that force nowhere.

Then I told them that for me the trouble with living only according to the don'ts is that you tend to be narrow and passive— a corpse in a narrow coffin is perfectly obedient to all the don'ts. A dead body does not murder or betray or hurt anyone. And the vast majorities who witness (or fail to bear witness to) the murders and humiliations of history without raising a finger to slow them, the silent majorities with clean hands and clear consciences—these proper people are obeying the negative demands of ethics to the very letter. They do not kill anyone, they do not get pregnant while they are addicted to drugs or alcohol, and they have washed their hands of those who do. They are comfortable, and they have their reward: a nice, clean, comfortable life. This is a good reward, but for some people it is not good enough.

The mysteriously enduring force of ethical demands that celebrate the ecstasies of living can say yes too. It can behoove you to help. It can urge you to go out of your way to diminish the murders and the humiliations that people perpetrate upon themselves and others. If you obey the demand to be your brother's keeper, to help a stranger, your actions resonate in people outside your own hide, and doing this sort of thing can be as uncomfortable as it can be risky. Still, the joys of helping (especially of helping the very young) are—at least for some people—wider and deeper than the cozy pleasures of people who stay put.

Having said this, I told the stories of the villagers of Le Chambon, of the ambiguous Maj. Julius Schmähling, and of great-handed Joshua James. As Emerson put it, these were people who would "rather die by the hatchet of a Pawnee, than sit all day and every day at a counting-room desk." These were people who were more wild than civil, more powerful than nice.

I ended with a warning: If we confine our attention to such extraordinary people, we are in danger of becoming passive admirers of statues on pedestals instead of active participants in the spreading of life. Devout hero-worshipers can look up too much and stumble through life, as Thales did when he kept his eyes on the stars. Too often we postpone work when we worship.

I told them that one day in the South of France, after I had been talking for a few hours with Magda Trocmé, I took a long walk in the countryside that Napoleon had once marched through with his Grande Armée. I had to get away from my obsession with her local, immense accomplishments. As I walked by the lush fields just north of Nice I tried to recall the decent things I had done. For the life of me I could find only ambiguity. I thought of my combat days when I helped stop Hitler, but I had been drafted, and I helped stop the mass murders by killing as many German soldiers as I could with my 155-millimeter artillery piece. I was a helpful killer who violated the negative demand against killing in order to obey the positive one to spread life. But Magda and her villagers! Their ethical purity was beyond me. They obeyed the negative demands of ethics by hating and hurting no one even *while* they obeyed the positive demands of ethics by saving about five thousand children!

Magda Trocmé made me feel like a cat looking up at a queen. She touched me, but I could not touch her. I remember that on that long afternoon walk through the valleys near Digne I even resented the tall trees for making me feel so small and so rootless.

I ended the talk by urging my audience to help the staff of the Women and Children's Center. I urged them to volunteer for the other everyday-life-size jobs that needed to be done there and in the six other addiction-fighting programs of The Connection. These, I said, were projects we could work at that had no hatred and no hurting in them, and that spread the joy of life here and now.

During most of the talk I avoided looking at a certain woman sitting in the middle of the audience. I avoided her eyes because I felt that I had nothing to tell her about help. She was the founder of The Connection, and fifteen years earlier she had all but pushed me into joining its board of directors.

Her name was Kätchen Coley. She had a wide, high forehead, wide-set eyes, and high cheekbones, but the bottom of her face was small, like the bottom of a heart. She was a combination of a child and a terror. Usually when you talked to her, she listened to you with every muscle of her face focused on you; then she started talking in her mildly rasping voice, and she talked, and she talked, and she talked. In recent years those of us who loved her had the know-how to silence her abruptly, but she could talk less experienced people into distraction. Still, for the twenty-five years I had known her, when she listened, she listened body and soul, and when she talked she often told unforgettable stories about helping the helpless here in the Connecticut Valley.

After the ceremony, in the crush of people at the refreshment table, she found her way to me, smiled mildly, nodded her approval with her full head of brown and graying hair, and left without saying anything and without any sign of affection. As I watched her still-voluptuous figure going away from the table without taking any food, I thought, That's Kätchen, slightly Germanic, slightly military Kätchen. To glance at her you'd never know how loving she is.

One evening at a party I had found myself sitting on the floor in front of a fireplace with Kätchen, both of us sober and hungry in that crowded living room. I looked at her sitting there erect, even on the floor among swaying, noisy people, and I leaned toward her and asked, "Kätchen, what in hell made you start The Connection in the first place, and stick with it?"

She turned those wide, childlike eyes on me, and said, "Well, duty. You know, duty. Ever since I can remember duty was important in our family. My father lived by it."

I remembered the stories I had heard about her young woman-hood in Germany, when her father—Maj. Truman Smith, a man who knew Adolf Hitler, Hermann Göring, and other leading Nazis—was the military attaché to the American Embassy in Berlin, in the years when Germany was getting ready to take on the world. Something slightly perverse made me say to her as we sat there, "But Kätchen, duty was what made Hitler's SS and his whole regime work. Duty made the Nazis follow orders and kill civilians with a clear conscience. Duty isn't enough."

Sitting there stiffly, staring at me with that rounded triangular face of hers, she said, without missing a beat, "Well, then, call me an SS maiden." There was no anger or bitterness in her voice.

Though her answer was what I deserved, it shocked me—and it filled me with remorse. Would I ever clear my mind of the years I have spent studying the Nazis? I realized for the hundredth time that the answer was no: Until the moment of my death the measuring stick of our capacity to be murderously cruel to one another would always be the story of the twelve years when the Nazis held power in Europe.

Immediately after she said, "Well, then, call me an SS maiden," she turned away from me to talk with somebody else. As I sat there alone in the crowd, I found myself thinking about a story she had once told me.

Between 1935 and 1939 her father, in his dual capacity as a spy and a diplomat in Berlin, had been studying the immense leap forward being made by the German air force. He saw the Luftwaffe becoming more powerful than all the other European air forces combined. Because he saw this expansion as a threat to the United States in particular and to world peace in general, he made and cultivated contacts with the leaders of the Luftwaffe, including Air Marshal Göring himself: He wanted to observe the explosive growth of Germany's air force from up close.

One afternoon Major and Mrs. Smith, in the company of Charles Lindbergh, whom Smith had invited to Berlin in order to get an expert's point of view on German air force expansion, went to a formal luncheon in Göring's Berlin residence. During the meal Göring had told Lindbergh about a pet lion he kept in the house, and Lindbergh had asked if he might see it. Göring had agreed to show it to him. After a splendid meal the party arose and went into the gleaming, wainscoted library. A few minutes later the doors were flung open, and into the room leaped a young lion, some three feet high and four feet long from the tip of its nose to the end of its tail.

At first the lion was startled by so many strangers, but when it saw its master seated in a big armchair, it recovered its wits, loped across the room, and leaped onto Göring's lap. It put its paws on his shoulders and started licking his face.

Kätchen's mother was standing behind Göring, a wide table safely between her and the air marshal, who was wearing his resplendent white-and-gold uniform. In the middle of the love play between the young lion and Göring, someone suddenly started laughing, and she wondered what the laughter was about. She soon found out: The lion in its excitement was urinating plentifully on its master's shining uniform.

Mrs. Smith saw Göring's wide neck go blood-red. He jumped to his feet and flung the young lion from him with so much force that the animal bounced off the wall. Then, his blue eyes shining with rage, he turned on his guests and asked, "Who did that?" He was referring to the one who had laughed during his humiliation. Silence.

Frau Göring rushed up to him, threw her arms around his neck, and in a loud whisper said, "Hermann, Hermann. It is like a little baby! There are too many people here!"

Göring softened and let the lion be led away. "Yes it is. It is like a little baby," he said, and the people in the room laughed uncomfortably.

Mrs. Smith turned to look for Lindbergh. She was convinced that Göring would never forgive Lindbergh for witnessing his humiliation. But Lindbergh had already sensed this, and he had been attentively asking an aide about a picture on the far wall from the moment the lion had started urinating.

When Kätchen had shown me her mother's diary entry that told the details of this story, the first phrase that jumped out at me was "like a little baby." I thought of the distance between that utterly civilized luncheon and the concentration camps of Central Europe, where no one was shown mercy for being "a little baby." I thought of the hundreds of thousands of children whom the Nazis would soon deliberately torture and destroy in concentration camps and "actions" on the Eastern Front.

But my next thought was of the immense gap between that whole upper-echelon Nazi world in which Kätchen was raised as a preteenage girl, and the Connecticut Valley world where I knew her as a champion of wandering addicts. What a chasm there is between the friends of the lost and the elegant, polite mass murderers of the world!

I left the party early, mainly because I was ashamed of what I had said to Kätchen about duty, and because I did not know how to apologize to her. Since she, typically, did not seem to have been hurt by my little sally about the Nazis, I felt that I ought to get away and apologize to myself for what I had said to her.

As soon as I got home I went into my study and pulled out copies of letters she had received years earlier from some of the people she had helped. As president of The Connection, I had been studying the history of the organization, and these letters were an essential part of that history. After I read some of the letters I thought that I might apologize to her after all: I would call her up and read one or two of them to this "SS maiden."

One of the earliest had been written in 1971 by a young man named Pooper—I have kept his spelling and punctuation—on a hand-made circular yellow card with pink, blue, and green flowers drawn around its edge. In the center of the round card was a picture of the sun shining above a dark cloud with rain falling from it. The words under the drawing read:

Dear Mrs. Coley

I have tryed to wright you a letter to think you for all the thing you have done for me but I can't think of enough words to say. So I holp can

see this as I feel it. This is one thought of mine of you, you are like the sun
you keep shining if it is cloudy or if it is raining

Love Pooper

I never read these notes to Kätchen. I decided to let this chapter
apologize for me.

2

In the middle of the state of Connecticut, across the Connecticut
River from Middletown, there is a high, broad hill that forms part of
the immense eastern wall of the Connecticut Valley. Spread out on
the top of that natural wall is the Connecticut Valley Hospital
(CVH), an array of white-trimmed redbrick buildings that have been
used for years to rehabilitate people suffering from mental disorders.
One of those buildings is Woodward Hall. In the rear of Woodward is
a driveway that is close to the elevator in the building and therefore
handy for transporting patients to and from ambulances.

One day in 1971 there was a burst of activity in Woodward. A
young man who had been convicted of armed robbery had struck a
nurse. He had been heavily sedated, strait-jacketed, and then locked
up. Dr. Edward Friedman, the chief of Alcohol and Drug Services at
CVH, and the other staff were waiting for a Department of Corrections ambulance to arrive and take Joe (that was the patient's
name) to the maximum security prison in Somers.

In the small Woodward facility the other inmates knew all about
this, and they were anxious about Joe's future, partly because they
were afraid of being sent to Somers themselves. They were all relatively young first offenders serving out sentences for substance-
related crimes by entering the Woodward treatment center instead
of going to jail. They were in various painful and confusing stages
of "drying out"; they were far from being blasé, hardened criminals.
Woodward was alive with their fear and anger over what was being
done to Joe.

Some inmates and volunteer staff of the hospital rushed to a
window when they heard the ambulance arriving in the courtyard.
They watched Joe—looking like a mannikin—being carried out on
a stretcher to the ambulance. Their anxiety for Joe and for their
own futures peaked.

Suddenly one of the volunteer staff rushed down the stairs, even though she did not yet know her way around the building, found the back door between the elevator and the ambulance, and ran outside just in time to grab Joe's hand before he was put into the ambulance to go to Somers prison. She held on to his hand as he was being pushed into the ambulance, and she called out with a mildly raucous, "Joe! Joe! I don't know if you can hear me, but I know that you are going away. I know where you are going, and I'll write you. Do your best, and take care of yourself. Remember: We are all thinking of you." And when the ambulance started moving, she ran after it for a while, calling out words of affection until it pulled out of the driveway.

As soon as the ambulance was gone, one of the nurses told Kätchen—for the volunteer who had run out to talk to Joe was Kätchen Coley—that Dr. Friedman wanted to talk to her immediately. She knew that Dr. Friedman had wanted Joe to be taken away as quietly and inconspicuously as possible, and she knew that her actions had ruined his plans.

In his office Dr. Friedman told her that he had been trying to keep a riot from happening. The patients were frantic about what was happening to Joe. They were going to go into depression having seen Kätchen rushing out to Joe and running after the ambulance as it left for Somers. All this was going to hurt the program. He told her that he was doing his best to make this new and precarious program work, and what she had done had imperiled it.

Kätchen expected that he would tell her to leave Woodward, but instead all he did was point out that the whole program depended on each action taken by the volunteers and the staff. Dr. Friedman, on the basis of his training and experience, believed that Joe was a bad apple who could ruin the program at Woodward and had to be removed. He told Kätchen that the success or failure of this brand-new project of keeping first-time, substance-involved offenders out of prison and under treatment depended on the staff working together and not undercutting one another's efforts by emotional outbursts.

But all Kätchen could do during the interview was think about Joe, who was being brought like a jacketed zombie to Somers, a place where he would find no compassion, no treatment for his alcoholism, but plenty of brotherly advice on how to be a criminal.

*   *   *

For the next twenty years of her life Kätchen continued to be
Kätchen, an amateur, not a health care professional. As Dr. Friedman puts it, she was an "enthusiastic personality," someone who
was always getting "sucked into the lives" of the people she helped.
She simply could not or would not adopt a clinical point of view
on people. Friedman was a staff psychologist whose brown-eyed
compassion was intense but whose training and long experience
gave him a certain clinical objectivity in his involvement with his
patients. He thought about them as patients who fit certain cate-
gories he had been examining and dealing with for years. And he
tried to handle them expeditiously, for everybody's sake. Some of
the young people called him "Fast Eddie."

He was also an administrator who had to oversee a number of
other professionals and who was responsible to other administrators of CVH. He was a professional, whose compassion was controlled.

Kätchen, on the other hand, was an amateur (which in its original French meant "lover"). She was neither trained nor paid for the
work she did. The help she offered mainly came with personal caring; the help Dr. Friedman and his paid staff offered was mental
health care. Once I asked him whether Kätchen and the other
unpaid and untrained volunteers harmed the Woodward program
more than they helped it. He answered: "There were some squab-
bles over who was in charge of the patients, the staff or the volunteers, because both wanted control. But the volunteers, and especially Kätchen, contributed so much to the morale of the patients
and to the speed of their growth that we never dreamed of doing
without them."

There was room—in fact a vital need—for both approaches.
Early in the history of the program a vivacious young woman
named Billie came to Woodward. She followed Friedman through
the halls, begging him for a teacher who would help her get her
high school equivalency degree. She insisted that in order for her to
get away from heroin—and from jail—she had to do something in
the time she was spending at Woodward, and what better thing was
there for her to do than get an education? But there were no teachers at Woodward. What could she do? Friedman had no funds for
teachers. What could *he* do?

He decided to turn to the person in charge of volunteer work for CVH, tall, blond, intense Johnsia Knapp. She was the wife of a professor of psychology at Wesleyan University, and so the first people she thought of were her friends among the faculty wives. And one of the first wives she thought of was Kätchen Coley.

Friedman was not sure that there would be enough continuity with these volunteers; he expected them to pull out of the program after a short time dealing with their unstable students. And so he screened them rather carefully before accepting their help. In fact some of the volunteers did stay only a short time. They got no pay; there was no organization, only a hit-or-miss one-on-one relationship between tutor and pupil. The volunteers did not know their students' detailed histories, nor would they have understood their psychological profiles if they had. A volunteer would arrange her day or her week so that she could meet with a student at Woodward, but the student might not turn up, might either forget the appointment or decide to drop the whole project of getting an equivalency degree. No records were kept, there was no way of disciplining the students, and there was always the erratic behavior of the drug or alcohol addict who, in a pinch, chose to satisfy his appetites rather than keep his promises. Moreover, some of the professional staff felt that these amateur do-gooders were not really helping their patients as much as they were being overwhelmed by their sad stories.

Yet Kätchen Coley persisted. She made and kept the most appointments with the students, and she kept the records of the tutorials of all the other volunteers. Her unending enthusiasm kept the whole program on the boil. She forgave and forgot all the broken promises. She was not a therapist, she was a mother and a big sister—a passionately devoted friend who kept believing that love would conquer all. And love almost defeated her.

3

One summer afternoon late in the sixties Kätchen found herself in the Middletown courthouse, facing the Connecticut River. Other than the judge and the bailiff, there were only two people left in the courtroom: Kätchen and a brown-haired man in his twenties who had just been convicted of robbing a gas station with a gun. Before the robbery the young man had been one of her tutees, and he had gotten his high school equivalency certificate. He had no friends and no relatives, and his case looked open and shut. Kätchen was not there to save the young man from prison. The judge would surely send him to Somers. All she saw was that he was alone, and that he needed companionship during this terrible experience that would probably doom him to a life of crime and addiction by imprisoning him with hardened criminals in a place where drugs were easy to get.

Before the judge passed sentence, Kätchen thought she would explain her presence in the room, and so she stood up and said to the judge: "Your honor, this young man has nobody to testify in this investigation, and I am here to keep him company because nobody else is here." Then she sat down.

The judge then had the accused stand up and receive sentence. To Kätchen's amazement the judge said: "Your record is very bad, and you should go up to Somers, but because there is this good woman here, who has faith in you, I'm going to give you one more chance. Case dismissed."

This was the last thing Kätchen had expected. She had not testified to the young man's character, she had not even mentioned his work with her for the high school equivalency, and she had never said that she had faith in him. But here he was, released simply because she was present in the courtroom with him!

At five o'clock that hot afternoon the two of them found themselves standing on the courthouse steps, staring out at the river across the highway. The young man had been held at the Sims Street pretrial jail in Hartford, where his wallet—with his money, identification, and driver's license—had been stolen from him by guards or other inmates. He owned nothing but the clothes on his back, and he had no place to stay. The YMCA demanded a two-week rent deposit, a job, and a driver's license—and it was five o'clock, the end of the working afternoon.

"Well," the young man said, "I do have ten cents on me. Thank you. Good-bye," and he started to walk down the steps.

Kätchen called down after him, "What are you going to do?"

He looked up at her and said, "I'll live on the street. I'll find a back porch."

Kätchen said, "You'll find a back porch, and you'll find one of your street friends who'll turn you on right away because he'll want to see somebody who's as bad off as he is."

Kätchen did not know what to do, but she did know that she could not abandon him. And so she told him to wait while she called home. When she got her husband, Bill, on the phone, she told him the story, except for the armed robbery part, and she half begged, half insisted that they keep him in their house one night until they could figure out what he might do. She didn't hang up until Bill agreed.

At the beginning of Kätchen's work at Woodward, Friedman and his staff had laid down an unbendable rule: Never give a patient your home address or phone number. On that one rule the well-being—in fact, the safety and possibly the very life—of the mental health care worker depended. Violate it, and for the rest of your life at that address and phone number you would be in danger. You would be at the mercy of your patient, who lived from crisis to crisis, from desperation to desperation, and you would be at the mercy of any criminals your patient knew.

This rule of anonymity is the moat that separates the erratic addict from the therapist. Violate it and you can become not a professional care provider but a codependent with an addict, a codependent whose life can be overwhelmed by the effects of addiction, just as relatives and friends of the client are. Violate it, and you can be caught in the hurricane.

Kätchen had learned this at Woodward, but Dr. Friedman and his staff had not even dreamed of inviting a client into their homes to spend the night. Robbery, murder, arson, anything is possible for an addict under your roof. This was the assumption that did not need to be put in the form of a rule. And this was the assumption Kätchen violated not only on a summer day in 1970 but for many days and nights for decades afterward. After Ron the armed robber, there came to Kätchen's house at Maple Shade Road Billie the heroin addict, and after Billie there came Mikey the perpetual pot smoker, and so on, and so on.

That summer evening she drew her reluctant husband along with her into the chaos of codependency with addict after addict, convicted thief after convicted thief. As the years went by, many of them turned up, and Kätchen could never say, "Sorry. You'll have to make other arrangements." If it was a man, he might have his current girlfriend with him, and they might stay for a week, sometimes planting daffodils in the garden for their keep, sometimes doing nothing.

Always they entered into the very center of the Coleys' lives, as only utterly dependent and moody houseguests can do. As Bill told me years later: "Her generosity approached martyrdom; and it's very hard to have a home life with somebody who is a martyr to the outside world." He believed that an intimate relationship had to be exclusive, private. He came to feel that he had no privileges in Kätchen's life. Time after time Kätchen and he spent the whole night up with what Bill called "a bunch of zombies in my life," and he had a class to teach at eight o'clock that morning. As far as Bill was concerned, there was not enough Kätchen to go around.

4

In the history of ethics there have been two kinds of "duty" or "obligation." One has been called "perfect" obligation. We have a perfect obligation, an unexceptionable obligation, for example, not to murder anyone. *Everybody* has the right not to be murdered. Another kind of ethical demand is usually called an "imperfect" obligation. We have an imperfect obligation to help people in need. It is imperfect because not everybody has the right to be helped by me. And this is so because I do not have the time or energy or money to help everybody. It is a physical and mental impossibility to help everybody in the world who needs help, and if something is impossible to do, I am under no obligation to do it, just as I can be under no obligation to fly by flapping my arms. Not every suffering child in distant lands, not every shelterless or sick person in our own, can have the *right* to be helped by me if it is utterly impossible for me to help them all. Everybody has the right not to be killed by me, but not everybody has the right to be helped by me. Our duty to help is a limited and a soft one.

Because help is an imperfect duty, there is pathos in the cry "Help!" That cry does not say, "I have the right, and you have the duty to help me!" It says, "Please! Help me if it pleases you to help me. Please!"

Now, some extraordinary people are so passionately and compassionately involved with every needy person they meet that they feel that he or she has the right to be helped, no matter what limitations there are on the helper's time, energy, or resources. The people who believe that helping is an imperfect, restricted obligation usually call such indiscriminate helpers "bleeding hearts," "soft touches," or "suckers." From the point of view of more selective souls, such people are always being "taken in" by a "sob story." They don't have the common sense to say no.

The soft touches cannot help everybody in the whole world—that is a physical and psychological impossibility—but they feel that they must help every desperate person in *their* world, every strung-out alcoholic or drug addict who comes up the pike. Kätchen was one of these people, and so was Magda Trocmé of Le Chambon, who said to every desperate refugee who came up to her door in the presbytery of the village, "Naturally! Come in. Come in." So was Joshua James, who tried to save every shipwrecked sailor off the coast of Nantasket for sixty years.

People like Kätchen and Magda cannot turn anybody away. Helping this person right here is for them an unexceptionable obligation. Bill Coley believed that rescue was an imperfect, exceptionable obligation, a demand that mainly had to do with one's family and friends. The eye of the hurricane was somewhat narrower for Bill than it was for Kätchen.

At three o'clock one morning the phone rang at the Coley home. Kätchen answered and heard Ron, the young man she had helped get out of jail, say, "Kätchen! They've arrested me! If they put me in jail I'll commit suicide! Help me!" Kätchen covered the phone and told Bill what she had just heard. Bill, just coming out of sleep, grumbled, "Well, tell him to commit suicide beween nine and five!" It was a witticism, of course, but the truth that it expressed was the truth that destroyed—or at least helped mightily to destroy—the Coley marriage.

It was this deep belief of Kätchen's that help is a perfect obligation here and now that had made her rush out at Woodward and reassure the young man in the straitjacket who was being taken to the maximum security prison at Somers. For her Joe's need was a *demand*, not just a request: He had a *right* to her help. She could not see the danger of such behavior on her part in front of all those explosive people looking down on them from the library window. All she could see was Joe's need there before her on that stretcher, in that jacket, on his way to a brutal prison; and all she could feel was the demand to give him what help she could. Bleeding hearts can have poor peripheral vision.

In the last years of their marriage, each of her "zombies" demanded her devotion more insistently than her husband did. She was, on the periphery of her awareness, conscious of her husband's growing exasperation, but her obligation to help someone who was destroying his life and the lives of others with alcohol or drugs remained perfect, unexceptionable. And so Bill left Kätchen in November 1973.

5

Kätchen was far from being eternally forgiving toward her young friends. When one of them betrayed her, her world could be shattered, and her sense of obligation to the betrayer could be destroyed.

One evening after the marriage had finished and Bill had moved out, he brought over an excellent stereo player to replace the one he had taken with him. The next day one of Kätchen's lost people, Bob, came for a visit, and Kätchen showed him her new stereo and told him how good it made her feel that Bill was so considerate, so generous, and that he was still a friend. The next day when she came back from work the stereo was gone.

She knew Bob had once stolen all of his mother's silver in order to feed his drug addiction, but the love and the trust she and Bob shared was the very axis of the world to Kätchen, and the thought that he might have stolen the stereo made her universe wobble. She wandered from room to room hoping to find the stereo, and she wept bitterly for hours.

The next day Bob called, and over the phone Kätchen sobbed out her misery—but she did not have the heart, or the evidence, to accuse him of taking the stereo. She simply sobbed over the destruction of the central reality in her life, the love and trust she shared with these people who needed her.

Apparently Bob was surprised and disturbed by the depth of her misery. When Kätchen cried out, "Bob, who could have done this? Who could have done this?" he promised that he would call some fences he knew who handled stolen merchandise in the Middletown area. They might be able to help. A few hours later he called up Kätchen and said that it would cost her fifty dollars to get the stereo back from one of the fences he knew. In a few minutes he came to Kätchen's home, took her in her car to a spot a few miles outside of Middletown, left her standing on the side of a country road, and came back with the stereo.

Years later he told her what she already knew, that he was the one who had stolen it.

Again and again I asked Kätchen what she feared the most while having all these volatile, dangerous people living in the very center of her life. She always answered: "I was afraid that someone would violate my trust in him." She felt that if anybody violated that trust her whole life would have been proved false, wrong, stupid. She felt that if this happened, then all those people who had told her over the years that she was only an ineffectual, empty-headed, sentimental do-good lady who had a tendency to go over-board—all those people would be right.

During the desperate long-distance collect calls from her addicts, during her visits with them in jails, during her nights and days spent weeping with them or celebrating their brief triumphs, she knew that mutual trust and caring were the central reality in her life. Anyone who betrayed that trust and that caring would explode that reality and destroy her main reason for living.

In the late sixties and early seventies—before hard drugs and hard-drug addiction took over so many lives—Kätchen and others found trust and caring to be good therapy. In those days when she met someone who needed help, she first saw to it that he or she spent time with her while sober and in control of his or her appetites. When he or she was in control the two of them could talk together, and Kätchen would find out what the person most deeply wanted from life. She would get an intuition, so to speak, of the person's soul and most enduring needs, of something deeper than his or her destructive deeds.

She cherished these conversations, which were full of passion and painful honesty, because she had very few, if any, such conver-sations with her friends in the academic world of Wesleyan Univer-sity. Faculty and faculty wives seldom if ever talked about their naked needs. Their terrifying weaknesses were the pornography, the dirty little secrets, of their lives. They usually wanted to display how quick-witted, how well read, and how up-to-date they were. Kätchen hardly ever read books, and she could not endure bookish or archly witty conversations. She thought in terms of the stories of people's actions and passions, and only personal, heartfelt communion meant anything to her. She found that if she opened her heart and mind to young addicts, they opened their hearts and minds to her and revealed their souls, just as she revealed hers. They were vastly more engrossing and in touch with the depths of human feelings than her Wesleyan friends were.

It is astonishing that she was betrayed so seldom, addiction being a condition that shatters all trust. But the fact is that only two people ever betrayed her. This fact remains the central mystery of Kätchen's life for me.

I have often asked myself how Le Chambon kept saving refugee children in large numbers for four years during the German occupation of France without being burned to the ground or destroyed by the Germans or their French puppets. It was generally known in the region that the worst enemies of the Nazis, the Jews, were being rescued by the village, and villages in France had been destroyed for doing far less than this. Sometimes much of the answer seems to lie in the good luck of the village in having Maj. Julius Schmähling as the commander of the occupying troops in the region. But the reason that is at the core of it all for me is that the villagers made violence irrelevant. They were nonviolent; they did not resort to arms; they were not an immediate threat to the German occupying troops; and so they were, for most of those four years, let be. In their refusal to hate or to kill they were "dis-arming," somewhat like the innocent face of a child.

And perhaps Kätchen Coley was betrayed so seldom because she had such unflagging innocence. But another reason had to be that she knew what she was doing. Somehow she knew the "souls" of the people she was trusting. She may not have been just a "bleeding heart" after all. She may have seen her young friends plainly and truly, except, perhaps, for Bob.

6

Once, early in the seventies, Kätchen found herself talking with a young man who was casually peeling the enamel off his teeth while she spoke to him. He was not only a heroin addict but also a "speed freak," heavily involved with amphetamines. Since these appetites were costly, he wrote bad checks, including checks on his father. He was living on Twinkies, like so many other addicts, because he didn't care about nutrition and wanted only a quick sugar fix. The drugs and the Twinkies interacted and detached the enamel from his teeth. He was always being taken to dentists, but there was very little they could do for him. The heroin deadened his toothaches, and the Twinkies kept him awake afterward. There was very little that one-on-one friendship could do for him. With such hard-drug cases Kätchen began to see people destroying their lives in ways that individual caring could not stop.

And so Kätchen started The Connection, an institution that could give structured, professional treatment—as well as friendship—to addicts. She created it just in time, in 1972, when addiction and our awareness of its life-destroying nature became intense and widespread.

There are various stories about how she started the first and largest drug-and-alcohol rehabilitation group in Connecticut. Kätchen remembers how, after she had talked with the young man who was peeling the enamel off his teeth, she started having talks in the library of Woodward Hall with her chief, Dr. Friedman. The problems of their young clients were getting too complex to be solved by only a tutorial program leading to a high school equivalency degree. One day at the end of 1971 Friedman said to her, "Why don't you see if you can get something else started besides this tutorial program?"

Nancy Flanner gives a different account of how it all began. Nan was Kätchen's closest friend at Woodward and one of the very few people who had stuck it out there with her for years. She was a quiet, steady woman, whose husband was a dentist in Durham, near Middletown. Her world was unlike the one Kätchen lived in: It was a cozy, traditionally New England, rather puritanical world, with none of the intellectual and moral trends that were always swaying the Wesleyan University community in neighboring Middletown. Quiet Nan Flanner fitted into that somewhat staid, unintellectual community somewhat better than Kätchen fitted into her intellectually faddish academic community.

The two old friends took an automobile trip to Maine in 1971, and on the way back they found themselves, as usual, discussing the problems of their young patients at Woodward. They agreed that one of the big problems was follow-up: Young alcohol and drug addicts, no matter how well they were tutored by the volunteers, had nowhere to go after Woodward. They had no way of reentering society after they had served their sentences. Many went right back into destroying their lives and the lives of their friends and relatives. Wouldn't it be fine, Kätchen and Nan asked themselves, if these young people could have a home in Middletown that would get them used to living a normal community life?

The staff of this transitional home would help them to stay off drugs by keeping them busy at various tasks, including cooking and cleaning, and would help them get interviews with various local merchants and businesspeople. The home would help these people connect with a physically, mentally, and financially healthy way of life. It would be especially helpful for people between the ages of sixteen and eighteen, who were being forgotten by the system after they served their alternative-incarceration sentences at Woodward.

Nan Flanner says that she and impulsive, talkative, persistent Kätchen worked very well together. Kätchen could have founded Connection House without her, but she could never have started it without Kätchen. "Kätchen has the *drive*," she says.

There seems to be some truth in what she says. It was Kätchen who called Catholic Charities and got advice; it was Kätchen who kept in close contact with the Red Cross in Hartford; and above all, it was Kätchen who found a man to write the crucial first grant application. She herself was incapable of writing such an application, mainly because her patience would run out when she had to deal with numbers. Her one great skill was badgering and attracting the right people to do the jobs she felt had to be done.

And so she ensconced one of her alcoholics, who had written various successful grant applications, in the guest room of her house on Maple Shade Road and fed him on steaks and Cokes—no alcohol, of course—until the application to the Law Enforcement Assistance people was done.

They got the money—a $28,000-dollar grant that would take effect in 1972, and go on, with a possibility of renewal, until 1975. But this was only the beginning of their problems.

She and Nan Flanner shared another trait besides caring: They were stubborn women. And in the rest of the early history of The Connection their persistence, and especially the persistent *drive* of Kätchen, won the battle against indifference and violence.

As soon as they got news of the grant, Kätchen and Nan started looking for a house. The first possibility was a residence on the road south to Saybrook. But when they applied for a zoning variance that would permit them to run the house there, the black dean of Middlesex Community College, a colonel in the army, organized a classic NIMBY (not in my back yard) attack, and the zoning variance was turned down. Kätchen had mistakenly assumed that the colonel would not do what had been so often done to his people—namely, exclude "the wrong people" from the neighborhood.

An old friend of Kätchen, a gentle, sweet-tempered man named Nick Saraceno, owned a house in a pleasant neighborhood on Washington Street, right across from Indian Hill Cemetery. He offered to rent it to her group. It was in bad shape, but if she was willing to repair it, she could have it for a very reasonable rental. It was perfect. Kätchen needed a centrally located, low-rent house in the center of Middletown so that her young people could get to and from work and so that she could use her grant funds for personnel, food, and equipment instead of exorbitant rent. Besides, painting and repairing the house would give her young people something to do until they found jobs, and would also give them a sense of pride in living in a house they had made pleasant.

However, it turned out that drug addicts had been hanging out in the house for months. There was trash in the basement, holes in the walls, and all the plumbing pipes were gone. One day she was lamenting all this to one of her alcoholic friends, when he whispered to her, "Kätchen! Don't tell anybody I've told you, but I know where the pipes are. They're piled up behind a barn on Milbrook Road. Some of the drug addicts ripped them out, and they're planning to sell them soon to feed their habit."

When she went out to Milbrook Road, sure enough she saw all of this valuable copper piled higgledy-piggledy behind a barn. She cajoled and begged Mr. Parmelee and his fellow plumbers to transport the pipes and to reinstall them. And then a Mrs. Reed, a friend of Kätchen's mother in Fairfield, out of the blue gave Kätchen three thousand dollars. They had a house, and money to fix it up.

The first director of Connection House was Joe Monroe, who had been head of the drug program at Somers prison while he was an inmate there. He was black, streetwise, and a recovered heroin addict. He had the disciplined, powerful energies that Kätchen, Nan, and Dr. Friedman respected. But his first job had nothing to do with counseling: He had to help repair and paint the dilapidated house across from the cemetery on Washington Street.

While the house was being prepared, Kätchen got a phone call from Somers prison. It was from the man she had consoled while he was being taken away from Woodward to Somers in a straitjacket. She told him that the house was not finished, and Joe Monroe and the volunteers were too busy working on it to give their time to counseling him. But he overrode her hesitation by begging her to let him come to Connection House, because he did not want to return to Waterbury, where he was sure to get back into the drug scene.

And so Nan Flanner and Kätchen found themselves in the waiting room in Somers prison, a room they both knew well. Even after all their visits they were both deeply depressed by the iron gates and the close surveillance. Finally the dark-haired, fiery Italian whom Kätchen had consoled at Woodward came through an iron gate into the waiting room, wearing a handsome dark blazer and a neat striped red tie, with fifty dollars in his pocket, his only bridge to the outside world. He had been in and out of prisons and treatment centers most of his life, and he was very thin.

Nan and Kätchen drove him straight to the Washington Street Connection House, across from the cemetery, and introduced him to Joe Monroe, whose clothes were spotted with paint and who looked nothing like a drug counselor.

The next day while he was helping Joe work in the house, he asked Joe if he could go out and have a drink at a bar down toward the river. Joe—well within the limits of authority—said, "No. We've got to get this house done, and you've got to stay dry or you can't stay with us."

Joe Monroe was standing at the foot of the stairs in the front entryway of the house while this conversation was going on, and the cadaverous Italian was farther up the stairs. At this moment Kätchen came in through the front door in time to see her violent Italian running down the stairs holding above his head a heavy board with a nail sticking out of it. Kätchen pushed Monroe out of the way just in time before the nail came down.

The young man did not spend another hour in the house. He was the first resident in Connection House, and after his one day there Kätchen never saw him again.

7

This happened in the spring of 1972, when Kätchen's marriage was near its end and when she started drinking too much. At night she would drink wine heavily, and occasionally an alcoholic or a drug addict living in her house or visiting saw her drunk. Kätchen's daughter Kitty was being driven out of their house by Kätchen's drinking, the fights, and the quiet antagonisms beween Kätchen and Bill. Often the teenager spent hours at Touch, "the drop-in center for young drop-outs" as Kätchen described it. For a while Kätchen directed Connection House, but she hated paperwork, and whenever somebody came into her little office with one more story of being fired for calling a boss a fucking asshole, the paperwork went unfinished. It was breaking her heart that she could not spend more time with the people who needed her.

But when she turned away from administration and went back to individuals, she became the terror of the directors of Connection House. She was always turning up in the middle of the day with endlessly detailed stories about the clients, or about people she wanted to admit as clients. Whenever one director caught sight of her car coming into the driveway, he disappeared out the back door. And when Kätchen could not find him in the building, she would think, Oh! He's neglecting my child! He's destroying my baby! My child is dying! Sometimes she even heard a director say, in the adjoining room, "If that woman comes around one more time I'm going to go crazy!"

Still, she had a deeper problem. In the early seventies, when The Connection began, there was a long-term treatment plan called "the Concept" that was in widespread use in corrections systems across the country. The Concept was basically a process of humiliation and enforced conformity, not unlike the boot camp of the U.S. Marines. Males' heads were shaved at the beginning of their training, and there were "expediters" in the system who served as an internal police force. If you conformed to the system you became an expediter, a policeman, and if you continued to conform you rose to higher ranks. If you were ever criticized seriously by your expediters you were humiliated by being assigned jobs like cleaning toilets, and you descended in the rigid pecking order.

The Concept worked, but only while you were in prison. When you left prison all you knew was the Concept. You did not know what to do next. You had no occupation and no preparation for dealing with the many choices in life that required sensitivity and self-confidence. Instead of being ready to live in a world of choices and affection, you were merely "concepted."

In her dealings with friends who went in and out of prisons, in and out of being "concepted," Kätchen became convinced that there had to be an alternative to producing people who were disconnected from ordinary personal and vocational life. In the first years of The Connection some of Kätchen's staff were graduates of the Concept program. They brought a narrow, rigid spirit with them, and Kätchen had to fight them every day. She wanted her staff to care, as she cared, for the individuals they were trying to help. Sometimes she took a client into her own home in order to remove him or her from the Concept after she had failed to remove the Concept from Connection House.

Such problems, combined with the end of her marriage, the bohemian life of her daughter, and her drinking made her life a horror.

In the middle of all this, throughout the seventies and eighties, she kept The Connection alive by pushing and cajoling and talking the ears off anyone who had control of any funds. Ron, the alcoholic who was so brilliant at writing grant applications that could squeeze blood from a turnip, had killed himself with an overdose of drugs and alcohol. Though executive directors of The Connection helped raise money, it was mainly Kätchen's obsessive, single-minded, exasperating *will* that kept the doors open.

In the middle of the institutional and personal whirlwind that was her life, she remained the enemy of the Concept and the friend of many of the clients. Peter Nucci, who is now executive director of The Connection, says that she kept it alive because "she identified people not in terms of abstract clinical classifications, but in terms of their own names, and in terms of her affectionate relationships with people."

Nucci tells how, in 1979, there was a conference with the head of a large funding group. The administrators of The Connection made their plea for funds, and then the head of the funding group said, "This is a nice project, but we have a budget crisis now, and we can really do nothing to help you. When we get some money, we'll help you out."

There was silence. It seemed that there was nothing more to be said. Then Nucci heard a disturbance. Kätchen was standing up as straight as an arrow in the back of the room. She was no longer an administrator in The Connection, but she couldn't keep away from her child. She started telling stories about their clients, just stories out of the blue that had no particular bearing on funding. Nucci says: "And the stories broke the ice—they gave the abstractions, the numbers that The Connection administrators had been parading, *life.*"

People started laughing at and with Kätchen as she told her stories. As Nucci put it, "She showed us that we could have fun doing these things with people, real, deep fun. She was the catalyst. Even though she could be a real pain in the neck with those endless stories."

The fact was that Kätchen was incapable of taking no for an answer. She was obsessively impulsive. Throughout this part of her life she was the soul, the vivifying spirit of The Connection. She kept exciting both the clients of The Connection and the health care professionals who now surrounded her into laughter, and exasperation. There were always those in the mental health care community in Connecticut who thought of drug or alcohol addiction as a disease that the objective, all-knowing professional could cure without any personal involvement of therapist with patient. There were always people who saw therapy on the model of a surgeon operating coolly on an anesthetized patient, or a doctor prescribing pills to a passive patient. And while addiction became more and more deadly, these people became more and more useful. But the present program director of The Connection, burly Bill Farrell, says that The Connection, with all its sophisticated, licensed professionals, still has "the Kätchen impetus—passionate caring."

8

Two stories that show what Farrell's phrase means.

In the early seventies, while Kätchen and Nan Flanner were still at Woodward, Dr. Friedman decided to show some people in the Connecticut Valley community what it meant to be addicted to drugs and what it meant to fight that addiction. And so he invited a young man from Harlem to come up and explain the physiological and emotional murderousness of drugs in the inner city. He was a well-dressed, lucid, powerful man who had escaped death from drug addiction by the skin of his teeth. When he was finished telling his violent and victorious story, a Middletown woman stood up and said, in all earnestness: "I just can't understand drug addiction. All *I* need in order to get high is to see a beautiful sunset." And she sat down.

The tall young man looked at her, then turned his eyes away toward the library window overlooking the grounds of the Connecticut Valley Hospital, and he said nothing. Nothing.

When Nan Flanner told me this story, I suggested that the word "insensitivity" might begin to explain this abysmal moment. She would not accept the word; she would not accept any word. Nan Flanner is a mistress of silence. She sees the abyss of ignorance that separated that dreamy, self-satisfied Connecticut Valley woman from that hard-as-nails inner-city man. She sees the dark space that separates intimate knowledge from smug gentility. And since the space is deep as well as dark, only silence expresses it.

But for me the space is crossed by caring, by listening to a story with every fiber of your mind and heart. Some people do not care enough to listen to and see and feel the story of a person's addiction.

The second story is also about Woodward. In the second year of her volunteer work there Kätchen started using the word "fucking" to express her feelings. Again and again in her tutorials and in her casual conversations with her young people, she would use the word. They—especially the young men—used the word in each other's presence to express a burst of passion, and the closer she came to them the more she felt their feelings and the more she used their language. The polite talk of her privileged youth and of Wesleyan University was no longer her home language; she was more at home in the language of lost young people.

The young people could not bear to have her that close, that intimate. They could not bear to see her give up the power, the superiority of a mother. They did not want her to be simply one of them. And so they put a big jar on her desk, and they told her that every time she used the word, she would have to put a nickel in the jar. And so Kätchen used the "f-word" less and less, and the conversations became more comfortable.

By that time her young people had gotten the message: She cared, and she cared passionately about what they were doing together at Woodward. She was not helping with her fingertips; she was responding to them with her heart's blood. They had not needed and they had not wanted her heart's blood, but now they saw that she was willing to give it. And so as the seventies passed she became more than a compassionate equal, a codependent, a cosufferer; she became someone who was both in and above the battle against drugs and alcohol.

9

In the sixties and seventies in Connecticut the so-called mental health system had large holes in it. One of these had to do with young people between sixteen and eighteen who had basic psychological problems and were addicted to drugs. No state service was willing to pay for helping them. At the end of the sixties, Dr. Friedman, as head of the drug and alcohol rehabilitation branch of CVH, admitted a sixteen-year-old named Mikey. He had been in various psychiatric programs across the state, and he had not been carefully diagnosed by anybody. He was a "spaced-out kid" who was passed haphazardly from program to program. He came into Woodward because he was trying to medicate himself with drugs, and this was the only excuse for referring him to Dr. Friedman. Unlike the other Woodward people he had not been convicted of any substance-related crime. He was just lost and wandering.

When he entered Woodward, Nancy Flanner and Kätchen Coley treated him like a son. But Nan soon lost her affection for him. "He observed no limits," she says, and no matter how hard she tried to get him to stop doing something he would keep doing it. For a while Nan tried to teach him how to drive a car, but he insisted on doing things his crazy way. When she told him to change, he ignored her. She felt that he was out of control, a loose cannon.

Kätchen stayed with him anyway. In fact, he became her favorite at Woodward, and later at Connection House. His almost-round baby face, his wide eyes, and his affectionate spirit, together with his wild unpredictability, won Kätchen's heart.

Late in 1972 Connection House, on the corner of Washington and Jackson streets, was beginning to function somewhat smoothly. Most of the rooms had been painted (in all sorts of extraordinary colors) by clients, as part of their payment for room and board; and gradually rules had begun to emerge and had begun to be enforced. And, most important, young people were beginning to get—and hold—jobs in and around Middletown.

Mikey did not have a felony problem, as many other clients had had, and he had been relatively harmless despite his addiction to marijuana; but he did have another serious problem: He was mad for driving. After Nan Flanner gave up on teaching him to drive, Kätchen (in her persistent way) took over and stayed with it, and he learned the rudiments as well as a wild boy could learn them. And so, since he, like all the other young people in Connection House, needed a job, Kätchen recommended him for work cutting grass (driving a tractor) in Indian Hill Cemetery, across the street. He was now seventeen years old.

One spring morning at about eleven o'clock, the house was quiet, and Kätchen was in her office wrestling with her endless, boring, triplicate paper duties. Mikey appeared at her office door with his baby face averted. Kätchen looked at him and at the clock, and asked, "What are you doing here this time of day?"

Mikey answered: "Well, I was mowing with that new tractor they've got, and I thought I'd have a joint." Kätchen stiffened: This was a violation of the basic rule of Connection House, the foundation of their whole treatment program: abstinence. Mikey went on: "Well, I guess I got stoned, because I rolled the tractor down the hill, and it's all banged up."

There was silence. Then Kätchen erupted: "Oh boy! That's the end of that job. This sort of thing makes me want to pull my hair out!"

Kätchen's expression of pain was more important to Mikey than the basic rule he had broken. The help she gave Mikey was personal, loving, trusting; the rules were only the distant boundaries, the guidelines of that love and that trust. A constant one-on-one flesh-and-blood relationship was at the heart of the matter.

Kätchen's stubborn affection for Mikey was enduring. Soon after the destruction of the new tractor, she got Mikey another job, this time as an assistant salad maker at a restaurant nearby. The restaurant was owned by a chunky man whose capacity for anger was as vast as his bulk. I have seen him turn purple and throw a customer out of his restaurant for complaining mildly about a piece of beef.

Mikey had been working for him for a week or so, when Kätchen got a phone call from the splenetic chef: "Get this kid out of here! He's bleeding all over my food!" Mikey had gotten high again, and he had almost cut his finger off while slicing vegetables. Kätchen spent the rest of the day with him in the emergency room of Middlesex Memorial Hospital having his finger sewed up. That was the end of that job, but it was not the end of Kätchen's stubborn faith in Mikey.

Like so many others, Mikey moved into the Coley home after he had failed at Connection House. It was this practice—the practice of taking Connection House dropouts into her own home—that was finishing off the marriage between Bill and Kätchen Coley. Bringing Woodward first offenders home was one thing, but bringing in all sorts of hardened dropouts from Connection House was another. On a deep level of her consciousness Kätchen knew that Connection House was finally ending her marriage, but her "duty," her persistent impulsiveness, her unrelenting need to help kept carrying her away, and kept bringing some of the most erratic young people in the Connecticut Valley into the very center of her life.

Then Mikey went beyond the boundaries. He was paying for his lodging by doing some cooking and cleaning in the house, and one evening she arranged with him to clean up after a dinner party. It was the night of the Wesleyan Art Center Ball, and so after the dinner Kätchen and her guests went to the ball. The next morning she had an early appointment. When she went out to her car, she could not open the door on the driver's side. Then she noticed that the side of the car was caved in, fenders, doors, and all. She came back to the house as if in a dream and called for Mikey. He was gone.

Mikey, in his passion to drive, had taken the car out while Kätchen was at the ball, and he had wrecked it. That was bad enough, but now he was gone. The wreck was an accident; it might have been caused by marijuana, but leaving the wreck at her door and running away, these were not accidents, and Kätchen felt the same deep betrayal as when her stereo had been stolen.

She called Nan Flanner and asked her to come over and move Mikey's belongings out of the house. She would have nothing more to do with him. The deep bond of trust was broken for her.

During the years that followed she kept getting phone calls from Mikey: For four or five years he worked for an asbestos-removal company that cleaned out nuclear plants in the region. He got married, drank, and fought with his wife until she left him. Finally he joined Alcoholics Anonymous, became one of their lecturers, formed his own asbestos-removal company, got back together with his wife, and was now thriving.

But the bond of trust and affection between them was gone. And now, though she has Mikey's phone number, she has not called him for years. Occasionally she is sad about not calling him, but she feels that he is now on his own. And though she is on the board of directors of The Connection, and is always there when we need her driving persistence, she feels that The Connection too is on its own. One gets older, and we go from loving to losing.

10

There are many stories like Mikey's, but with no neat closure, stories that do not end in a cure, that do not save the addict from self-destruction. But helping addicts is not the same as saving human lives from persecution, as the people of Le Chambon saved lives, nor is it the same as saving human lives from the hurricanes that visit coastal villages like Hull.

Oh, there are stories about addicts that have happy endings. For instance, there is the story of Billie, the young woman who came to Woodward Hall in the late sixties and persuaded Dr. Friedman to call in volunteers to help her and the other inmates get high school equivalency diplomas. In the eighties Kätchen met Billie on Middletown's broad Main Street, and "she was looking like a million dollars," as Kätchen puts it. She was selling real estate, very successfully, and she had not touched drugs or drunk much alcohol for years. And there is the story of the young man who used to stutter so horribly during his addiction so that he could not pronounce more than two words without a spasm. One day she was crossing Main Street and found herself in front of a big truck with a young man leaning out of the driver's side, waving wildly at her, and yelling, "Hey Kätchen! Kätchen! How you doin'? Look at me now! Talking a mile a minute!"

Such stories are rare, however. If you ask any of the early volunteers in Woodward Hall and The Connection, "Did you ever really *succeed* with any of your young people, so that you could send them out with your blessings and with high hopes?" you always get the same answer: "Not really." They will tell you that perhaps some people have succeeded the way Billie did, but many have not. Recently Nan Flanner told me that she believes that most of them "went back into the pits, back into their terrible lives, and are probably dead by now."

For years it has been fashionable—and sometimes even useful—to speak of addiction as if it were simply a disease, like smallpox or tuberculosis. Such diseases we can cure. But a person is never "cured" of addiction. He gets only a reprieve from it. It can go to sleep inside you, but it can always rise again, at any moment of your life. It takes the right circumstances and a firm will to keep it in remission. Lacking those circumstances and lacking that will, one action, at any moment, can bring on the hurricane. The overwhelming desire to feel yourself coming wildly *alive* again can rise within you and tempt you, and you are back in the double life of oblivion and disgust.

The people of Le Chambon and the people of Hull could speak of "saving" people, but the Kätchen Coleys can never talk this way. The people who were saved in Le Chambon or off Nantasket were passive recipients of help: All they needed to do was lie low, and their benefactors would do the rest. But "recovering" addicts have to keep making the right choices, have to keep entering the right circumstances if their lives are to be redeemed. Their benefactors can do just so much. In the end helping drug and alcohol addicts is a perfect instance of the adage, "God helps those who help themselves." There are no passive, no cured addicts; they are all active in a struggle whose victories and defeats come in moments, not once and forever.

The clients of Woodward and Connection House carried their own hurricanes within them. The refugees who were saved in Le Chambon and the shipwrecked people who were saved off Hull had physical winds and waves and moral monsters around them, and when they were sheltered from these alien threats they were saved, once and for all. It is not so with people who engage in what is now often called "excessive appetitive behavior." The enemy is within, and it is not a germ that can be wiped out like the germ of a physical disease: The enemy must be fought, and fought, and fought, and fought, and there is no predicting the outcome of the battle.

This being the case, what keeps people like Kätchen Coley from throwing up their hands and giving up? How can they keep on giving so much and keep on getting so little?

The answer is the momentary victories, momentary successes. At Woodward Hall a young person would reach out her hands and receive her high school equivalency diploma, and—for perhaps the first time in her life—she was not a loser. She had accomplished something that no hangover or strung-out morning could destroy, and she knew it: She could see her knowledge confirmed in Kätchen's eyes and in the eyes of all those around her who had helped her to come to this moment.

There were often celebrations of these little, vast achievements, and the celebrations lived in everyone's memories. Once two carloads of Woodward young people went with Kätchen and Nan to Meriden, just west of the Connecticut Valley. They arrived at a tiny apartment, the home of a young man who had just received his general equivalency diploma. They were greeted at the door by his plump little mother, and they crowded around a table for an Italian meal—with no wine. It was, as Nan remembers, "a glorious meal," and when it was over the mother who alone had created it, and who was still covered with sweat, embraced Nan and Kätchen and all the young people as they left the one-room apartment.

Moments count too. The world changes, and our lives change, but our lives are made of those moments, though they flee. Kätchen and Nan, and the few others who kept working with young addicts in the valley before The Connection became a professionally run institution, shared with the people moments when there were no drugs and no drinks, only people feeling clean and free of the smell of death. In those moments people felt that they were all at their best with one another, and it was a joy to be together.

Of course in such moments there was always a hope that *this* moment was the beginning of a lifetime of such moments. But the moment is not simply anticipatory; it is real in its own right, it is earned. It contains the past and supersedes it, and it dreams of the future, but it supersedes it too, because it has the virgin vivacity of the now.

In the days at Woodward Hall, and in the first years of Connection House, the help that was given and received was not "professional." It was not the therapy that comes from cool, detached, objective skills and knowledge; it was the therapy that comes when people laugh and cry with one another, and are enraged with one another and are overjoyed with one another for a precious little while.

<h2 style="text-align:center">11</h2>

There is help, and there is help. And the main difference I have found between them has something to do with mutuality, with the helper and the helped exchanging places, so that the helped one participates in the depths of his or her being with the spreading of life.

Mutual help in the Connecticut Valley in those years had more to do with friendship than with science, skill, or condescension. For me, the very heart of Aristotle's *Ethics* is the topic of friendship. Friendship for Aristotle is not a one-way street. Goodwill may be a one-way street. Wishing good things for somebody who does not wish good things for you has its own joys. But it is not what we usually mean by friendship. Friendship is mutual loving, mutual caring. As Aristotle puts it, it is "reciprocated goodwill." That abundant Italian meal in the tiny apartment—like the embraces of the woman who created it—was an act of friendship. You cannot be a friend of someone who is no friend of yours. Even a tree that we befriend seems friendly to us.

Friendship involves wishing good things—like a cumulatively joyous and tranquil life—for one another, but it also involves being there for one another, in misery and in joy. It involves spending time with one another, the way the staff and mothers of The Connection's Women and Children's Center spend time with one another. The misery of the struggle against addiction, and the moment-to-moment joys of succeeding in that struggle, and of childbearing, are what all of them share in that house on the lip of the Connecticut Valley.

And the women in the Women and Children's Center share conversation with one another. They think together with each other by talking together. They question one another and themselves, and they struggle to answer their questions together; they tell stories and listen to stories together. Their friendship is not simply an emotional bath—it is an enterprise in understanding—understanding the stories of their own lives and understanding the stories of those who are living with them.

Of course there was more than friendship in the relationships of staff or volunteers with "clients." The young people at Woodward or in Connection House were not there mainly to help the volunteers: The volunteers were there mainly to help the clients. The volunteers usually took the initiative in establishing programs: They were the helpers, not the helped. And so there was not the same kind of mutuality between the two parties that there is between two people who are good friends outside of any therapeutic or institutional confines. But some of the volunteers had warmer hearts than others, and a stronger desire to be there emotionally whenever the client needed them. Such helpers and their clients dwelt in a large, joyous, and painful area between therapy and friendship. And Kätchen was the queen of that area in the Connecticut River Valley.

12

People can be treated by other people in ways that look benign but are really destructive. Give a shelterless woman a coin with a condescending, self-congratulatory smile on your face, and you are giving an insult as surely as you are giving money. There is a way of helping people that fills their hands but breaks their hearts. What is kindness to the helper can be cruelty to the helped, because helping people mentally is a matter of perspective.

So is evil—do not ask the slaveholder if he is being kind to the slave; ask the slave. Do not ask the sword if it is inflicting pain; ask the victim of the sword. The same holds for goodness. Do not ask the supposed benefactor whether he or she is redeeming a life; ask the one who is supposed to be the beneficiary.

When somebody is being rescued from a visible, palpable harm, the point of view of the beneficiary is usually very close indeed to that of the benefactor. No refugee saved in Le Chambon ever suggested to me or anybody else I know that he or she was cruelly treated by being rescued from the Nazis, nor, to my knowledge, has anybody who was saved by Joshua James and his "boys" ever accused Joshua James of cruelty.

Nonetheless, in help that does not save a person from an external catastrophe, the kindness of the helper can be cruelty to the recipient. And so in many kinds of "help" you must look closely into the eyes of that recipient if you would know whether help has really happened.

This is why the letters young people wrote to Kätchen after they left Woodward or Connection House are so revealing to me. They reveal that here help happened, however fleetingly. Again and again I reread a letter from a young man named Ralph, written after he left Woodward in 1971. It is here as he wrote it to Kätchen:

Dear Mrs. Coley:

Her hair is that of a queen. Her brown hair covers a small face like a small jewled crown. Her eyes tell a story that she hopes for peace, comfort, and love for her fellow man. Her features are that of a Dove that glides through the air in search of those who seek her help. On her flight her love and friendship are unbendable as the cold frigid air of hate despair and mistrust and all of mankind's foes address her. She is for man a light of hope as she is for you and me my friend. Take heed though my friend for she can be destroyed by a Ruthless arrow of mankinds hatered. Lets gather around her and protect her with a sheild of love and a Flaming sword of friendship, for in this way she can continue on her flight, trying to show mankin his faults and hates, lets pray she will be able to carry on forever for man as is mankind is lost without such a dove as HER. . . .

                                                          Love,
                                                          Ralph

AFTERWORD

by Doris A. Hallie

Philip was not finished with his quest. Even after the telling of these tales, he continued to pursue his concerns intensely. He had made a new discovery about good and evil, help and harm during his final year and a half. He told me again and again that he felt that it was very important. He was giving the action of *help* a new dimension as he was seeing the need for a partnership between the helper and the helped. These ongoing thoughts did not detract from his pursuit of the tales here.

Philip loved writing this book. Oh, he had the pain that comes with the creative moments of inspiration and with the driving need to tell these tales right. But he was comfortable with these people—Magda, Julius, Joshua, Kätchen, and even Thoreau. They did good deeds as they lived with their human frailties.

For a year now I have been reading through Philip's journals and notes, and through his poetry, which he called "extempore effusions." These writings and entries span the fifty-one years from his stint as a soldier in World War II in 1943 to his final year, 1994. Philip yearned for a oneness with humankind and with nature. He loved his moments of joy—*jouissance*—as he called it, but he was forever aware of the dark side, that hurricane.

Philip wrote many of his "extempore effusions" during the summer of 1963, while living on the Connecticut shore. One called out to me as I read through them:

CONSPIRACY

Among the Mermaid's toe-nails and Mussels
I found one whitened Atlantic slipper
The smallest yet, and the purest white:
A young one, with a hole in it.

I was no friend to this alien creature,
And I am no friend to it now
As it lies on my fingers, with only some pink
On its punctured shell.

But I can conspire with it, two castaways
Amidst the life in death, the pain in peace,
Of the mothering sea; I can conspire with it
Against the gods.

Neptune, Jehovah, Jesus,
Tell me no stories with strange meanings;
Look at us two, the young and the old
So cold, so indifferent to the stop and go of each other's blood.

I am ready to stop my muttering against this life in death.
But I can never forgive the cold indifference between this shell and me.

Those who knew Philip and worked with him realized the conflicts within him and were often grateful for the intensity of his feelings. A Wesleyan colleague wrote to me after Philip's death, describing a trip they had taken together. What it revealed was quintessential Philip:

Dear Doris,

Both Vicky and I have been recalling fondly warm memories of Phil. One especially powerful and vivid recollection: Sometime in the early 1970s I drove to Boston with Phil to attend the wedding of a former student. On the way up and back we talked about Jewish sources that Phil could read that argued for the power of good over evil. That was a period when Phil seemed to be carrying the burden of the reality of evil. He was open, as usual, about how depressing it was for him to plumb the depths of evil. And he clearly was allowing himself to struggle with his own sense of pain and sorrow. What struck me that day was what went on at the wedding and reception in between these two conversations. Phil danced with his usual energy and abandon, a man enthusiastically dancing his blues away. Over the years, I came to see how characteristic that was of Phil. He allowed himself to experience in a full-bodied way whatever unhappiness is our due. And he willed himself also to climb out of these darker moods to experience joy and to celebrate life. For me that has been a splendid lesson for which I will always be grateful to Phil. . . .

I discovered in one of his wartime diaries, written when he was twenty-one, before he had studied philosophy, before he had penetrated the problem of good and evil, that he was already grappling with the issue of a connection between his sensuous/sensual self and his rational/intellectual self. And always he was trying to express the need he felt for that life-giving, critical connection with others and with nature.

On July 4, 1943, on an army base somewhere in the southern United States, he wrote:

Settled! After the wanderings, the sloppily conducted interviews, after the unknowing hours and days, after the examinations that couldn't examine; after all of this and more, I am a specialist in the Field Artillery. The army is rough on a boy, stimulating to a man. The army contains much of me now, but I still reserve a love for fine words that are convex on the concavity of reality. This for the army and its personnel have been a kind of purifying agent in the cleansing of my muddy attitudes. For instance, even my palate has been conditioned to a kind of Spartan purity: I enjoy water only now, and drink nothing else, except for some milk, and even the milk is not quite right. The water provides me with the deepest most transparent satisfaction I have every known; and (like Lawrence of Arabia, you know) I can tell the difference between waters of different wells and locale.

As to intellectual purification, I've found all my problems laid bare for me. There is a good chance that I may go overseas sooner that I had planned: I've found myself asking perhaps the most basic of all questions "Why live?" And the answers are bare and sharp, free from the lacy, Blue Boyish language of the dilettante "student of life." Some of the answers I find before me are: I live because if I die now my mother would feel great pain, great misery, and then she would die too. I do not want my mother to suffer and die. Another answer: I live for the wonderful eyes a person can find in the faces of his dear friends. . . .

Then, also, I live for the closeness I can feel to one human being, the thrilling nearness of a sensitive, passionate woman. I live too for the many, many odors and fragrances that burn up from living things. . . . I live for blue, green, brown, scarlet colors, for pure white and transparent liquids. I live for the sound of a woman's voice—gentle, a wonderful thing in woman; I live for the brusque, deep-voiced admission of sentimentality in men I know. I live for raindrops—the sight, feel, sound of them—each a globule experience in itself. But behind it all I live for the heavily moving stream of immortality that flows and throbs through all of nature and art, in fact. I live for a passion and an action—living.

And then on July 10, 1943, he writes:

The feel of the water is rich and shining within me. Spoke of moral support by means of two foxholes connected by a trench. Life is very much like this: each man follows the configurations of his own personality, but on one wall there is a passage leading to his fellows.

Fighting makes this all stark and clear—you need that passage way and find support by it.

Oh, but most of these comparisons are so horizontal! I must use a language that moves obliquely.

Fifty years later Philip was facing the specter of living or dying once again. The setting was different. While recuperating in our home from a broken back caused by myeloma as well as the aftermath of chemotherapy and radiation therapy, he writes once more in a journal about the purpose of his life. I do not know if he had remembered asking that same question and writing about it before being sent to battle on the Western Front.

August 20, 1993
. . . it dawned on me: I have a purpose in life, a purpose I often acknowledge in the breach, but a purpose that willy-nilly (despite my deliberate construction of it) is my purpose, my joy, my reason

for living: solidarity with the world of life and non-life, with other parts of nature, and most specifically solidarity among people who need help—or simply solidarity among people. Only stories or visions of transcending personal isolation and indifference can move me. Only acts of help and, in short, communion deeply move me to joyous tears. My first thesis (the flop at Oxford) was an out-thereness in all the senses, and the solitudes of Montaigne. But these were only the beginning—with my work on cruelty and then Chambon showing me that my deepest yearning was for communion. OUT THERENESS is *out-hereness*, communion. Exteriority is internal, or could be or should be. I yearned for touch and sex when I was younger in Oxford; I felt the solitude of my motorcycle there, and I lived for *my* pleasure—but always the solitude and the communion (sexual, friendly) worked together.

I wanted to be *in touch* but separation was my love as well.

But all my research for fifteen years has been in communion, and Emerson, after my heart attack, said it [for me] in back-to-back [essays] "Self-Reliance" and "Oversoul"—there is an overarching, undergirding, but often hidden communion—or I feel there must be.

Now that I have a disease that may go into long-term remission, or may kill me, I have felt myself as alone, separate; but Doris, my children, the doctors, friends like Alvin Silverdeal [Silverman] and Edwin Sanders, have come to me and have almost forced me by their love to realize that the only real joy in living is in communion, mutuality, solidarity.

And so . . . I close my eyes and open them to the darkly floating, quivering leaves and Louie at the round little table toward the kitchen, and Doris sweeping the floor of the kitchen and laughing at Louie with his hanging red shirt and bare feet and my scratchy throat—solitude and communion—and hope, joy lie only in the transcendence of self-absorption—in expansion.

. . . When you are in trouble you want help, communion. These extraordinary occasions show us reality as clearly, even more clearly than our usual indifference and separate bags. The purpose of my life is overcoming and living in separateness—for oneself and others amidst my monstrous selfishness.

During those two years of recuperating and after he had finished the first and even second drafts of this book, Philip now began to expand his vision of "help." He was questioning the distinction sometimes made between covenantal and contractual help, where the first is purely voluntary and ethical and the second is enforced by financial or legal constraints. In a correspondence with his good friend Theodore Sarbin, a psychologist in California, he wrote about his current thinking on this problem. In an e-mail on December 29, 1993, he wrote:

Dear Ted. . . . It feels wonderful to be communicating with permanent and fleeing objects across 3000 or so miles straight into the eyes and minds of dear friends. And so, dazed, I have nothing to say, except that Doris and I are feeling well for the age we're in and under the circumstances. The weather is gray but warmish. Joshua James the Coast Guard founder was both deeply covenantal and mildly contractual (toward the end of his career), but the Chambonnais were totally covenantal, but in this case they had a covenant with the God Trocmé taught them about, or to put it more accurately fed them love that was an imitation of Christ's love. Schmähling the German who protected Chambon had both a contract with the German government (to keep the rugged area quiet) and a covenant (with no hope of return, and very little military expertise).

Well, that's enough mystification for now—what I'm trying to say is that the covenant-contract distinction should have some shadings, nuances, gray areas—eh?

We love you both dearly, and it's a joy to be in real touch with you.
Doris and Phil

He continued the conversation with Ted Sarbin in an e-mail on January 29, 1994:

My dear Ted: It was gratifying to get your note. I was delighted that Genevieve is now symptom-free after that Bursus injection. I'm sure she'll be able to get into the swing of her golf quite readily—once an athlete always an athlete, if only in spirit. . . . Yes, I got your letter about Faust—and I am thinking hard along the lines of Covenant/Contract, so hard that it means that I'm reconceiving, rewriting my book on help around the distinction. What it amounts to me, in common-sense shorthand, is this: why is it that quid pro quo payment for expert and life-saving, etc. services, why is it that this sort of transaction is not strictly a moral phenomenon, while covenantal caring with usually little expertise, but lots of gratuitous helping, and no quid pro quo, why is the latter involved with a moral "ought" or moral, self-and-other-serving duty? Why is the covenantal so morally interesting, so moral? What's wrong with a bit of commercialism—I don't mind the commercialism of Christmas—as long as people are giving of their best to show their caring for others, whether or not somebody's getting rich or paid in the whole megillah of gift-buying and gift-giving. What is so covenantally attractive or admirable about moral transactions, and what is so neutral or "merely commercial" in quid pro quo helping? Is there a distinction between self-serving and altruism here? That's a messy distinction for me—whom do we serve if we serve not ourselves, whomever else we may be serving?

We love you and we rejoice in Genevieve's return to the sporting life.

In a couple of hours we go off to see Luce's "The Women" in the Hartford Stage production, and a Japanese dinner afterwards, Sushi, etc. plus Tempura, which I really love almost as much as Sushi. We're going with the Scheibes, and we'll give them your love, as I'm sure they give their love to you.

Pinichus [Philip's Hebrew name]

He pursued the subject for the last time on March 16, 1994:

Dear Ted,

. . . what is more important . . . to me (at present) is: why is contractual help morally neutral vis-à-vis covenantal help? What's so morally neutral about giving or receiving payment for (let's say) life-enhancing help? Why is quid pro quo morally neutral? What's so neutral about payment when great life-giving help has been given? I am deeply grateful to my doctors, whom I have payed well, and the gratitude involves moral approbation—they did what they morally ought to have done even though they were payed for it. . . .

Anyway, please acknowledge this. I'm delighted the Bronchitis is licked; tell us how Genevieve is faring—okay? I'm thriving mightily, just wrote a memoir-essay on my friendship with Camus—it would interest you, I am sure, and I'll pass it on to you later.

Love, Phil

Even when Philip wrote this final letter to Ted Sarbin in March 1994, his thinking was moving beyond the problem arising from that distinction between covenantal and contractual help. He began to see the importance of the helpees, in their relationship with the helper. Not all the helpees or victims would be forced to stay quiet like the Jews in Chambon or be "like tubs of butter" during the rescue efforts of Joshua James. Over the years as Philip worked with the addicts and clientele of The Connection, he came to think about the responsibility of the helpee to do his or her part in the rescue effort. Little help would be achieved without an active response and commitment from these young people to their social workers and to the volunteers like Kätchen Coley.

But it was during his illness that Philip most felt the importance of the active participation of the person being helped in a relationship with the helper. I would hear him talking to the visiting nurses and to the home health aides about their roles as helpers and his appreciation of their care, but he would continue to say that he knew he had to have a role in his own recovery. His thinking was taking him to new insights in this ethics of help. His concern with covenantal and contractual help seemed to be only a stepping stone to his deeper thoughts on the helper/helpee relationship.

He was excited about these new revelations. He was ready to go further and deeper into penetrating their importance. Philip discussed their moral implications with his therapist and with Edwin Sanders in their many philosophical and spiritual discussions. And he wrote down these thoughts that were grabbing him in a happenstance letter to a friend of our son, Louie. I say happenstance because Louie just happened to have his friend write to Philip, and Philip happened to respond quickly, which was not always his wont. I think he *had* to write down his current thoughts, and they went to Jay rather than to his journal.

This letter was the last writing Philip was to do.

From: Philip Paul Hallie
To: Jay L. Millen

April 25, 1994, 2:29 PM

Dear Jay: What a pleasure it was to read your letter! Many things in it interested me, [especially] the comment about the convergence of Louie's, Michael's and your careers. Your comment on this had a special twist to it for me: for years now I've been working on a book on help, on taking care of strangers. Le Chambon set me thinking about this, and so did the remarkable career of one Joshua James of Hull, Mass., who saved the lives of hundreds of people on hurricane-seas off the Cape around the turn of the century. In the course of my studies and thoughts about these people who helped strangers and put their own lives at risk in doing so, I found out that help is not the one-way street (the helper is active, and the helped person is passive) that it appears in the above cases. When I got sick I found that not only my immune system, etc., had to pitch in if the doctors and medicines were to help me, but also my attitudes, my optimism or despair, my buoyancy or willingness-to-sink into death, these mental or spiritual factors entered in too. It was not just a matter of an active doctor and a "passive" patient, it was a matter of a partnership, a two-way street, where both parties had to be active. (In the back of my mind I started thinking about certain countries—possibly Bosnia, Somalia, and possibly many others—who could not be helped because they were not capable of helping themselves, of being healthy like a good immune system or a reasonably healthy body. If they do not have resources to keep their own lives normal, it will be hard indeed to export economic and political help to them without smashing their identities or exacerbating their internal often tribal struggles.) Anyway, I've found that basically there is one-way street help and two-way street help, and the difference applies to many many interpersonal ways of behaving. I certainly had to do a lot of self-help to get out of the funk I was in after my month in hospital and my myeloma diagnosis. But Joshua James and the Chambonnais could help people without the people helping themselves very much. Joshua James used to say (he founded the Search and Rescue Service of the U.S. Coastguard) that all he wanted from the people he saved during horrific hurricanes, all he wanted from them was that they should sit in his life-boat "like a tub of butter." And the Jews in Chambon—all they had to do was hide and be quiet—but two-way street help is as dramatic as one-way street help, and just as important in everyday life, as well as in critical medical situations. . . . Well, I just thought I'd share this idea with you— thanks for writing, and especially thanks for writing so warmly and interestingly.

  Cordially, Phil Hallie

  Philip Hallie died on August 7, 1994, from heart failure and complications that followed an eighteen-month struggle with myeloma. The manuscript of this book, as published here with only slight editorial clarifications, was largely finished shortly before the diagnosis of his disease. He worked on it briefly during his convalescence. Throughout the planning and writing of this book he frequently talked about it with Doris Hallie, his wife of forty years.

INDEX